STRATEGIES FOR READING JAPANESE

Strategies

for
reading
Japanese

A Rational Approach to the Japanese Sentence

Setsuko Aihara

with Graham Parkes

JAPAN PUBLICATIONS TRADING COMPANY • Tokyo, Japan

Grateful acknowledgment is made to the following publishers for permission to reproduce material as example sentences:

Chūōkōronsha: *Nihon no meicho 7 Dōgen* (Tokyo, 1974).

Harvard University Press: *Modern Japanese: A Basic Reader*, vol. 2 (Cambridge MA, 1967).

Iwanami Shoten: *Iwanami Shinsho 367, Nihon Bunka-shi* (Tokyo, 1971).

Iwanami Shoten: *Iwanami Shinsho 719, Kan'ami to Zeami* (Tokyo, 1976).

International Christian University Press: *Modern Japanese for University Students, Part 2* (Tokyo, 1974).

Kōdansha: *Gendaishinsho 300, Tekiō no Jōken* (Tokyo, 1972).

Mainichi Shinbunsha

P.H.P. Kenkyūjo: *Hawai wa shizumitsutsu nishi e ugoku* (Tokyo, 1986).

Shinchōsha: *Gogo no eikō* (Tokyo, 1986).

Sōbunsha: *Nishitani Keiji Chōsakushū*, vol. 8 (Tokyo 1986).

Tōkyō Daigaku Shuppankai: *Kamen no kaishakugaku* (Tokyo, 1987).

Published by JAPAN PUBLICATIONS TRADING CO., LTD.
1-2-1 Sarugaku-chō, Chiyoda-ku, Tokyo, 101 Japan

Distributors:
UNITED STATES: *Kodansha America, Inc.* through *Farrar, Straus & Giroux, 19 Union Square West, New York, N. Y. 10003.*
CANADA: *Fitzhenry & Whiteside Ltd., 91 Granton Drive, Richmond Hill, Ontario L4B 2N5.*
BRITISH ISLES AND EUROPEAN CONTINENT: *Premier Book Marketing Ltd., 1 Gower Street, London WC1E 6HA.*
AUSTRALIA AND NEW ZEALAND: *Bookwise International, 54 Crittenden Road, Findon, South Australia 5023.*
THE FAR EAST AND JAPAN: *Japan Publications Trading Co., Ltd., 1-2-1 Sarugaku-chō, Chiyoda-ku, Tokyo, 101 Japan.*

First edition: May 1992 (First printing)

ISBN 0-87040-894-1

Printed in Japan

Contents

Introduction xi

Abbreviations xv

***Chapter One:* Basic Structures** 1

   1. SENTENCE PATTERNS 5
     1.1 Basic Sentence Patterns 6
     1.2 Variations and Expansions 9
   2. PREDICATES ENDING A SENTENCE 12
   3. PREDICATES WITHIN A SENTENCE 15
     3.1 Plain Forms 16
     3.1.1 Noun Modifier and *Toiu* Clauses 17
     3.1.1A Modifier Clauses (in which *ga/no* occurs, but not *wa*) . . . 17
       Single Modifiers 21
       V-Plain Forms + *no* 22
       Noun Modifier + Adverbial Phrase 23
     3.1.1B *Toiu* Clauses (in which *wa* can appear as well as *ga*) 27
     3.1.2 Quotation and Interrogative Clauses 30
     3.1.2A Quotation Clauses 30
     3.1.2B Interrogative Clauses as Noun Clauses 32
     3.1.3 Other Subordinate Clauses 34
       to "when/if . . ." 34
       nara(ba) "if/in case . . ." 38
       kara/node "since/because . . ." 38
       keredo(mo) "although . . ." 39
       noni/nimokakawarazu "in spite of . . ." 40
     3.2 Non-Plain Forms 41

3.2.1 Subordinate Clauses 41

tara(ba): Condition and Subjunctive 41

(r)eba : Provision and Subjunctive 42

. . . *temo* "even though . . ." 43

. . . *V-te kara* "since/after . . ." 43

3.2.2 Multiple Predicates 44

-te Form 44

V-te, V-naide/zuni 45

ADJ-kute, N/AN de 46

Variations of the *-te* Form 48

Other Types of Multiple Predicate 51

Chapter Two: Developing Strategies 53

STRATEGIC EXERCISE A

1. . . . *da.* 57

2. . . . *V.* 62

3. . . . *shirabeta.* 65

4. . . . *itte-ita.* 69

5. . . . *to ieru.* 76

6. . . . *to omawareru.* 79

STRATEGIC EXERCISE B

Sentence 1 85

Sentence 2 88

Sentence 3 91

Sentence 4 96

Sentence 5 101

Sentence 6 104

Sentence 7 111

Sentence 8 115

Chapter Three: Problematic Sentences 121

1. AMBIGUITY 126

1.1 Noun Modification 126

1.1.1 Modifier Clause + *N no N* 126

1.1.2 *ADJ + N no N* 129

1.1.3 *AN na + N no N* 130

1.1.4 Irregular Modifier Clauses 130

1.2 Plurality of the Noun 133

2. MULTIPLE PREDICATES 136
  2.1 Variations and Irregular Cases 136
    2.1.1 *N de, V* 137
    2.1.2 *AN de, V* 138
  2.2 Grouping Multiple Predicates 139
  2.3 Tense, Aspect, etc. and Final Predicate 142
3. IRREGULAR USAGES OF TENSE 148
  3.1 Past Tense 148
  3.2 Non-Past Tense 149
4. COMPLEX STRUCTURES 151
5. WORD MEANING 157
  5.1 *Hitei* 157
  5.2 *ni taishite*: "regarding" or "opposing" 159
  5.3 *-ka*: "transformation" 161
  5.4 *tettei(teki)*: "thorough, exhaustive" 163
6. THE ROLE OF CONTEXT 168
  6.1 Omitted Elements 168
    6.1.1 Topic Omission 169
    6.1.2 Subject Omission 171
    6.1.3 Omission of Indirect Object 172
    6.1.4 Omisssion of *V-te* 173
    6.1.5 Predicate reduced to *no* 174
    6.1.6 Omission of *da/dearu* 175
  6.2 Specification of Antecedents 177
7. METAPHOR 179
8. LOGICALITY 183
9. CULTURE 188
  9.1 Sociological 189
  9.2 Indirectness in Writing Style 192

***Chapter Four:* Grammar Guide** 199

1. PARTS OF SPEECH: OVERVIEW 202
2. VERBS 207
  2.1 Conjugation (Verb Forms) 207
    2.1.1 Consonant Verbs 207
    2.1.2 Vowel Verbs 211
    2.1.3 Irregular Verbs 213
    2.1.4 Negative Forms of Suffixes 213

2.1.5 Passive, Causative, and Potential Froms 214

2.2 Transitive and Intransitive Verbs 214

2.3 Passive and Spontaneous Forms 215

2.3.1 Passive Voice 215

2.3.2 Spontaneous Form 216

2.4 Tense and Verb Types 218

2.4.1 Tense 218

2.4.2 Verb Types 220

2.5 *-te* Forms 221

2.5.1 *V-te-iru* 221

2.5.2 *V-te-aru* 223

2.5.3 *V-te-iku/kuru* 225

2.5.4 *V-te-shimau* 226

2.5.5 *V-te-oku* 226

2.5.6 *V-te-miru* 227

2.6 V-stem 227

2.7 Verbalizers 229

3. NOUNS 232

3.1 Derivation of Nouns 232

3.2 Verbal Nouns 233

3.3 Time Words 234

3.4 Nouns used as Adverbs of Quantity 234

3.5 Loan Words 235

3.6 Pronouns 235

3.6.1 Personal Pronouns 235

3.6.2 K-S-A-D Series 236

4. ADJECTIVAL NOUNS 239

4.1 Special ANs: *-yō, -sō,* and *-ge* 239

4.1.1 *-yō da/na/ni* "appearance, state, shape, way" 239

4.1.2 *-sō da* and *-ge da* 239

5. THE USES OF *WA, GA,* AND *MO* 242

5.1 *Wa* 242

5.1.1. Topic *wa* 242

5.1.2 Contrast *wa* 244

5.2 *Ga* 247

5.2.1 Immediate Description of a Scene or Event 247

5.2.2 Subject Emphasis 247

5.2.3 Subject in a Location Sentence with *aru/iru* 248

5.2.4 Other Cases requiring Subject *ga* 249

5.3 *Mo* 250

5.3.1 "Also," "both . . . and," "neither . . . nor" 250

5.3.2 Emphasis *mo* 251

6. THE USES OF *NO* 255

6.1 *N no N* 255

6.1.1 "of" or connecting two nouns 255

6.1.2 Possessive 255

6.1.3 Copula *da* is changed to *no/dearu* after *N* 256

6.2 Subject in a Modifier Clause (equivalent of *ga*) 257

6.3 Sentence-Final Particle in Informal Speech Style 257

6.4 Emphasis or Softener in a Predicate 257

6.5 Pronominal: "one (person, thing, place, etc.)" 259

6.6 Nominalizer: Plain V (nonpast) + *no* 259

7. THE PARTICLE *NI* 260

7.1 Time 260

7.2 Location + *aru/iru* 260

7.3 Location + Other Verbs 261

7.4 Direction or Goal 262

7.5 Purpose 264

7.6 Manner Adv: *X* + *ni* 265

7.7 Subject for *dekiru* and *wakaru* 265

7.8 Addition 265

7.9 Sentence-Ending for Wish or Prayer 266

7.10 "per [number]" 266

7.11 Honorific: *o*-V-stem, *ni naru* 266

7.12 Partial List of other verbs that take *ni* 267

8. THE PARTICLE *TO* 270

8.1 Quotation Particle 270

8.2 Manner: . . . + *to* 270

8.3 Other Functions of *to* 273

9. THE USE OF *MONO* 277

10. THE USE OF *TOKORO* 280

10.1 *tokoro*: "place, point, residence" 280

10.2 *V* + *tokoro*: "at the point where . . ." 281

10.3 Other Uses of *tokoro* 282

11. THE USE OF *WAKE* 284
12. EMPHATIC PARTICLES 287
   12.1 Restrictives: "only" (*dake, nomi, kiri, bakari, shika*) 287
   12.2 Non-restrictives (*koso, sae, sura, made, demo*) 290
13. *-TE MO* AND *-TE WA* 293
14. SENTENCE-ENDING EXPRESSIONS 295
   14.1 Basic 295
   14.2 Other Endings that can be attached to the Predicate 299

Appendix 305

1. IDIOMATIC EXPRESSIONS 307
2. IDIOMS USING *V-TE* FORMS 337
   2.1 Idiomatic Phrases 337
   2.2 Idiomatic Constructions 342
3. COMPOUNDS USING V-STEM 345
   3.1 V-stem + V 345
   3.2 Other V-stem Compounds and Phrases 359
4. GRAMMAR LISTS 362
   4.1 Transitive/Intransitive Verb Pairs 362
   4.2 *-i* (Vowel) Verbs 365
   4.3 Momentary Verbs 369
   4.4 Adjectival Nouns 371
   4.5 Conjunctions 377
5. OLD KANA 379

About the Authors 381

Introduction

I N ORDER TO LEARN To read Japanese, two things are necessary (aside from the learning of the relevant vocabulary and idioms). First, one has to master the Japanese writing system consisting of kanji, hiragana, and katakana. Numerous books are available that teach one how to do this.[1] The other thing is to learn the grammatical structure of the language, so that one can correctly construe the relationships among the various elements in a sentence. There are no books available, as far as I know, that systematically teach one how to understand the grammatical structure of Japanese for the specific purposes of reading comprehension. The present book is designed precisely to fill this gap.

Assuming an understanding of the Japanese writing system and that the reader knows (or is learning) the necessary vocabulary, this book will impart the knack of "decoding" Japanese sentence structure—such that a few months of industrious study will enable him or her to become a fluent reader of Japanese. It teaches a rational approach to the grammatical structure of Japanese texts in such a way that it can be used with equal success in classes in Japanese reading comprehension and also as a "self-study course" on one's own.

Since the sentence structure of Japanese is quite different from that of most Indo-European languages, one of the major difficulties confronting a beginning reader faced with a long Japanese sentence concerns *where to begin* in trying to make sense of it. A special feature of this book—which is unique in this respect—is that it teaches one how to understand the way in which the subordinate clauses within a complex sentence are "nested" one within the other. Such an understanding allows one to see the overall structure of the sentence and thus to know where to begin in rendering it into English (or French, German, or whatever).

People who have learned enough Japanese to be able to read have presumably internalized a set of strategies for understanding grammatical structure of

---

[1] Especially recommended are those authored by James Heisig. *Remembering the Kanji* (vols. I and II), *Remembering the Hiragana*, and *Remembering the Katakana*.

the language—although the employment of those strategies will generally remain unconscious during the process of construing the sense while actually reading. What this book does is to make these kinds of strategies *explicit*, in order to allow the beginning reader to attain fluency more quickly and effectively. Thus it may also be helpful for people who can already read fairly well—insofar as it will enable them to read more fluently and with more precise understanding.

The prerequisite for using the present book effectively is only a minimal prior acquaintance with Japanese—of the kind that could be acquired through an introductory course in the language or through spending time with an audio cassette that gives the pronunciation of the language. In most Japanese language programs, students go through a year or two (or more) of instruction in the spoken language before beginning serious reading. However, my experience has shown that such a long preparation may not be necessary. Students who are willing to work hard at mastering grammatical structure and acquiring vocabulary can profitably begin to learn to read with only a minimal knowledge of how the language is spoken.

This means that the book can be helpful to readers with a broad range of prior abilities and in a variety of contexts. It can be used in college level reading courses in Japanese from beginning through advanced levels. Beginning students will be able to learn almost all the grammar they need to know from this text, while more advanced students will be able to use the chapters on grammar as a reference resource in order to brush up their understanding and fill in any gaps. Since the later chapters teach one how to decipher some fiendishly complex sentences, the book will be especially useful for graduate students who want to be able to read scholarly writing in their particular field(s) of interest and who may be required to take language exams in reading modern Japanese for their degrees.

It can also be used by people who want to be able to read materials relating to their particular professions—whether law or business, or science, medicine, or technology—either in formal courses or as a self-study guide.

While this book is intended to be instructive in several of the areas relevant to reading comprehension—knowledge of vocabulary and idiomatic constructions, grammatical understanding, and an acquaintance with certain aspects of Japanese culture—its primary focus is on strategies for decoding sentence structures, as elaborated in the "strategic exercises" of Chapter Two. These are designed to train students to discern the structure of sentences more or less independently of word meanings, by having them work with sentences in which all the words except those that function as structural clues are at first kept concealed. Learners will then appropriate the strategies in a way that somewhat parallels the approach taken by computer translation, with the help of guiding questions and notes.

As an introduction to Chapter Two, the first chapter presents some basic features of Japanese grammar concerning the *predicate* which work as structural clues. Chapter Three elaborates the strategies of the previous chapter into areas of greater difficulty and complexity, dealing with such things as modifying relationships, multiple predicates, omitted elements, and cultural context. Chapter Four presents a comprehensive grammar specifically oriented toward reading comprehension, which can serve as a review for students familiar with basic grammar and as a practical reference guide for readers. Much of the book is based on an analysis of the most common errors made by students over the years as well as on formal linguistic inquiry. (However, linguistic and theoretical explanations have been avoided unless they actually aid reading comprehension.)

The Appendix provides some lists of frequently encountered idiomatic expressions and constructions. While the book is aimed at reading modern Japanese rather than classical texts, some features of the classical grammar survive in modern literary style, and these have been mentioned where appropriate. Since one also comes across some old kana used in (especially scholarly) writing up until around the middle of this century, a guide to these forms has been included in the Appendix. Limitations of space made it impossible to include a second appendix of vocabulary peculiar to written Japanese, most of which are Sino-Japanese compounds that students are not exposed to in learning the spoken language. The project of producing a list of such vocabulary items as a companion to the present volume is one that I hope to undertake in the near future.

Gratitude is due to a number of people who have helped in the creation of this book—primarily to my students, from whom I have learned most over the course of the years. James Heisig, Director of the Nanzan Institute for Religion and Culture in Nagoya, serenely assumed what turned out to be the enormous burden of designing and typesetting the entire book. Without this help and the encouragement afforded by his energetic wit and humor, this text would probably never have seen the light of day.

Whatever effectiveness I may have attained as a teacher is based on the solid foundation in teaching methodology I received in the Department of Japanese at International Christian University, especially from Professor Tazuko Ueno. I am also thankful for the kind support of Professor Fumiko Koide, who founded the program there. I am indebted, too, to Professor Samuel Martin who was later my thesis adviser, and from whom I have learned a great deal about Japanese linguistics.

Part of the research for the book was generously funded by the Japan Studies Endowment at the University of Hawaii, through a grant from the Japanese government. I also wish to thank my colleague of many years, Mrs Kakuko Shoji, who provided numerous helpful suggestions on points of grammar. Mr Dennis Ogawa read an early draft of the first two chapters, which benefited from his meticulous annotations; while Professor Valdo Viglielmo also took time away from his busy schedule in order to read the manuscript. I am grateful to several other colleagues at the University of Hawaii: Professor Sharon Minichiello, for her warm encouragement throughout the duration of the project, and Professors George Grace and Ann Peters, who guided my linguistic and psycholinguistic inquiries into the comprehension process.

Among others who in various ways helped this manuscript to completion, I should like to mention: Professors Michiko Asai, Carl Becker, Tom Dean, Tom Kasulis, Megumi Sakabe, Eiko Uehara, Seiko Yoshinaga, Dr Benton Chun, and several students in my Japanese 301 class.

Todd Fukushima helped by typing in Japanese at great speed late into Christmas Eve. Tanya Sienko provided some helpful comments at the eleventh hour; while Mr Kazuyoshi Terao and Ms Fumiko Fujibe prevented serious damage to my eyes by taking over the task of stripping in the kanji. Helen Parkes and Mrs Hideko Aihara were supportive and understanding during the difficult throes of finishing up the manuscript.

Lastly, I wish to express my greatest appreciation to Graham Parkes for his invaluable contributions at every stage of the project, not to mention his unflagging encouragement at times when it simply didn't seem worth while continuing.

Setsuko Aihara
Nagoya, January 1992

Abbreviations

THE FOLLOWING abbreviations will be used (especially at the penultimate stage of translating example sentences) to designate the grammatical functions of sentence components:

ADJ	adjective	**OMIT**	omitted
ADV	adverb	**ONG**	on-going action
AN	adjectival noun	**Ō**	V-ō form
APP	apposition	**PASS**	passive
CAUS	causative	**POT**	potential
COND	condition	**PRED**	predicate
CONJ	conjunction	**PRON**	pronominal
CONT	contrast	**QUES**	question particle
COP	copula	**QUOT**	quotation particle
DRN	direction	**RSN**	reason
EMPH	emphasis	**SEQ**	Sequence
INQ	inquiry	**SOFT**	softener
INST	instrumental	**SPON**	spontaneous
LIST	listing out	**SUBJ**	subject
LOCN	location	**TOP**	topic
MNR	manner	**V**	verb
N	Noun	**Vi**	intransitive verb
NOM	nominalizer	**Vt**	transitive verb.
OBJ	(direct) object		

Chapter One

Basic Structures

1. SENTENCE PATTERNS 5

   1.1 Basic Sentence Patterns 6

   1.2 Variations and Expansions 9

2. PREDICATES ENDING A SENTENCE 12

3. PREDICATES WITHIN A SENTENCE 15

   3.1 Plain Forms 16

      3.1.1 Noun Modifier and *TOIU* Clauses 17

      3.1.2 Quotation and Interrogative Clauses 30

      3.1.3 Other Subordinate Clauses 34

   3.2 Non-Plain Forms 41

      3.2.1 Subordinate Clauses 41

      3.2.2 Multiple Predicates 44

Basic Structures

A SOUND KNOWLEDGE OF grammar and the ability to make full use of it are of crucial importance in learning to read a foreign language. By relating words to one another, grammatical understanding permits a narrowing of the various potential meanings of each word to its actual meaning in a particular context, thereby enabling the reader to construe the sense of the entire sentence. Even at the level of single words, a knowledge of parts of speech and grammatical categories contributes to an understanding of sentence structure.

In the case of a verb, for example, one can ask whether it is intransitive or transitive, a momentary verb or durative, and so on. If it is intransitive one will not expect a noun for a direct object followed by the particle *o*, but will rather be on the watch for a subject particle *ga*. And if the expected subject noun followed by *ga* does not appear in the text, one knows that there are two possibilities: either the subject has been omitted (in which case one has to determine what it is), or else the subject particle *ga* has been replaced by the contrast *wa* or the particle *mo*. If the verb is a momentary verb, one knows that the *V-te-iru* construction will not signify an on-going action but rather a state; and so forth. The more one can narrow down the possibilities on the basis of grammatical clues in this way, the more quickly and reliably one will arrive at correct construal of the sentence.

As far as grammar is concerned, native speakers generally have only "knowledge how" of their language (they communicate by means of it, but they know little about how it works), while adult learners of the language have primarily "knowledge that," which takes time to be developed into working condition. There are two types of "knowledge that" with respect to grammar: one concerns grammar as used in describing the language as coherently as possible by way of a linguistic theory, while the other has to do with grammar as working knowledge at the performance level of production or comprehension — and thus gradually shades into "knowledge how." It is the latter, which might be called pedagogical grammar, that is our concern in this book, since it is this kind of grammatical understanding that undergirds all competence in reading comprehension.

Sound grammatical knowledge enables the reader to make a variety of predictions. If the mesh of your net (grammatical knowledge) is fine you catch more fish (understanding of content); if the net is coarse or has holes in it, you may lose fish. The more precise and extensive your predictions are, the sooner you are likely to attain a thorough understanding of the sentence. Thus **readers need in addition to a thorough knowledge of grammar the skills or strategies for making effective use of this knowledge.**

This book attempts to present the necessary grammar in as simple and systematic a way as possible from the learner's point of view, so that s/he may bring his or her understanding of grammar up to the level of "knowledge how." The grammar is therefore arranged quite differently from the grammars found in most language textbooks. The relevant features have been divided into those of a more "structural" nature and those of a more "idiomatic" nature (that is, peculiar to the language in question). The first can be compared to the basic structure of a house—consisting of vertical supports, beams, cross-spars, staircases, etc.—while the second would correspond to more detailed features—shape and size of windows, style of doors, and so on.

In acquiring "structural" grammar one learns sets of rules that are applicable to the broad ways in which sentences are constructed, whereas "idiomatic" grammatical features simply have to be learned instance by instance. Through the former the learner comes to read, as it were, a basic architectural plan of the house; in becoming familiar with the "idiomatic" features one comes to see the detailed specifications (these windows are hinged at the side and open inwards), thus getting a much better idea of how the house will actually look and function.

For example, one finds in Japanese grammar a number of Verb-Verb constructions: *V-te* + Verb, for example, or V-stem + Verb. Since these constructions have no counterpart in English, one has first to learn the structural meanings of the various types of combinations, and then to fill out this understanding with knowledge of the relevant "idiomatic" features. In addition to learning the various ways the *V-te* form functions, one needs to become familiar with the meanings of (for example) *V-te shimau*, *V-te oku*, or *V-te ageru* independently.

Chapter 1 presents features that may be used as structural clues at the sentence level, while chapter 4 presents a more comprehensive grammar which both elaborates structural features in detail and also includes more idiomatic grammatical points. A list of particular idiomatic phrases and expressions is given in the appendix. The strategy exercises in chapters 2 and 3 will help readers to develop skills and techniques to put their knowledge of grammar to use in "decoding" the sentence structure of written Japanese. The development of such skills will eventually provide the reader with the grammatical "knowledge how" that is necessary for reading Japanese with full comprehension.

1. Sentence patterns

DIFFERENT TYPES OF sentences reflect different types of predication: statements of identity or equivalence which relate two items or phenomena—as in "This **is a book**," descriptions of the condition of something using adjectives—as in "This book **is good**"—or descriptions of an action or movement by way of verbs as—in "The baby **cries**." Since each language has different ways of structuring and categorizing its words and sentences, it depends on the language how different types of predication are actualized structurally.

In Japanese **the most important element is the predicate**. While in English the predicate (= words in bold letters in the above example sentences) follows the subject of the sentence, in Japanese **it comes right at the end**. When subsentences appear within a larger sentence, they are called **clauses**. In clauses, too, the predicate appears at the end. **By identifying the type of the final predicate of a sentence one can determine the sentence pattern.**

PREDICATE TYPES

For the purpose of distinguishing types of predicate, adjectives can be understood as being like verbs (verbals) in that they inflect and can stand alone as a predicate, whereas nonverbals (nouns and adjectival nouns) cannot and have to be supported by the copula *da* which has its own inflection. (See below, § 2, and ch. 4, § 14.)

We can thus distinguish two main types of predication (See ch. 4, § 1 for parts of speech):

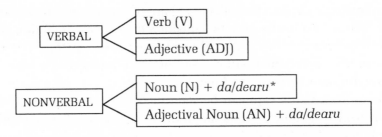

* *Dearu* is a more literary form that is frequently used in scholarly writing.

1.1 Basic Sentence Patterns

Basically all sentences can be reduced to one of the following patterns:

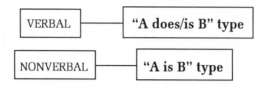

VERBAL: "A does B" type : X *wa* (Y *ga*) V.

*Hanako **wa** aruku.*	Hanako walks.

"Hanako walks" is an example of the simplest kind of predication in English: a subject-predicate sentence in which "Hanako" is the subject and it is predicated of her that she "walks." In the Japanese sentence, however, "Hanako" is **the topic** of the sentence rather than the subject. Japanese distinguishes between the topic (indicated by the following particle *wa*) and **the subject** (followed by the particle *ga*).

In Japanese sentences the topic is more frequently used than the subject, and in most cases the subject in an English sentence will correspond to the topic in Japanese. This simple **Topic** *wa* **Predicate** form may be regarded as a contraction of an original **Topic** *wa* **Subject** *ga* **Predicate** structure, thus:

X *wa* V	is a contraction of	X *wa* Y *ga* V

So "Hanako walks" would originally have been construed as:

*Hanako **wa** Hanako **ga** aruku.*	As for Hanako (TOPIC), Hanako (SUBJECT) walks.

When the topic (X) and the subject (Y) are the same, only one of them appears. Thus *Hanako wa aruku* may be considered as an abbreviation of *Hanako wa Hanako ga aruku*, with the *Hanako ga* having been omitted. Whether the topic or the subject is retained will depend on the context. If the topic and the subject are different both are retained.

This original structure can be seen in constructions using the intransitive verb *wakaru* ("be understandable, understand") as well as the verb *dekiru* ("be do-able, be able to") and the potential forms of a number of transitive verbs. Such verbs take a subject word followed by *ga* rather than a direct object followed by *o*. (See below, § 1.2 for the expansions and variations of the basic sentence patterns involving *N + o* and transitive verbs.)

Thus "Hanako understands French" is:

| *Hanako **wa** furansugo **ga** wakaru.* | As for Hanako, French is understandable. |

And "Hanako can play tennis" is:

| *Hanako **wa** tenisu **ga** dekiru.* | As for Hanako, tennis is do-able/playable. |

"Hanako can read English" is:

| *Hanako **wa** eigo **ga** yomeru.* | As for Hanako, English is readable. |

A similar construction is used with certain "verbal" adjectives:

VERBAL: "A is B" type : X *wa* (Y *ga*) ADJ.

In Japanese, "X wants (to do) Y" is expressed by adjectives that function very much like verbs: *hoshii* ("is desirable/desired, wants") and the *V-tai* ending ("want to V").

Thus "Hanako wants a car" is:

| *Hanako **wa** kuruma **ga** hoshii.* | As for Hanako, a car is desired. |

And "Hanako wants to buy a car" is:

| *Hanako **wa** kuruma **ga** kai-tai.* | As for Hanako, buying a car is desirable. |

⮡ The expressions . . . *hoshii* and . . . *V-tai* are nowadays often used with the direct object particle *o* (in a way that more closely corresponds to the English): *Hanako **wa** kuruma **o** hoshii* and *Hanako **wa** kuruma **o** kaitai.*

The **Y ga** construction is used for more simple types of predication using adjectives:

"Hanako is tall" is translated:

*Hanako **wa** se **ga** takai.*	As for Hanako, her height is high.

"Hanako is black-haired" is translated:

*Hanako **wa** kami **ga** kuroi.*	As for Hanako, her hair is black.

The simplest type of verbal-adjectival predication, in which the subject has been omitted, leaving only the topic, is:

*Hanako **wa** omoshiroi.*	Hanako is interesting.

NONVERBAL: "A is B" type : X *wa* (Y *ga*) N/AN *da*

N: **X** *wa (Y ga)* **N** *da.*

*Hanako **wa** gakusei da.*	Hanako is a student.
*Hanako **wa** okāsan **ga** isha da.*	As for Hanako, her mother is a doctor. (= H's mother is a doctor).

AN: **X** *wa* (Y *ga*) **AN** *da.*

(For an explanation of adjectival nouns, see ch. 4, § 4.)

*Hanako **wa** genki da.*	Hanako is healthy/full of energy.
*Hanako **wa** me **ga** kirei da.*	As for Hanako, her eyes are beautiful. (= H's eyes are beautiful)
*Hanako **wa** tenisu **ga** jōzu da.*	Hanako is good at tennis.

| *Hanako **wa** kudamono **ga** suki da.* | As for Hanako, fruit is likable. (= H likes fruit) |

↪ Occasionally **particle** + *da* appears as a predicate, where the *da* stands for a predicate that has been omitted:

| *Kono basu wa Tōkyō kara **da** (= kita).* | This bus is (= came) from Tokyo. |
| *(Sore wa) ame ga futta kara **da** (= komatta, ikanakatta, etc.).* | It's because it rained (that I was inconvenienced, didn't go, etc.) |

1.2 Variations and Expansions

Sentences can be expanded by the use of various particles of place, time, direction or goal, means, and so on, depending on the nature of the predicate.

➥ The verb can be either **transitive** (Vt) or **intransitive** (Vi). Vt normally takes a direct object (OBJ) word followed by the particle *o*. Vi normally goes with a subject and has no direct object. (See ch. 4, § 2.2.)

Expansion with DIRECT OBJ + *o*:

| *Hanako **wa** hon **o** yomu.* | Hanako reads a book. |

Expansion with INDIRECT OBJ + *ni*:

| *Hanako **wa** Tarō **ni** hon **o** ageta.* | Hanako gave Taro a book. |
| *Hanako **wa** Tarō **ni** eigo o oshieta.* | Hanako taught Taro English. |

* See ch. 4, § 7.4 for verbs of giving and receiving.

Expansion with PLACE + *de*, INSTRUMENTAL + *de*, and INDIRECT OBJ + *ni*:

*Hanako **wa** heya **de** furansugo **de** kodomo **ni** hon **o** yomu.*	Hanako reads a book in French to her child in the room.

➥ V can be a **motion** verb, a kind of Vi that can take DEPARTING POINT + *kara*, DIRECTION + *e* or TERMINAL POINT + *ni/made*, and INSTRUMENTAL + *de*:

*Hanako **wa** Tōkyō **kara** Ōsaka **made** hikōki **de** itta.*	Hanako went from Tokyo to Osaka by plane.

➥ There are some Vi's that take the particle *ni*:

*Hanako **wa** Tōkyō **de** sensei **ni** naru.*	Hanako will become a teacher in Tokyo.
*Hanako **wa** Shinjuku **de** densha **ni** noru.*	Hanako gets on the train at Shinjuku.
*Hanako **wa** Waikiki **de** hoteru **ni** tomaru.**	Hanako stays at a hotel in Waikiki.

> * When two places appear in one sentence, *de* is used for the larger area while *ni* denotes a more restricted location or specific place. (See ch. 4, § 7 for more verbs that take *ni*.)

➥ V can be the verb of **existence** (*aru/iru*), which takes a subject and LOCATION + *ni*.

*Asoko **ni** uchi **ga** aru.*	There is a house over there.

If the subject is an **activity** or **event** rather than a thing, where it takes place is indicated by *de* instead of *ni*.

*Kono heya **de** miitingu **ga** aru.*	There is (will be) a meeting in this room.

When the subject is topicalized, it is normally placed at the beginning of the sentence and followed by *wa*.

*Uchi **wa** asoko **ni** aru.*	The house is over there.
*Miitingu **wa** kono heya **de** aru.*	The meeting will be (held) in this room.

➥ Passive, Causative, and Causative-Passive constructions

(See ch. 4, § 2.1 for these forms.)

*Inu **ga** kuruma **ni** hikareta.*	The dog was run over by a car.

The particle *ni* indicates the agent who does the action. It was the subject of the original active sentence: ***Kuruma** ga inu o hiita.*

*Hanako **ga** hisho **ni** tegami **o** taipu saseta.*	Hanako had her secretary type the letter.
*Kodomo **ga** okāsan **ni** hon **o** yomaserareta.*	The child was made to read a book by the mother.

The subject in the above sentences can be topicalized and be followed by *wa*, as in the last two examples in the previous section. This yields a sentence of the form: *Inu **wa** kuruma ni hikareta.*

Sentences can be expanded further by adding modifiers as well as phrases or subordinate clauses for time, place, reason, manner, and so on. They may also be expanded by using *V-te* forms to create multiple predicates (as discussed below in § 3.2.2). Even in the case of a complex sentence containing several subordinate clauses, the patterns outlined above will be found within each individual clause.

2. Predicates ending a sentence

T HE MAIN PREDICATE of the entire sentence (thus of the main clause, if there is more than one clause) is placed at the end of the sentence in Japanese, while predicates of subordinate clauses are placed at the ends of their respective clauses. Main predicates may take either a formal form (. . . *desu* or -*masu* form) or a plain or informal form (*kaku* rather than *kakimasu*). The basic forms are given in the following tables:

FORMAL

	NONPAST		PAST	
	AFFIRMATIVE	NEGATIVE	AFFIRMATIVE	NEGATIVE
V	*kaki-masu*	*kaki-masen*	*kaki-mashita*	*kaki-masendeshita*
ADJ	*ii-desu*	*yoku-arimasen*	*yokatta-desu*	*yoku-arimasendeshita*
N	*hon desu*	*hon dewa*[1] *arimasen*	*hon deshita*	*hon dewa arimasendeshita*
AN	*hen desu*	*hen dewa arimasen*	*hen deshita*	*hen dewa arimasendeshita*

[1] *Dewa* can be contracted to *ja* in the informal speech style.

PLAIN (INFORMAL)

V	*kaku*[1]	*kak-anai*	*ka-ita*	*kak-anakatta*
ADJ	*ii*	*yo-kunai*	*yo-katta*	*yo-kunakatta*
N	*hon da/dearu*	*hon dewa nai*	*hon datta/deatta*[2]	*hon dewa nakatta*
AN	*hen da/dearu*	*hen dewa nai*	*hen datta/deatta*	*hen dewa nakatta*

[1] The nonpast plain affirmative form is also called the "dictionary form" and corresponds to the infinitive form of the verb in English.

[2] Like *dearu* in relation to *da*, *deatta* is a more literary form of *datta.*.

OTHER FORMS (See also ch. 4, § 2.1)
FORMAL

VERB	CONSONANT VERB[1]	VOWEL VERB
Passive	*kak-aremasu*	*tabe-raremasu*
Causative	*kak-asemasu*	*tabe-sasemasu*
Causative-passive	*kak-aseraremasu*	*tabe-saseraremasu*
Potential	*kak-emasu*	*tabe-raremasu*
Imperative	*kak-inasai*[2]	*tabe-nasai*
-ō form	*kak-imashō*	*tabe-mashō*

[1] Consonant verbs are verbs whose roots end with a consonant, while the roots of vowel verbs end with a vowel. (See ch. 4, §§ 2.1.1 and 2.1.2 for details, and § 2.1.3 for irregular verbs.)

[2] The imperative ending of *masu* is *mase/mashi*. However, V-stem + *nasai* is normally used for the formal (= *masu* form) imperative form in modern Japanese. *Nasai* is the root of the honorific verb *nasaru* "to do."

ADJ & AN	
-ō form	· *akai/kirei deshō*

PLAIN

VERB	CONSONANT VERB	VOWEL VERB
Passive	*kak-areru*	*tabe-rareru*
Causative	*kak-aseru*	*tabe-saseru*
Causative-passive	*kak-aseru*	*tabe-saseru*
Potential	*kak-eru*	*tabe-rareru*
Imperative	*kak-e*	*tabe-ro*
-ō form	*kak-ō*	*tabe-yō*

ADJ & AN	
-ō form	*akai/kirei darō* (or *dearō*)

(See ch. 4, § 14 for examples of this form.)

⮑ Note that the *-(r)eba* and *-tara* forms are not included here since they cannot stand as the main predicate of a sentence, though they can constitute clauses. (See below, § 3.2.1.)

Formal forms are used in the formal speech style both in writing and in conversation at formal occasions, or in talking to someone one does not know well. Plain forms are used in the informal speech style in talking to close friends or to one's family members in informal situations. In written Japanese the most common literary style is the plain style in which sentence endings are all in the plain form. The plain style is used in official documents, articles in newspapers and magazines, academic writing, and so on.

Regarding the use of the copula, there are two slightly different styles: one that uses *da* and another using *dearu*. The *dearu* style tends to be used more in official documents or in academic writing. However, the formal style, often called the *desu/-masu* style, is also used widely in literature as well as in writing in everyday situations.

3. Predicates within a sentence

SENTENCES MAY BE complex, containing several clauses, each one of which may contain smaller, subordinate clauses within it. The fact that the word order of Japanese is quite different from that of English creates considerable difficulty in reading comprehension, particularly for English-speaking students. Japanese is a S-O-V language in which the verb (the main predicate) comes at the end of the sentence and the direct object precedes the verb.

Kodomo ga uta o utatta.

The child   a song   sang   "The child sang a song."

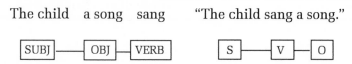

Japanese is also **post**positional rather than **pre**positional, which means that **a particle follows** rather than precedes **the noun to be modified**, and **the noun to be modified follows the clause that modifies it.**

[Jon ga tateta]   *uchi*   *e*   *iku.*

John built   a house   to   go

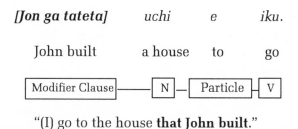

"(I) go to the house **that John built.**"

The burden of transposing back and forth long chunks of meaning when trying to comprehend Japanese can be exhausting. For smoother decoding of structural meaning, it is important to develop the skill of accurately identifying clauses and their relationship to the rest of the sentence. For this reason **predicates appearing within a sentence** are significant, since they **mark the ends of clauses** and thus help one distinguish "chunks of meaning" within the context of the larger sentence.

3.1 Plain Forms

Most of the predicates that appear in subordinate clauses within sentences are in the plain form instead of the *-masu* form (even in the formal speech style), except for the following cases:

In very polite speech:

*Sochira e magari**masu** to sugu de gozaimasu.*	If you turn that way, you'll get there soon.

In clauses ending with other forms such as *-tara*, *-(r)eba*, *-temo*, and *-te kara*:

*Ame ga fut**tara** ikanai.*	If it rains (I) won't go.
*Kono kusuri o nom**eba** kitto naoru.*	If (you) take this medicine you will surely get better.

(See below, § 3.2.1 for further examples.)

⤳ *-nara* clauses have conditional meanings similar to those of *-tara* and *-ba* clauses, but since they follow V-plain form they will be discussed later in this section.

Plain forms within sentences, including the various forms presented above in § 2, **are usually predicates**, and they normally mark the end of subordinate clauses except in the cases of . . . *shi* "moreover, on top of that" and . . . *bakaridenaku/nominarazu* "not only does one . . . (but . . .)," which are cases of multiple predicates (see below, § 3.2.2).

It is a good idea, when you read a text, to make it a habit to mark possible endings of subordinate clauses every time you come across a plain form within a sentence.

BASIC FORMS

V*(r)u*	V-*nai*	V-*ta*	V-*nakatta*
ADJ-*i*	ADJ-*kunai*	ADJ-*katta*	ADJ-*kunakatta*
AN *da/dearu*	AN *dewa nai*	AN *datta/deatta*	AN *dewa nakatta*

3.1.1 NOUN MODIFIER AND *TOIU* CLAUSES

Since modifier and *toiu* clauses precede the noun, the predicate—as indicated by a **V-plain form**—of the clause **appears to the left of the noun** (or above it when the text is written vertically):

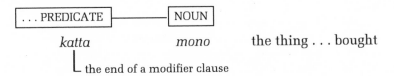

| ...PREDICATE | — | NOUN |

katta   *mono*   the thing ... bought

└ the end of a modifier clause

In a noun modifier clause a subject + *ga/no* occurs, while in a *toiu* clause a topic + *wa* can occur as well as a subject + *ga*.

A. *Modifier Clauses (in which ga/no occurs but not wa)*

➥ These clauses contain a subject + *ga/no* rather than a topic + *wa*. If one finds a topic + *wa* in a sentence containing a modifier clause, it will be the topic for the entire sentence.

A topic + *wa* **normally goes with the main predicate**, which comes **at the end of a sentence**, and **governs the entire sentence**. It is thus good practice to mark the topic + *wa* and the main predicate when first scanning a complex sentence. In general **a subject + *ga* goes with the predicate** (normally the closest one to its right) **of a subordinate clause** and governs only a part of the sentence (the part inside the clause). Therefore, **inside ordinary noun modifier clauses *wa* does not occur**.

| *Tarō **wa** [Hanako **ga** kaita]* tegami o yonda.* | Taro read the letter that Hanako wrote. |

* [   ] indicates a clause.

Tarō is the topic for the main predicate *yonda*, while *Hanako* is the subject for the predicate *kaita* in the modifier clause.

↪ It seems that originally both *ga* and *no* had the function of relating a noun to a following noun or verbal. There are, at any rate, cases in the modern language where each seems to assume the other's function:

An example of *ga* followed by N to denote possession:

wa ("I") *ga kuni*	my country

This kind of classical usage survives as an idiomatic expression in modern Japanese:

waga sha	my company
waga kō	my school

An example from classical Japanese of *no* followed by V to denote the subject of a clause:

[otome no ikakuru] oka	a hill where a maiden hides

Theorists suppose that since *ga* was used more often with verbals than to relate two nouns, it came to assume the function of the subject marker. But since a primary use of *no* was to relate nouns, when used as a subject marker it still required a following noun or noun-like form, and thus it came to be used in a subordinate clause as a subject marker as shown in the above example: *otome* (N) *no ikakuru oka* (N).

Examine the following:

    a. *Watakushi **ga** kita toki inakatta.*
    b. *Watakushi **wa** kita toki inakatta.*
    c. *Watakushi **wa** kita toki mita.*

Toki is a noun meaning "the time" and is modified by a modifier clause in each of the above sentences. The surface ambiguity is clarified if we examine the respective ranges of *wa* and *ga*. In sentences (b) and (c), *watakushi* is the topic for the main predicate, *inakatta* and *mita* respectively.

[Watakushi ga *kita*] *toki (**X** wa)* **inakatta.**	When I came, X wasn't there.
Watakushi wa [*(X ga) kita*] *toki* **inakatta.**	When X came, I wasn't there.
Watakushi wa [[*(watakushi **ga***) *kita*] *toki* **mita.**	When I came, I saw (it).

➥ A noun modifier clause in which *ga/no* occurs but not *wa* is the same kind of "restrictive" type of relative clause that we find in English, and this type can have a subject word (*N* + *ga/no*) but not a topic word (*N* + *wa*).

Compare the following:

RESTRICTIVE ⟶ *kare ga/no iwanakatta] koto*

the thing he didn't say (among the things he did say)

NON-RESTRICTIVE ⟶ *kare ga/wa* iwanakatta] (toiu)** koto*

the fact that he didn't say . . .

> * Note that *wa* can occur in non-restrictive clauses. This type will be referred to as a *toiu* clause and is discussed in the following section.
>
> ** This *toiu* after a clause is often omitted in the non-restrictive type clause. If the *toiu* is omitted, there is no way to tell whether the clause is restrictive or non-restrictive except from the overall context: *kare ga iwanakatta koto* could mean either "the thing he didn't say" or else "the fact that he didn't say . . ."

⇨ From the point of view of function, such non-restrictive clauses are what are called "complement clauses" and should be distinguished from noun-modifier clauses. (See the next section, B.)

➥ **Neither the *-ō* form nor the imperative (*-e/ro*) form of the verb appears as the predicate in a modifier clause,** (while they may in *toiu* clauses and quotation clauses), although the *-ō* form of the copula may do so:

*[. . . to kangaeru **dearō**] hitobito*	people who may think . . .

The classical *-ō* form of ADJ may also be used at the end of a clause in literary style:

*[kaidoku no muzukashi**karō**] bunshō*	sentences the decoding of which may be difficult

➥ Here are some examples of modifier clauses containing V, ADJ, N, and AN in their respective predicates:

V	*[Hanako ga/no **katta**]*	*hon*	the book that Hanako bought
	PRED (V)	N	

ADJ	*[okāsan ga/no **omoshiroi**] gakusei* PRED (ADJ) N	a student whose mother is interesting

Special attention must be given to cases where the predicate of a clause consists of *N/AN + da/dearu*, since the copula *da/dearu* normally appears as *no* after a noun and as *na* after an adjectival noun in restrictive modifier clauses — but does not do so in *toiu* (non-restrictive) clauses.

The original sentence ⟶ *wa/ga N da/dearu*

becomes in a modifier clause ⟶ *ga/no N no/dearu] N*

N	*Okāsan wa/ga nihonjin da/dearu.*	The mother is Japanese.
	[okāsan ga/(no)* nihonjin no/(dearu)] gakusei PRED (N + *da*) N	a student whose mother is Japanese

> * *No* tends not to be used when the predicate of the modifier clause is *N + no (=da)*, probably because the [*N **no** N no*] *N* construction becomes rather confusing insofar as the first *no* can easily be mistaken for the possessive *no* — as in: **okāsan no** *nihonjin no* **gakusei** ("**mother's** Japanese **student**").

Similarly with ANs:

The original sentence ⟶ *wa/ga AN da/dearu*

becomes in a modifier clause ⟶ *ga/no AN no/dearu] N*

AN	*Okāsan wa/ga kirei da/dearu.*	The mother is beautiful.
	*[okāsan ga/no **kirei** na/(dearu)] gakusei* PRED (AN + *da*) N	a student whose mother is beautiful

In the case of a *toiu* clause the copula remains as *da/dearu*:

*[Hanako no okāsan ga sensei **da/dearu**] toiu koto*	the fact that Hanako's mother is a teacher.

☞ In some rare cases *naru*, which is the noun-following form of the classical copula *nari*, may be used in place of *no* or *na* after N or AN respectively at the end of a modifier clause (a relic from classical usage):

[(myōji ga/no) Tanaka (N) naru] mono	a person who(se name) is Tanaka
[sugata ga/no iyō (AN) naru] onna	a woman whose appearance is strange

SINGLE MODIFIERS

In cases where there is no subject word followed by *ga/no* to the left of a predicate within a sentence, either the subject has been omitted or the predicate is being used as a single modifier. The single modifiers are adjectives, adjectival nouns (followed by *na*), and verbs in the past tense (= past participles in English). They can be considered structurally as predicates representing modifier clauses, although it is not necessary to mark them as predicates.

For example, in *akai hon* "a red book," the adjective *akai* is a single modifier, although it can be considered as the predicate of a modifier clause and thus as representing a clause by itself, the subject of which has been omitted. For example:

[(hyōshi ga) akai] hon	a book (the cover of which) is red *or*: a red book

In a phrase such as *sugureta/sugurete-iru gakusha*, "an excellent scholar," *sugureta* is the past tense of the verb *sugureru* "to excel," and *sugurete-iru* is the *V-te* construction indicating a state "is excellent" (see ch. 4, § 2.5.1). These verb forms are used as independent modifiers to refer to a certain state (although they could be regarded as having been originally the predicate of a clause by itself).

Some other single modifiers derived from *V-ta* are: *michitarita* "contented," *kawatta* "strange, eccentric," *yaseta* "slim, skinny," *futotta* "fat," *gakkari shita* "disappointed," *machigaeta* "wrong," *magatta* "bent, winding, unjust," *sunda* "clear, pure," *nigotta* "murky," *hakkiri (to) shita* "clear," *yuttari (to) shita* "relaxed, loose," *pittari (to) shita* "tight fitting."

➥ If the topic particle *wa* appears rather than *ga* or *no* to the left of the predicate, and if the topic word is not for the final predicate (= the end of the sentence), the clause is not a restrictive modifier clause and is either a quotation clause for certain verbs such as "to think," "to hear," "to write" (see below, § 3.1.2) or else a *toiu* clause (see the next section, B)

If you do not find the particle *to* after the predicate in either case, and the verb is not the kind that takes a quotation particle, then the topic word **should not**

be included in this particular clause. It should be regarded as the topic for a predicate outside this particular clause—perhaps for the main predicate of the entire sentence.

[kare ga iwanakatta] koto [SUBJ PRED] N CLAUSE	the thing he didn't say

OMITTED SUBJ PRED *kare wa [(kare ga) iwanakatta] koto ga aru* TOPIC CLAUSE N-SUBJ MAIN PRED	As for him, there is something he didn't say.

In this example the topic of the sentence and the subject of the clause coincide. The *wa* indicates the topic for the main predicate, *aru*.

⇨ This construction may also be used idiomatically, with the slightly different sense of "having had the experience of . . .":

Kare wa [(kare ga) Nihon e itta] koto ga aru.*	(As for him) He has been to Japan.

* See Appendix § 1 for the . . . *koto ga aru* and similar constructions.

CONSTRUCTIONS INVOLVING V-PLAIN FORMS FOLLOWED BY *NO*

The nominalizer *no** following a verb plain form:

Kanojo wa [nomu] **no** *ga suki da.*	She likes to drink (drinking).
[Tori ga tobu] **no** *o mita.*	(I) saw a bird flying.

* See ch. 4, § 6.6.

The pronominal *no** following a verb plain form:

[Hanako ga katta] **no** *wa kore da.*	The one Hanako bought is this.
[Hanako ga itta] **no** *wa Hokkaidō da.*	The place Hanako went is Hokkaido.

* See ch. 4, § 6.5.

⤷ The clauses in the two preceding sentences are noun modifier clauses, while the clause in this next sentence is not:

[Kare ga sore o iwanakatta] *no* ga ikenai.*	It is bad that he didn't say it.

> * This *no* represents *koto* "the fact" and is the equivalent of [. . .] *toiu koto ga ikenai.* This clause is not a restrictive modifier clause but is a *toiu* clause, even though the topic particle *wa* is not used in the clause. (See the following section, B.)

There are many other idiomatic constructions involving V-plain forms. If a V-plain form fits none of the cases discussed so far, one should consider it as an idiom but not a predicate of a clause. A partial list of such idiomatic constructions is provided in the appendix.

NOUN MODIFIER + ADVERBIAL PHRASE

[hikōki ga deru] toki (ni)	(at the time) when the plane leaves

The above clause is considered as a noun modifier modifying *toki*, with the time particle *ni* being attached to form an adverbial phrase indicating "the time when . . ."

[Denwa ga tōi] **toki** *(ni) wa* *kakenaosu.*	When I cannot hear well on the phone, I re-dial.
[Karada no chōshi ga hen na] **toki** *(ni) wa nomanai yō ni suru.*	When my health is not good, I try not to drink.
[Shingō ga kiiro no] **toki** *(ni)* *michi o watatta.*	I crossed the street when the signal was yellow.

⤷ Other particles can be attached to *toki* such as *kara*, *made*, and so on.

There are numerous adverbial constructions like the above, consisting of a noun modifier clause and a following noun often followed by a specific particle:

[. . .] *aida* "while" (throughout the time that an action or state continues)

[Hanako ga hanashite-iru] *aida Tarō wa damatte-ita.*	While Hanako was speaking, Taro kept silent.

[. . .] *aida ni* "while" (at some point during an action or state)

[Hanako ga hanashite-iru] aida ni Tarō wa shokuji o shite-shimatta.	While Hanako was talking, Taro finished eating.

[. . .] *baai (ni)* "in case of . . ."

[Kaji ga okotta] baai ni wa 119-ban e renraku shite-kudasai.	In case of fire please contact 119.

[. . .] *hodo/kurai* "to the extent, so . . . that" EXTENT

Soko wa [uo ga mina shini-ta-eru] hodo kitanai kawa ni natta.	It became such a polluted river that all the fish died off.
Kare wa [maijikan kurasu no ato de sensei ni shitsumon suru] kurai nesshin datta.	He was so enthusiastic that he asked the teacher questions after every class.

[. . .] *kagiri* "as long as . . ."

Seiseki wa [kurasu o yohodo yasumanai] kagiri daijōbu da.	As for the grade, it will be all right as long as one doesn't miss too many classes.
[Shachō ga konai] kagiri shiki wa hajimaranai.	So long as the president doesn't come, the ceremony won't begin.

(See Appendix § 1 for more expressions with *kagiri*.)

[. . .] *koro (ni)* "about the time when . . ."

Tarō wa [yūbinya ga kuru] koro ni soto ni deta.	Taro went outside about the time the mailman came.

[. . .] *mae ni* "before . . ."

Tarō wa [Hanako ga kuru] mae ni heya o sōji shita.	Taro cleaned the room before Hanako came.

[. . .] *sai (ni)* "at the time, upon doing . . ."

[Kasai ga okita] sai ni wa kono deguchi kara dete-kudasai.	In case fire breaks out please leave through this exit.

[. . .] *saichū ni* "in the middle of doing . . ."

[Jon ga tabete-iru] saichū ni denwa ga natta.	The telephone rang while John was (in the middle of) eating.

[. . .] *tame (ni)* CAUSE or PURPOSE

[Ōyuki ga futta] **tame ni** *kisha ga okureta.* (CAUSE)	Owing to a heavy snowfall the train was late.
[Kenkō o iji suru] **tame ni** *mainichi joggingu o suru.* (PURPOSE)	In order to maintain my health I jog everyday.

[. . .] *tokoro de* PLACE (of an action or event)

[Kinō Jon ga tabeta] tokoro de watakushi mo tabeta.	I, too, ate at the (same) place where John ate yesterday.

[. . .] *tokoro ni* LOCATION

[Kikō ga ii] tokoro ni sumitai.	I want to live in a place where the climate is good.

(See also ch. 4, § 10 for more on *tokoro*.)

[. . .] *uchi ni* "while . . ."

[Atsui] uchi ni nonde-kudasai.	Please drink while it's hot.
[Kuraku **naranai*** *] uchi ni kaerimashō.*	Let's go home before it **gets** dark.

* The negative form is used with *uchi ni* when the speaker feels that s/he will be troubled or disadvantaged if a certain situation occurs. In this second example, the approaching darkness is perceived as negative.

(See Appendix for more adverbial constructions of this kind.)

⤷ Note that although *aida, aida ni, uchi ni* and V-stem-*nagara* can all be translated as "while," the meanings are somewhat different.

In the case of V-stem + *nagara*, the subject of the verb must be the same as the
subject or topic of the main predicate, since V-stem *nagara* does not by itself
constitute a clause:

Jon wa (Jon ga) terebi o minagara tabete-ita.	John was eating while (he was) watching television.

In the case of *aida (ni)* and *uchi ni*, the subject of the clause and the subject or
topic of the main predicate need not be the same.

Watakushi wa [(watakushi ga) sono hanashi o kiite-iru] uchi ni namida ga dete-kita.	I started to weep as **I** was listening to the story.
Jon wa [Hanako ga tabete-iru] aida terebi o mite-ita.	While **Hanako** was eating, **John** was watching TV.
Jon wa [Hanako ga tabete-iru] aida ni dekaketa.	While **Hanako** was eating, **John** went out.
Jon wa [(Jon ga) nemuku naranai] uchi ni shukudai o shita.	**John** did his homework (during the time) before **he** got sleepy.
[Haha ga ki ga tsukanai] uchi ni watakushi wa kowareta osara o sutete-shimatta.	I threw away the broken plate while **my mother** wasn't noticing (= before she noticed).

The following take only *V-ta* form as the predicate of a modifier clause:

[. . . *V-ta*] *ato de* "after . . . did . . ."

[Minna ga tabeta] ato de hanasō.	Let's talk after everyone has eaten.

[. . . *V-ta*] *totan ni* "at the moment when . . ."

[Uchi ni tsuita] totan ni ame ga furi-dashita.	The moment I got to the house it began raining.

B. *TOIU* Clauses (in which *wa* can appear as well as *ga*)

Toiu clauses (often called appositive or complement clauses) give the content of the following noun, as in "the fact/story **that . . .**" They are normally translated as "that . . ." Either the subject particle *ga* or the topic particle *wa*, or both *wa* and *ga*, can appear in this kind of clause. However, the subject particle *ga* cannot be replaced by *no*. Basically *toiu*, which consists of the quotation particle *to* and the verb *iu* "to say," is inserted after the predicate—though it is often omitted.

⇨ The quotation particle *to* is normally contracted to *-(t)te* in spoken Japanese:

Nan teiu hito?	What is the person called?
Ame ga furu tte itta.	(He) said that it's going to rain.

(See ch. 4, § 8 for other functions of *to*.)

N and AN are followed by *da/dearu* but not by *no* or *na* at the end of *toiu* clauses:

[Jon no hahaoya wa nihon-jin (N) *da/dearu] toiu uwasa*	the rumor that John's mother is Japanese
[Jon no hahaoya wa genki (AN) *da/dearu] toiu henji*	the reply that John's mother is well

The *toiu* is often omitted:

[[Mō sugu kare wa shinu (V) *]* unmei ni aru* (V)*]* koto o shiranai.*	He doesn't know that he is destined to die soon.

> * The *toiu* has been omitted after the clauses "(that) he will die soon" and "(the fact that) he is destined . . ."

➥ When the *toiu* is omitted, *toiu* clauses look similar in structure to noun modifier clauses. However, **Noun Modifier Clauses** refers to "restrictive type" relative clauses discussed in the preceding section.

➥ *Toiu* clauses are not restrictive clauses.

[takara ga kare ni ataerareta] toiu unmei	the fate that the treasure was given to him

However, [*kare ni ataerareta*] *unmei* "the fate that was given him" is not a *toiu* clause but a restrictive and therefore noun modifier clause (discussed in the previous section).

⮕ The *-ō* and imperative (*-e/ro*) form may appear as the predicate of a *toiu* clause. The *toiu* cannot be omitted when following these forms.

[Tōhyō shinaosō] **toiu** *teian ga atta.*	There was a suggestion to revote.
Musuko ni [sugu uchi e kaere] **toiu** *denwa o shita.*	(I) made a phone call to my son to come home immediately.

⮕ Examples of *toiu* clauses:

[hito wa kanarazu shinu (V)] toiu unmei	the fate that the human being is bound to die
[Jon ga jikishachoo (N) da/dearu] toiu uwasa	the rumor that John is going to be the next company president
[josei wa ippan ni dansei yori jumyō ga nagai (ADJ)] toiu koto	the fact that in general the life span of women is longer than men's

Although any noun can follow *toiu*, the more common ones are: *koto* "fact, matter," *jijitsu* "fact," *hanashi* "story," *uwasa* "rumor," and *kibō* "hope." Although the *toiu* is often omitted after a clause, it is obligatory in the phrase N_1 *toiu* N_2, "N_2 called N_1": *Yamada toiu hito* "a man called Yamada."

Here are some more examples of *toiu* clauses:

[Kare no kōi wa rippa (AN) da/dearu] toiu iken ga aru.	There is an opinion that his action was admirable.
[Keiji wa A ga yōgisha (N) da/dearu] toiu hōkoku o shita.	The detective reported that A is the suspect.
Keiji wa [yōgisha ga sono jikoku ni gaishutsu shite-ita (V)] (toiu) jijitsu o tsukitometa.	The detective discovered the fact that the suspect had gone out at that time.

| Jon wa [(jibun ga) itsuka kokyō ni kaereru (V)] (toiu) kibō o idaite-ita. | John had the hope that some day (he) would be able to go back to his homeland. |

(See Appendix § 1 for idiomatic expressions involving *toiu*.)

➡ The content of a *toiu* clause can be a question.

↪ Note that the *toiu* after interrogative clauses cannot be omitted:

[naze mono ga shita e ochiru (V) ka] **toiu** gimon	the question of why things fall
[chikyū wa marui (ADJ) ka] **toiu** shitsumon	the question of whether the earth is round
[Tarō wa nihonjin (N) dearu* ka] **toiu** shitsumon	the question of whether Taro is Japanese
[Tarō wa genki (AN) dearu* ka] **toiu** shitsumon	the question of whether Taro is well

*Da after N/AN is omitted before *ka*, though *dearu* is not.

➡ *To itta (yō na)* can be used in place of *toiu* after a quoted N or a clause: . . . *to itta* "such as . . ." or . . . *to itta yō na* "something like . . ." The latter has a connotation of greater indirectness or vagueness.

| ekonomikku animaru to itta adana | a nickname such as "economic animal" |
| [An ōjo ga rikon suru] to itta yō na uwasa | a rumor to the effect that Princess Anne may divorce |

3.1.2 QUOTATION AND INTERROGATIVE CLAUSES

Just as in a *toiu* clause, **the topic particle** *wa* **or the subject particle** *ga* **(or both) can occur in quotation and interrogative clauses, but the subject** *ga* **cannot be replaced by** *no*.

A. Quotation Clauses

Quotation clauses consist of discourse quoted indirectly and followed by the particle *to*. Direct quotations enclosed in quotation marks (「   」) are also followed by *to*; but whereas in indirect quotation the predicate in the quoted clause must be in the plain form, in the case of direct quotation the predicate can be in either the formal or the plain form. Any of the plain forms can occur at the end of these clauses, including *-ō* forms and imperative (*-e/ro*) forms.

The contents of thoughts and feelings are also conveyed as indirect discourse through the use of the quotation particle. Quotation clauses are followed by such verbs as: *iu* "to say," *kiku* "to hear," *kaku* "to write," *omou* "to think/feel," *kanjiru* "to feel, "*kangaeru* "to think," *rikai suru* "to understand," and *setsumei suru* "to explain."

⇨ *. . . to suru* "to make it that . . ." is an expression used to denote a hypothetical situation: *A o B to suru* "suppose A is B," or *[teki ga kita] to suru* "suppose that the enemy has come." *. . . (mono) to shite-iru* means "consider that":

Karera wa [kaigi wa seikō shita (mono)] to shiteiru	They consider that the conference was a success.

(See also below § 3.1.3 and ch. 4, § 8 for other functions of *to*.)

Examples of quotation clauses:

Sono hito wa [tsugi no basu wa niji ni kuru (V)] to itta.	The man said that the next bus will come at two o'clock.
Garireo wa [chikyū wa marui (ADJ)] to itta.	Galileo said that the earth is round.
Jon wa [ashita mata ikō (V)] to teian shita.	John suggested that we go again tomorrow.

Chichi wa [sugu uchi e kaere (V)] to itta.	The father said to come home immediately.
Jon wa [jibun wa Amerikajin (N) da/ dearu] to itta.	John said that he is American.
Jon wa [Hokkaidō wa kirei (AN) da/ dearu] to omotta.	John thought that Hokkaido was beautiful.

⇨ N/AN is followed by *da/dearu* but not *no/na*.

The content of a quotation clause is rendered more indefinite by inserting a *ka*:
    . . . *to **ka** itta/kiita/kaita* "said/heard/wrote . . . or something like that."

| Hanako wa [Jon ga Amerika e kaette-shimatta (N)] to **ka** itta. | Hanako said that John has gone back to America or something to that effect. |

When the quoted clause is a question,

(1) *to* can be omitted:

| Watakushi wa Jon ni [itsu kuru ka] (to) kiita. | I asked John when he is coming. |

(2) *da* is omitted (but not *dearu*) after N/AN and before the question particle *ka*:

| Watakushi wa Jon ni [hahaoya wa/ga nihonjin (N) ka] (to) kiita. | I asked John if his mother is Japanese. |

and (3) when *ka dō ka* "whether or not" is used, the *to* is usually dropped:

| Watakushi wa Jon ni [okāsan ga nihonjin (N) ka dō ka] kiita. | I asked John whether or not his mother is Japanese. |

B. Interrogative Clauses as Noun Clauses

Interrogative clauses can serve as Ns. In such cases the clause either contains an interrogative word such as *dare, doko, itsu* and *nani*, or else it ends with *ka dō ka* "whether or not." *Da* after N/AN is omitted in interrogative clauses, while particles following such clauses may or may not be omitted.

N as Direct Object:

Watakushi wa [Jon no hahaoya wa/ga nihonjin (N) dearu ka dō ka] (o) shirabeta.	I checked whether or not John's mother is Japanese.
Watakushi wa [Jon ga doko e iku (V) ka] (o) shitte-iru.	I know where John is going.

Compare this with Indirect Quotation:

Watakushi wa Jon ni [doko e iku ka] (to) kiita.	I asked John where he was going.

N as Topic:

[Dare ga kaigi ni deru (V) ka] wa mondai dewa nai.	Who is going to attend the conference is not an issue.

N as Subject:

[Ashita Jon ga kuru ka dō ka] (ga) wakaranai.	(I) don't know whether John is coming tomorrow or not.

Other:

[Sore ga seikō suru ka dō ka] wa [Jon ga kuwawaru ka dō ka] ni kakatte-iru.	Whether or not (we) will succeed in this all depends on whether or not John will join (us).

⤷ It is also possible to interpret all the above examples as cases of *toiu* clauses in which *toiu koto* "the fact that . . ." has been omitted:

Watakushi wa [Jon ga doko e iku ka] (toiu koto) (o) shitte-iru.	I know (the matter concerning) where John is going.

However, in this book the kinds of interrogative clause discussed in this section are treated as N clauses rather than as *toiu* clauses.

See also "sentence-ending expressions" in ch. 4, § 14. When a sentence-ending expression is added to a sentence in order to qualify it in some way, any *wa* or *ga* occurring in the original sentence is retained.

Summary of Noun Modifier, Quotation, and Interrogative Clauses in Terms of Particles and Forms of Predicates

N Modifier Clauses:

[*ga/no V*/ADJ, N/AN dearu, N no,* or *AN na*] *N*

  **Imperative (-*e/ro*) form and *-ō* form do not appear.

***Toiu* Clauses:**

[*wa/ga V/ADJ, N/AN da/dearu*] *(toiu) N*

Interrogative: [*wa/ga V/ADJ, N/AN dearu* ka*] *toiu N*

  * *Da* is omitted before *ka*.

Quotation Clauses:

[*wa/ga V/ADJ, N/AN da/dearu*] *to iu/kangaeru,* etc.

Interrogative: [*wa/ga V/ADJ, N/AN dearu ka**] *to kiku*

  * *Ka dō ka* can be used when an interrogative word is not used in the clause. *Da* is omitted before *ka*.

Interrogative Clauses as N Clauses:

with an interrogative word:

[*wa/ga* V/ADJ, N/AN dearu ka*] *wa/ga/o/mo*

  * When an interrogative word appears as a subject it is followed by *ga* but not by *wa*; *dare ga, doko ga, dono N ga,* etc.

without an interrogative word:

[*wa/ga V/ADJ, N/AN dearu ka dō ka*] *wa/ga/o/mo*

3.1.3 OTHER SUBORDINATE CLAUSES

There are numerous expressions in Japanese which contain V-plain forms that are not followed by a noun—and so are not noun modifier clauses. These clauses may contain a subject + *ga* or a contrast *wa*, but not *no* or a topic *wa*. If the word following a V-plain form is not a noun followed by a particle such as *wa* (topic), *ga* (subject), *o* (object), or *ni* (indirect object), it is probably part of an idiomatic expression. In this case one has to consult a dictionary or a reference book to check the special meaning of the expression or construction. (Some of the more frequently used expressions are included in the appendix.)

... + *to** "when/if"

[. . . Plain Nonpast] *to* "when"

*[Sono ishi o mochiagete-miru (v)] **to** iroirona mushi ga ita.*	When I tried lifting that stone, there were various insects [under it].
Kodomo wa [hahaoya (N) da] to iukoto o kiku.	The child listens when it is the mother (who is speaking).

[. . . V-*(r)u/ta*] *to dōji ni* "at the same time as . . ."

*[Beru ga nari-owaru] **to** dōji ni densha ga deta.*	As soon as the bell stopped ringing, the train departed.

[. . . V-*(r)u*] *to sugu (ni)* "when . . ., immediately after . . ."
[. . . V-*(r)u*] *to totsuzen/totan ni* "at the moment when . . ."

*[Chōshoku o taberu] **to** sugu dekaketa.*	When (I) finished eating breakfast (I) went out (immediately).
*[Tamatebako no futa o akeru] **to** totsuzen naka kara shiroi kemuri ga dete-kita.*	The moment (he) opened the treasure box, white smoke suddenly came out.

↳ [. . . *V-ta*] *totan ni* is a noun modifier type adverbial clause (see above) and has a similar meaning to the above: [. . . *aketa*] *totan ni* "at the moment when he opened . . ."

[. . . Plain Nonpast] *to (itsumo/kanarazu)*
"if/when(ever) . . . , always. . ."

This construction is used to assert regular **sequential occurrences**: when A happens B always follows. The clause preceding *to* and the main predicate stand in a constant sequential relationship.

*[Koko o hineru (V)] **to** mizu ga deru.*	When you turn this, water comes out.
*Maitoshi [harusaki ni naru (V)] **to** kanarazu koshi ga itaku naru.*	Every year when spring approaches, my lower back aches without fail.
*Hanako wa [tesuto no ten ga yokunai (ADJ)] **to** kigen ga waruku naru.*	Hanako gets into a bad mood whenever her test score isn't good.
*[Aite ga meue no hito (N) da] **to** kinchō suru.*	(I) become nervous when the other party is older (than I).
*[Karada no chōshi ga hen (AN) da] **to** amari nomenai.*	When my health isn't good, I can't drink very much.

⇨ *-tara(ba)* and *-(r)eba* (see below, § 3.2.1) can be used in all the above examples. However, *-tara* conveys a greater sense of a causal relationship between the two events, while *to* simply presents them as sequential. The *-(r)eba* construction has the connotation of either causal or sequential occurrences.

SEQUENCE	*Haru ga kuru **to** hana ga saku.*	Whenever spring comes, flowers bloom.
CAUSAL	*Haru ga ki**tara** hana ga saku.*	When (if) spring comes, then flowers bloom.
EITHER	*Haru ga ku**reba** hana ga saku.*	When/if/every time spring comes, flowers bloom.

⇨ Note that . . . *toki (ni)* "(at the time) when . . ." is a N-modifier construction (see above, § 3.1.1A) rather than an adverbial clause.

[. . . Plain Nonpast] *to* "if"

*[Kono kusuri o nomu (v)] **to** naoru.*	If you take this medicine you will get better.
*[Shiken ga amari muzukashii (ADJ)] **to** komaru.*	If the exam is too hard I'll be in trouble.
*[Kondo no doyōbi ni Jon mo hima (AN) da] **to** tsugō ga ii.*	It would be convenient if John, too, is free this coming Saturday.

➦ If the main predicate consists of **a request, invitation, command, or volitional,** *to* is **not used** at the end of the preceding subordinate clause; rather *toki ni* or **a** *tara* **construction is used** instead. **This is because *to* is used for repeated occurrences,** while a request, command, or invitation is a one-time event. Compare the following examples.

*Tōkyō e iku **to** (**itsumo**) yōfuku o kaitaku naru.*	Whenever I go to Tokyo, I feel like buying clothes.

REQUEST:

*Tōkyō e itta **toki (ni)**/**ittara** yōfuku o katte kudasai.*	Please buy clothes when you go to Tokyo.

COMMAND:

*Shigoto ga owatta **toki (ni)**/ owa**ttara** denwa shinasai.*	Give me a call when you finish your work.

INVITATION:

*Tōkyō e kita **toki (ni)**/**kitara** uchi e yorimasenka.*	Won't you stop by our house next time you come to Tokyo?

VOLITIONAL:

*Mi ga akaku natta **toki (ni)**/ **nattara** torimashō.*	Let's pick the fruit when it becomes red.

[. . .] *to suru to* or *to suru nara* "supposing . . ." HYPOTHETICAL

The first *to* in this expression is the quotation particle, while the second *to* is a conjunction.

[Rokuji ni deru (V)] **to suru to** *goji ni wa okinakutewa ikenai.*	Supposing we are to leave at six, then we should get up at five.
[Kare ga hannin (N) da] **to suru to** *doko de kyōki o te ni ireta no darō ka.*	Supposing he is the culprit, I wonder where he got the weapon?
[Rokuji ni deta* (V)] **to suru to** *mō tsuku koro da.*	Supposing he left at six, he should be here by now.

    * The past tense can also be used with *to suru to.*

[Kare ga dekinai] **to suru nara** *hoka ni dare ga dekiru darō ka.*	Supposing he isn't able to do it, I wonder who else could?

    (See Appendix for . . . *(mono)* **to** *shite,* . . .
    to *shite mo* and . . . **to** *shitara/sureba.*)

[. . . Plain Nonpast] *to* WISH

[Kono uchi ga motto ōkii] **to** *ii noni.**	I wish this house were a lot bigger.

    * *Noni* literally means "although, in spite of" and is attached at the end
of this kind of wish-expression (=subjunctive) to express a condition that
is contrary to reality. What is omitted here is: *(genjitsu ni wa) ōkikunai*
"(in reality) it is not big." Other such exclamatory phrases are *mono o* or
no da ga/keredo(mo).

Nara (in the next section) and NON-PLAIN forms such as *-tara* and *-(r)eba* (below, § 3.2.1) are also used to give a subjunctive sense.

. . . *nara(ba)* "if/in case . . ." CONDITION

[Kare ga iku (V)] **nara** *watakushi wa ikitakunai.*	If he is going, I don't want to go.
[Te ga tsumetai (ADJ)] **nara** *tebukuro o shitara ii.*	If your hands are cold, it would be good if you wore gloves.
[Heya ga kirei (AN) dearu*] **nara** *sōji shinakutemo ii.*	If the room is clean, you don't have to clean it.
[Ochiau jikan ga sanji (N) dearu*] **nara** *daijōbu da.*	If the time to meet is three o'clock, it's all right.

> * The nonpast affirmative form of the copula *da* after N/AN does not appear before *nara* in the above sentences, while its negative form does: *kirei* **de(wa) nai** *nara.*

[Sanji (N) de(wa) nai] **nara** *ikanai.*	If it is not three o'clock, I won't go.
Moshi [watashi ga tori (N) dearu] **nara** *tonde-iku noni.*	If I were a bird, I would fly there.

The ending *noni* here gives this sentence a subjunctive sense.

. . . *kara/node* or *yue(ni)* "since/because . . ." REASON

Kara tends to be slightly less formal and used widely in speaking, while *node* tends to be used in writing and as well as in very polite speech. *Yue ni* is highly literary.

FORMAL SPEECH STYLE

[Kaze o hiita] **kara** *shigoto o yasumimasu.*	I will not (come to) work because I have caught a cold.

VERY POLITE FORMAL SPEECH STYLE

*[Kaze o hiki**mashita***]* **node/kara** *yasumasete-itadakimasu.*	I would like you to allow me to miss work since I have caught a cold.

* In polite speech the V-*masu* form can be used within a sentence.

WRITING

[Kaze o hiita (V)] **node/kara** *shigoto o yasunda.*	I missed work because I caught a cold.
*[Senkō ga nihonshi (N) **da/dearu**] **kara** nihongo o benkyō suru.*	Since my major is Japanese history, I study Japanese.
*[Kyō wa doyōbi (N) **na/dearu***]* **node** *hannichi shika hatarakanai.*	Since today is Saturday, (I) work for only half a day.

* The nonpast form of the copula *da* after N/AN appears as **na/dearu** (but not *da*) before *node* and *yueni*.

*Kare wa [chichi ga amari ni genkaku (AN) **na/dearu***]* **yueni** *kaette hankō shite-iru.*	He is rebelling all the more because his father is so strict.

⮕ *V-te kara* means "after doing . . ."; see below, § 3.2.1.

⬛ *. . . keredo(mo)** "although . . ."

[Ame ga futte-inakatta (V)] **keredo(mo)** *kasa o motte-itta.*	Although it wasn't raining, I took an umbrella with me.

* The *mo* is often omitted.

⮕ The conjunction *ga* may be used in place of *keredo(mo)* in the above sentence. However, it will be different structurally because *ga* connects two sentences while *keredo(mo)* follows a subordinate clause:

PLAIN STYLE

Ame ga/wa futte-inakatta ga, kasa o motte-itta.

SENTENCE₁ + *ga*,   SENTENCE₂

FORMAL SPEECH STYLE

Ame ga/wa futte-imasendeshita ga, kasa o motte-ikimashita.

SENTENCE₁ + *ga*,   SENTENCE₂

Keredomo cannot be used in this second example, since it must follow a clause. (An exception to this rule is the use of *keredomo* in the very polite speech style, where it may follow a sentence ending in the *-masu* or *desu* form.) In other words it can only follow the plain form predicate (*futte-inakatta*).

... *noni/nimokakawarazu* "in spite of the fact that"

[Ame ga futte-ita (V)] **noni/ nimokakawarazu** *dekaketa.*	In spite of the fact that it was raining, (I) went out.
[Kaze o hiite-ita (V)] **noni/ nimokakawarazu** *oyogi ni itta.*	In spite of the fact that (I) had a cold, I went for a swim.
Kare wa [sore ga kirai (AN) **na/ dearu*]** **noni** *sō ienakatta.*	In spite of the fact that he didn't like it, he couldn't say so.

* The nonpast form of the copula *da* after N/AN appears as **na/dearu** before *noni*.

Kare wa [nichiyōbi (N) **dearu*] nimokakawarazu** *shukkin shita.*	He went to work in spite of the fact that it was Sunday.

* The nonpast form of the copula *da* after N/AN appears as **dearu** before *nimokakawarazu*.

(See below, § 3.2.1 for V-*temo* "even if.")

3.2 Non-Plain Forms

3.2.1 SUBORDINATE CLAUSES

While many subordinate clauses end in plain forms, some end in other forms such as -tara(ba), -(r)eba, -temo, and -te kara.

. . . -tara(ba)   Condition and Subjunctive

V-tara/nakattara
ADJ-kattara/kunakattara
N/AN deattara (dattara)/denakattara
"if/when something happens"

[Niji ni nattara (V)] hajimeyō.	Let's begin at (when it becomes) two o'clock.
[Kawa ga katakattara (ADJ)] muita hō ga ii.	If the skin is tough, it is better to peel it off.
[Tsugi no densha ga kyūkō (N) denakattara] noranai.	If the next train is not the express, I won't take it.
[(Moshi mangaichi) tenki ga hen dattara (AN)] yame ni suru.*	Should the weather not be good, we will cancel (the event).

* *Mangaichi* literally means "one ten-thousandth" and is translated "if something should happen."

[(Moshi) hane ga attara (V)] soko e tonde iku noni.	If I had wings, I would fly there.

[(Moshi) [kare ga Amerika e iku] to shitara(V)] itsu iku no ka.	If he is to go to America, when is he going?

. . . -(r)eba   Provision and Subjunctive

V-(r)eba/nakereba
ADJ-kereba/kunakereba
N/AN deareba/de(wa)nakereba:
"if, provided that . . ."

[(Moshi*) ame ga fureba (V)] ikanai.	If it should rain, I won't go.

* *Moshi* "if" is often omitted.

[(Moshi) mi ga akakereba (ADJ)] taberareru.	Provided that the fruit is red, we can eat it.
[(Moshi) jikan ga motto areba (V)] Kōbe made ashi ga nobaseru no da ga* . . .	If (I) had more time, I could extend my trip to Kobe.

* The conjunction *ga* is used here to imply "but" followed by an omitted sentence such as *jikan ga nai kara ikenai* "since there isn't time, I can't go."

[(Moshi) okāsan ga byōki deareba (N)] shikata ga nai ga.	If it is the case that your mother is ill, it cannot be helped.
[(Moshi) soko ga fuben deareba (AN)] karinai.	If it is the case that that place is inconvenient, (I) will not rent it.
[Kon'na uchi ni sumereba (V)] ii no da ga.	I wish I could live in this kind of house.

Note the following unusual use of the conditional:

[Koko made kureba/kitara] mō daijōbu da.	Since we have come this far, we are safe.

In this example our coming this far has already taken place and should therefore have been expressed as *koko made kita kara* "because we have come this far." The conditional form is used in this case even though the condition has actually been fulfilled. The meaning is something like: "If we make it this far (and in fact we have made it this far), then we are safe."

(*ikura**) . . . *-temo* "even though/if . . ."

> *V-temo/nakutemo**\
> *ADJ-kutemo/nakutemo*\
> *N/AN demo* or *deattemo/de(wa) nakutemo*

> * This adds the meaning of "no matter how much . . . may . . ." when attached to the examples below. Other such words are: *donnani* "how much," *nando/nankai* "how many times."

> ** *-temo* is sometimes replaced by these classical forms: *V-(e)domo, ADJ-keredomo, N/AN dearedomo.*

[Ame ga futte mo (V)] itta.	Even though it rained, I went.
[Mi ga aokutemo (ADJ)] tabeta.	Even though the fruit was green, I ate it.
[Kodomo ga byōki demo (N)] dekaketa.	Even though the child was sick, I went out.
[Tenki ga hen (AN)] demo iku.	Even if the weather is not good, I will go.
[Ikura ame ga futtemo] mada tarinai.	No matter how much it rains, it still won't be sufficient.
[Kare ga nando kiitemo] kuwashii kotae ga erarenakatta.	No matter how many times he asked, he couldn't get a clear answer.

Certain *V-te* forms expressing permission, negative permission, prohibition, and obligation contain clauses from the structural point of view, but since they are simple constructions of a more idiomatic nature they need not be marked as clauses. (See ch. 4, § 2.5.)

. . . *V-te kara* "since/after . . ."

[Jon ga kite] kara tabeyō.	Let's eat after John comes.

[Seiyō no bunka ga haittekite] kara nihongo wa kawatta.	The Japanese language has changed since Western culture came in.

3.2.2 MULTIPLE PREDICATES

Two or more sentences can be put together into one sentence. This means that a sentence can have more than one predicate, as can a clause. Multiple predicates can either share the same topic or subject, or else they can have different ones.

-*te* Form

AFFIRMATIVE: *V-te*
 ADJ-kute
 N/AN de/deari/deatte

NEGATIVE: *V-naide/zuni*
 ADJ-kunakute
 N/AN de(wa) nakute
 (*V-nakute*)

The *V-te* form within a sentence is used to connect two sub-sentences in certain ways. It can be considered as the predicate of the first sentence, while the second predicate can be the predicate of the second sentence or of the main sentence. Sometimes more than one *-te* form occurs within a sentence. It is important to group such *-te* forms carefully, examining the context and function of each one thoroughly. One should bear in mind that *-te* forms do not necessarily share the same topic or subject. (See, for example, some of the sentences on the next page.)

The tense of the final predicate determines the tense of *V-te*'s that are grouped together in previous clauses or sub-sentences. When the final predicate includes auxiliaries for aspect* and various moods, these normally affect the other *-te*'s in the same group. (See ch. 3, § 2.3.)

* The aspect of the verb indicates, for example, the state resulting from an action's having taken place:

Kare wa nihon e itte-iru.	He has gone to Japan (= is now in the state of being there).

Kare wa nihon e itta.	He went to Japan (but may have come back or gone on elsewhere).
Kare wa nihon e itte benkyō o hajimete-iru.	He **has gone** to Japan and **has begun** studying.

The aspect "has done . . ." is attached to both verbs in this last example.

(See ch. 4, § 2.5 and Appendix for *V-te* constructions that do not serve as multiple predicates.)

> *V-te* (gerund form), *V-naide/zuni*

SEQUENCE* or LISTING OUT

* In order to emphasize sequence, *V-te kara* or *V-te sorekara* is used.

Ha o migaite kao o arau. PRED₁ PRED₂	(I) **brush** my teeth and then **wash** my face.

Daigaku e itte,
   PRED₁
kurasu e ikanaide/ikazuni,
   PRED₂
(sono mama) toshokan e itta.
      PRED₃
	Having gone to the university, I **didn't go** to class but **went** (straight) to the library.
	
	Or: I went to the library instead of going to class.

Ninjin wa, kawa o mukanaide/mukazuni kiru. PRED₁ PRED₂	As for the carrots, **not peeling** the skin, (I) **slice** them.*

* This could be considered a "manner" construction with the meaning of "slice them without peeling the skin." (See next page.)

↳ The V-*nakute* form can also be used in listing out:

Ninjin wa kawa o mukanaide/mukazuni/ *mukanakute, jagaimo wa kawa o muku.* PRED₁ PRED₂	With carrots I don't peel the skin, but with potatoes I do.

REASON

A comma tends to be used after the reason *V-te.*

Ame ga futte, michi ga waruku natta. 　　PRED₁　　　　　　PRED₂	Because it **rained**, the road **became** muddy.

☞ The V-*nakute* can be used to give a negative reason:

Ame ga furanaide/furazuni/furanakute, 　　　　　　　　PRED₁ *nōmin ga komatte-iru.* 　　PRED₂	Because it **doesn't rain**, the farmers **are in trouble**.

MANNER

Basu ni notte iku. 　　PRED₁ PRED₂	(I) **go** by (**riding** the) bus.
Bentō o motanaide/motazuni 　　　　　　　PRED₁ *dekaketa.* 　　PRED₂	(I) **went out without taking** a boxed lunch.

ADJ-kute, ADJ-kunakute and *N/AN-de, N/AN-dewa nakute*

LISTING OUT similar features*

　　* Normally features are listed in groups of similar (favorable or unfavor-
　　able) qualities: *hirokute utsukushii niwa* "a spacious and beautiful gar-
　　den," rather than *semakute utsukushii niwa* "an unspacious and beautiful
　　garden." The latter would be *semai keredomo utsukushii niwa* "a beautiful
　　garden though small."

ADJ-kute ADJ

Kono momo wa ōkikute amai. 　　　　　　　PRED₁　PRED₂	This peach **is big** and **sweet**.

Kono momo wa amakunakute
          PRED₁
mi* mo katai.
          PRED₂
	This peach **is not sweet** and also the flesh **is hard.**

* *mi* is "fruit, content, what is inside."

AN de ADJ:

Ano hito wa kirei* de omoshiroi. PRED₁ PRED₂	That woman **is beautiful** and **interesting.**

* *Kirei* when used of a person normally refers to a woman. In the case of men one uses *hansamu na* (AN) or *bidanshi* (N).

Sono hito wa kirei dewa nakute
                    PRED₁
hin mo warui.
          PRED₂
	That woman **is not beautiful** and also **is not refined.**

N de N da:

Kare wa Itariajin de* gaka da. PRED₁ PRED₂	He **is Italian** and **is a painter.**

* This *de* should be distinguished from the instrumental particle *de*, "by means of, with," and from the place particle meaning "at, in."

Kare wa itariajin dewa nakute
                    PRED₁
gaka de mo* nai.
          PRED₂
	He **is not Italian** nor **is he a painter.**

* *Mo* has replaced the original *wa*.

REASON

ADJ-kute V:

Kore wa muzukashikute wakaranai. PRED₁ PRED₂	Since this **is difficult**, I don't **understand** it.

Kore wa amakunakute taberarenai. PRED₁　　PRED₂	Since this **is not sweet**, I **can't eat** it.

AN de V:

Bureeki ga hen de 　　　PRED₁ *shūri shite-moratta.* 　PRED₂	Because the brakes **were bad**, I **had** them **repaired**.
Koko wa shizuka ja nakute 　　　　PRED₁ *benkyō dekinai.* 　PRED₂	Since this place **is not quiet**, I **can't study**.

N de V:

Kare wa kawarimono de 　　　　PRED₁ *kirawarete-iru.* 　PRED₂	Because he **is eccentric**, he is **disliked**.
Koko wa kankōchi ja nakute 　　　　PRED₁ *amari konde-inai.* 　PRED₂	Because this **isn't a tourist place it isn't crowded**.
Setsumei ga eigo de wakaranai. 　　　PRED₁　PRED₂	Since the explanation **is** (in) English I **don't understand** it.

↪ The predicates in this last sentence share the same subject but not the same topic. *Watakushi* "I" is the topic for PRED₂ but not for PRED₁.

> Variations of the *-te* form

➡ In many cases the **V-stem** (the form that results from dropping the suffix *-masu*) is used instead of *V-te*, in which case it is almost always **followed by a comma**. In the case of *ADJ-kute* the *te* may be omitted, though the *de* of *AN-de* may not be. The V-stem tends to be used in literary style and to show the reason for the main verb, while *V-te* without a following comma rather denotes manner. However, both forms can be used to show sequence as well. In this book the V-stem used by itself within a sentence in place of *V-te* is treated as *V-te*.

*Kare no kokoku chibetto wa nairiku ni **ari** (= atte)* (LISTING OUT), *irioiro na minzoku ni kakomarete-iru bakaridenaku, sono mura ga taishōrūto ni ichishite-**ori****(REASON), *sono sonchōsan ni totte wa, kotonaru shisutemu no hitobito ni sessuru toiu koto wa, nichijō sahanji **deari** (LISTING OUT), nanra no teikō o motsu mono de wa nakatta no dearu.*	His home country, Tibet, is inland, **and** not only is it surrounded by various peoples, but also his village is located on the caravan route, **and so** for the village chief to have contact with people involved in different systems was an everyday event **and** (=to which) he did not have any resistance

* *Ori* is the stem of the humble verb *oru* "to be" (*ori* "to be [animate]" in classical Japanese). However, it is used here in place of *ite*, the -*te* form of *iru* to show the state: *ichishite-iru* "is being located." This usage is common in written Japanese and does not convey a humble sense when used with *V-te*.

Kono (= 1884) shigatsu ni wa Also sprach Zarathustra *no daisanbu ga shuppan sarete-**ori**, Niiche wa kono daisanbu o motte* Zarathustra *wa ichiō kanketsu shita mono to kangaete-ita.*	In April (of 1884) Part Three of *Also sprach Zarathustra* had been published, **and so** Nietzsche was thinking that *Zarathustra* had been more or less completed with this third part.

V-te-oru is also used in story telling:

Tsuru wa mainichi hata o otte-orimashita.	Tsuru was weaving everyday.

*Ekonomikku-animaru-ron ni wa, gaikokujin gawa kara no nihonjin e no hinan, kōgeki no katachi o torumono to, sore o **uke** (SEQUENCE) nihonkokunai ni oite nihonjin no kokorogamae toka, shisei nitsuite no giron no futatsu ga aru.*	As for the idea of [the Japanese being] Economic Animals, there are two arguments: one that takes the form of criticism or an attack from the side of foreigners, and the other, **in response to the above**, argued domestically [=from among Japanese people themselves] concerning their mental attitude or attitude (in general)."

⮕ In the case of verbal nouns (ch. 4, § 3.2) consisting of a "head noun" (normally of Chinese origin) and the verb *suru* "to do," the *shite* or even V-stem *shi* may be omitted, especially in official reports or newspaper articles. These forms will be followed by a comma. Such verbal head nouns are also treated as *V-te* forms in this book.

| *Monbushō wa . . . o **kikaku** (shi-te), jikkō ni utsushita.* | The Ministry of Education planned . . . and carried it out. |

Even if there are no apparent *-te* forms of verbs, as in the above examples, readers should carefully examine all elements of the sentence so that they can successfully group them together as multiple predicates. Learners should always **be alert for possible *-te* forms.**

⮕ The V-*zu* form normally takes *ni* and means "without doing . . ." or "instead of doing . . ." Note that the *-zu* form of the verb *suru* "to do" is *sezu*. (See also ch. 4, § 2.1.3.)

The negative *-te* form of the verb *aru* "to exist (inanimate)" is not *naide* but *nakute*:

| *Okane ga nakute . . .* | I didn't have any money, so . . . |

⮕ The *de* of N/AN *de* has alternative forms, *deari* and *deatte*, which are the stem and *-te* forms of *dearu* respectively (*deari* being derived from *nite* "in, at" and *ari* "exist" in classical Japanese).

| *Kare wa gakusha deari/deatte seijika demo aru.* | He is a scholar and is also a statesman. |

⮕ Special literary form of *-te*:

> *V-zu shite = V-naide/nakute*
> *ADJ-ku shite = ADJ-kute*
> *N/AN ni shite/nite = N/AN de*

| *Yomazu shite wakaru hazu ga nai.* | There is no reason to expect that one can understand (it) without reading (it). |
| *Kare wa wakaku shite kono yo o satta.* | He died (left this world) young. |

fukuzatsu ni shite nankai na setsumei	an explanation that is compli-cated and difficult to understand

Other Types of Multiple Predicate

X *tari* Y *tari*

"do things like X or Y" or "sometimes . . . is X or Y, among other things"

Kenkō o tamotsu tame ni oyo-idari (V) hashittari (V) suru.	In order to maintain my health I do things like swimming or running.
Shūnyū wa ōkattari (ADJ) sukunakattari (ADJ) suru.	As for income, sometimes it is large and other times it is small.
Kyōshi wa Nihonjin (N) deattari Amerikajin (N) deattari suru.	As for the teacher, it can be Japanese or American (among other nationalities).

The following examples contain different subjects for each predicate:

*Tokidoki koe no **chōshi** ga hen (AN) dattari **atama** ga itakatttari (ADJ) suru.*	Sometimes the condition of my voice is bad or else I get a headache (among other things).
*Sono kodomo wa totemo yowakute, **isha** ga hinpan ni yobaretari (V) **uba** ga yatowaretari (V) shita.*	Since the child was very weak, a doctor was frequently called on or else a nanny was hired (among other things that had to be done).

The following constructions involving multiple predicates take plain forms:

X *bakari/dake/nomi de naku* Y *mo* OR: X *nominarazu* Y *mo*

"not only X but also Y"

Jon wa Chūgokugo o benkyō shita (V) bakari de naku Nihongo mo wakaru (V).	John not only studied Chinese, but he also understands Japanese.

Tomodachi wa mina shinsetsu de Tarō ga kagu o hakonde-kureta (V) bakari de naku Hanako ga uchi no sōji mo tetsudatte kureta (V).	Friends were all kind, and not only did Taro carry the furniture (for me) but also Hanako helped me clean the house.
Kono ume wa hana ga utsu-kushii (ADJ) bakari de naku edaburi mo (= ga) migoto (AN) da.	Not only does this plum tree have beautiful flowers, but its branches also grow beautifully (= in a beautiful shape).

(See Appendix § 1, under *bakari*, for a case where X and Y are nouns.)

X *shi* Y *mo suru/aru* (or any predicate)

"X and, moreover, Y . . ."

Jinkō ga amari ni fueru to hitobito wa hinkon ni naru (V) shi shizenkankyō mo (= ga) hakai sareru (V).	When the population increases excessively, people become poor and, moreover, the natural environment is destroyed.
Mangō wa amai (ADJ) shi kaori mo (= ga) dokutoku da.	Mangoes are sweet and, what's more, the fragrance is unique.
Kare wa mikake wa/ga/mo rippa da (AN) shi jinkaku mo (= ga) subarashii.	His appearance is grand and, moreover, his personality is also wonderful.
Tarō wa Nihonjin da (N) shi nihonkokuseki mo (= o) motte-iru (V).	Taro is not only Japanese but also has Japanese nationality.

Chapter Two

Developing Strategies

STRATEGIC EXERCISE A

1. *. . . da* 57
2. *. . . V* 62
3. *. . . shirabeta* 65
4. *. . . itte-ita* 69
5. *. . . to ieru* 76
6. *. . . to omowareru* 79

STRATEGIC EXERCISE B

Sentence 1 85
Sentence 2 88
Sentence 3 91
Sentence 4 96
Sentence 5 101
Sentence 6 104
Sentence 7 111
Sentence 8 115

Developing Strategies

READING COMPREHENSION is a process of decoding sentences according to their contexts, to which each sentence in turn contributes. At the sentence level it involves **two types of decoding**: decoding of **the structure of the sentence** and of **the meaning of words placed in a particular context**. These two types of decoding take place concurrently, mutually interacting, until one finally arrives at an understanding of the entire sentence. While the structure of the sentence will determine the meanings of the words in it, the words in turn also help to constitute the structure. However, since the surface meanings of words are relatively easy to come by, through the reader's memory or information given by a dictionary, students tend to be over-dependent on such readily available meanings—and thus to ignore the importance of analyzing the structure.

In this chapter, students are **encouraged to ignore the meanings of the words temporarily**, so that they may **focus** instead **on the structure of the sentence**. More specifically, students will learn how to "**read the structure,**" to utilize structural clues to analyze sentences, in such a way that they can develop the skill of decoding the structure of the written sentence. They will develop techniques to identify the major elements of a sentence in order to determine the sentence pattern, to identify subordinate clauses accurately and grasp their relation to the major elements, and to develop strategies for analyzing particularly problematic structures.

In order for students to be able to focus on the structure, this section presents artificial sentences in which the actual words are hidden, except for predicates, particles, some nouns and other elements that are structurally significant. Sentences are written in Romanization in this chapter since the objective is to learn strategies rather than getting used to the actual reading of *kana* and *kanji*. In Strategic Exercise A, students are expected to develop strategic techniques by answering guided questions and reading relevant structural notes while each sentence expands to its full length. The actual words are given when necessary.

In Strategic Exercise B, entire sentences are given in which the actual words in the sentence are replaced by letters of the alphabet, as in mathematical formulas which represent only the abstract relationships among various possible numbers. Students are expected to develop further strategic techniques with the help of guiding questions similar to those in Exercise A. The meanings of the words will again be given, so that students may continue to focus on strategies.

In both sections the sentences are translated into English, first as they are, and then with the actual words. The reader will thus learn how to integrate consciously the two levels of meaning, structural and non-structural. Throughout this chapter students are encouraged to consult or review relevant grammatical points in chapter 1 and chapter 4 so that they can develop their knowledge of grammar into good working condition. The next chapter will present structurally problematic sentences that provide the opportunity for students to apply and develop the strategies and techniques learned in this chapter.

Strategic exercise A

$$\boxed{\textbf{1.} \quad \ldots DA}$$

This is the end of the first sentence to be considered. In actual reading, one recognizes quite a few words and begins to make sense of them, even on a first reading. This is of course an important process in comprehension, but for now let us ignore the words entirely and assume that . . . *da* is all we see. Our focus here is the sentence ending, the PREDICATE of the sentence. The copula *da* may be preceded by a N or AN. It can also follow a *no* of EMPHASIS or SOFTENER (see ch. 4, § 6.4): *V/ADJ* + *no* or *N/AN* + *na* + *no*. Occasionally *da* may follow a particle (as in: . . . **kara** *da* ". . . is because"; see ch. 1, § 1.1). We now look to the left of *da*:

1 ... *N da.*

The main predicate of this sentence is: *N da*: "(Something/someone) is N" as in (*Kore wa*) *hon da* "(This) is a book." The pattern of this kind of sentence is *N wa N da*.

➥ **Look for the topic of the sentence.** In order to find the topic word **look for the topic particle** *wa*, which should be somewhere **to the left (ahead) of the predicate.**

2 ... N_1 *wa** ... N_2 *da*. "N_1 is N_2."

Nouns can be modified by:

    a. an *ADJ*, *N* + *no*, or *AN* + *na*

    b. a noun modifier clause** the ending (predicate) of which will be in plain form: *V, ADJ, N/AN dearu, N* + *no*, or *AN* + *na*

c. a *toiu* clause — or else by a combination of these three.

> * There is the possibility that N₁ could be an emphasized subject followed by the subject emphasis particle *ga* (ch. 4, § 5.2.2). The meaning of the sentence would then be "It is N₁ that is N₂," instead of "N₁ is N₂." However, at this stage it would be difficult to determine whether a *ga* to the left of the predicate is the emphasis particle for the subject of the main predicate or the subject particle in a modifier clause for N₂.
>
> ** It is of crucial importance to be thoroughly familiar with the different possible constructions that may be found within these two different types of clause. Please review §§ 3.1.1 A and B of ch. 1.

➥ Are there any modifiers for these nouns? Look immediately* to the left of N₁ and N₂ respectively for any plain forms.

> * It is possible for modifiers such as *ADJ, N no, AN na* — or even another modifier clause — to be inserted before the noun to be modified. Such is the case with multiple modifiers: e.g. **N no ADJ** + N (*Jon no atarashii shigoto* "John's new job") or **[ ] N no ADJ** + N ([*Amerika e kaetta*] *Jon no atarashii shigoto* "the new job of John's, who went back to America").

A V-plain form that does not come immediately before the noun to be modified could be one of those multiple modifiers; or else it could be the predicate of a subordinate clause in an adverbial construction (see ch. 1, § 3.1.3) or of an adverbial clause (ch. 1, § 3.2). But for now let us assume that this sentence does not contain such adverbial clauses or multiple modifiers.

3 ... **katta** (Vt) *N₁ wa* ... **ii** (ADJ) *N₂ da.*
     bought   good

Katta is the verb plain form and is therefore the predicate of a modifier clause for N₁.

> ➥ **Is there a subject** for this predicate *katta*? **Look to the left** of *katta* **for a subject particle** *ga* **or** *no.* If the topic particle *wa* occurs, then this is a *toiu* clause from which the *toiu* has been omitted.

4 > [... *N₃* **ga** ... *katta*] *N₁ wa* ... *ii N₂ da.*
        SUBJ   PRED

> ➤   indicates the beginning of the sentence.

The closest subject and predicate are normally grouped together to form a clause; therefore, it is unlikely that N_3 would be the subject for N_2 *da*, the main predicate.

TRANSLATION: "N_1 which N_3 bought is . . . good N_2"

5 . . . ii N_2 da

Ii is an ADJ modifying N_2. It could be the predicate of a modifier clause.

➥ **Is there a subject for this ADJ?** Look for *ga* or *no* to its left.

6 [N_4 no . . . *ii*] N_2

This *no* could indicate:

a. the subject in this modifier clause — or else it is
b. part of a Noun Phrase construction, X *no* Y, in which case the possibilities are:

    1. "Y **of** X" (*Tōkyō no chizu* "a map of Tokyo"), or simply connecting two Ns (*futari no musuko* "two sons")
    2. "X**'s** Y" (POSSESSIVE) (*Jon no uchi* "John's house")
    3. X and Y in APPOSITION (*tomodachi no Jon* "my friend John")
    4. the copula as a predicate representing any predication of X with respect to Y (see immediately below).

(See ch. 4, § 6 for the functions of *no*.)

No may also represent in a subordinate clause the copula *da* standing for a variety of predicates, as in: [*unagi* **no**] *Tanakasan* "Mr. Tanaka who eats (or dislikes, ordered, bought, etc.) eel" (see ch. 4, § 6.1.3B).

If Y is omitted (*X no*), the meaning is simply "of N_1" or "N_1's." However, we can assume at this point that N_4 *no* is not followed by a N; nor has a following N been omitted, since if it had been, there would still be a subject particle for this *N no* — but there is no other *ga* or *no* (the topic particle *wa* does not appear in a modifier clause).

There is still a possibility that N_4 *no* and N_2 constitute X *no* Y, and that a modifier has been inserted before N_2: N_4 *no* . . . N_2 as in, for example, **Jon no** *totemo ii* **tomodachi** "**John's** very good **friend**."

However, let us assume for now that N_4 is the subject for the closest predicate *ii*. CHECK this later.

TRANSLATION: "N_2, the N_4 of which is good"

7 [. . . *N₃ ga . . . katta*] **N₁** *wa* [*N₄ no . . . ii*] **N₂** *da.*

"**N₁** which N₃ bought . . . **is N₂** the N₄ of which . . . is good."

8 Filling in

Let us now begin to fill in the actual words and add other terms that have been left out. These will most likely be adverbials or phrases of time, place, manner, and so forth.

[*Kinō* N₃ ga Shinjuku de katta*]* *N₁ wa* [*N₄ no totemo ii*] *N₂ da.*
TIME SUBJ   PLACE PRED TOP SUBJ   ADV PRED MAIN PRED

"N₁ which N₃ bought in Shinjuku yesterday is N₂ the N₄ of which is very good."

> * Structurally, the TIME word could also modify the main predicate. However, this possibility is eliminated because the tense of the main predicate is nonpast.

N₁=*jisho* "dictionary" N₂=*jisho* "dictionary" N₃=*otōto* "younger brother" N₄=*setsumei* "explanation"

Substitute for N₁ to N₄ the actual words given above.

> **The dictionary** which my brother bought in Shinjuku yesterday **is a dictionary** the explanations in which are very good.
>
> The dictionary my brother bought in Shinjuku yesterday is one that has very good explanations.

CHECKLIST:

√ From (6): It is confirmed that N₄ *setsumei* "an explanation" is the subject for the predicate, *ii* "good," in the modifier clause for N₂ *jisho* "a dictionary": "a dictionary the explanations in which are very good."

9 Variations and other possibilities

9.1 This sentence could have an emphasized subject in place of the topic. Compare the following sentences.

    A. . . . *N₃ ga . . . katta N₁ wa N₄ no . . . ii* **N₂** *da.*

    B. . . . *N₃ ga . . . katta* **N₁ ga** *N₄ no . . . ii* **N₂** *da.*

In sentence B two subject particles (*ga*) appear. Normally a subject goes with the closest predicate to its right. Therefore, N_3 *ga* is immediately connected to the predicate *katta*, thus forming the clause [N_3 *ga katta*] modifying N_1.

N_1 could be either the subject in an immediate description: "N_1 is N_2," or else an emphasized subject: "**It is N_1** that is N_2" (see ch. 4, §§ 5.2.1 and 2 for the "immediate description" use of *ga*). However, this case is likely to be one of subject emphasis, since sentences of immediate description tend to be comparatively short and simple.

Ultimately, however, the context will determine this question, where the context could be the phrase, clause, or sentence in which the element is located, the sentences before and after, the paragraph, the book — or even something as broad as the reader's general knowledge about the world.

> [. . . *N_3 ga* . . . *katta*] N_1 *ga* [*N_4 no* . . . *ii*] N_2 *da.*
> └ EMPHASIZED SUBJ

> "**It is N_1** which N_3 bought . . . **that is the N_2** the N_4 of which is . . . good."

> [*Jon ga katta*] *jisho ga* [*setsumei ga ii*] *jisho da.*

> "**It is the dictionary** John bought **that is the dictionary** with the good explanations."

9.2 N could be preceded by a *toiu* clause (ch. 1, § 3.1.1B). While the topic particle *wa* cannot occur in a N modifier clause and occurs only rarely in adverbial clauses, **the topic *wa* can occur in a *toiu* clause.** Do not take the *iu* of *toiu* as a predicate, on the assumption that it is the plain form of the verb "to say" and indicates the end of a clause. *Toiu* is not itself a predicate or a clause ending. The clause ending (= the predicate) comes before *toiu* in this case.

> [. . . *N_3 wa* . . . *V*] **TOIU*** *N_1 wa* [*N_4 no* . . . *ADJ*] N_2 *da.*

> * If this *toiu* clause is to modify N_1, the *toiu* usually comes immediately
> before N_1; in such cases, what follows *toiu* tends to be a noun such as
> *koto, jijitsu, uwasa, hanashi, dekigoto,* etc. (See ch. 1, § 4.1.1B)

> [*Jon wa Amerika e kaeranai*] **toiu hanashi** *wa* [*shinpyōsei no nai*] *uwasa da.*

> "**The story that** John is not going back to the U.S. is a rumor with no credibility."

9.3 . . . *N_3 ga* . . . **katta no** (=N_1) *wa* . . . *N_4 no* . . . *ii* N_2 *da.*

N_1 could be *no*. This *no* would not be the particle "of" as in *N no N*, because the preceding word is not a noun but a verb. Since this *no* is followed by a particle (*wa* in this case) it has to be a kind of noun, either the pronominal *no* or the nominalizer *no* (ch. 4, § § 6.5 and 6).

However, the nominalizer *no* would have to follow the plain nonpast affirmative form *kau* to make *kau no* "to buy, buying"; therefore, the *no* of *katta no* is not a nominalizer but a pronominal. [. . . N₃ *ga katta*] *no* must mean "**the one** which N₃ bought."

> ## 2. . . . V.

In the sentence we just looked at, the adverbial phrases *kinō* (TIME) and *Shinjuku de* (PLACE) were both connected with the predicate of the clause, *katta*. However, there are cases in which an adverbial is connected with the main predicate.

1 . . . V.

The predicate is V: "Somebody does something," "Something happens," or "There is something." V can be either Vi or Vt (ch. 4, § 2.2). If it is Vi, the expected structure is: . . . *ga Vi* (or if the subject is topicalized or contrasted: . . . *wa Vi*). If it is Vt, the expected structure is: . . . *wa* . . . *o Vt* (or in the case of a subject or emphasized subject instead of a topic: . . . *ga* . . . *o Vt*).

2 . . . *kaeru* (Vi).
　　return

➥ "Return" to where? **Look** to the left for **a particle for direction or terminal point** (*e* or *ni/made*). Also expect a subject or topic: **look for *ga* or *wa* to the left**.

. . . *ga kaeru.* IMMEDIATE DESCRIPTION or SUBJ EMPHASIS (ch. 4, § 5.2), or

. . . *wa kaeru.* TOPIC or CONTRAST (ch. 4, § 5.1)

3 . . . *N₁* **wa** *N₂* **e** *kaeru.* "N₁ returns to N₂."

➥ Is N₁ modified? See sentence 1, step 2 above, for possible modifiers for N.

4 . . . *oshieta* (Vt) *N₁*
     taught

YES, there is a plain form of a verb before N₁. This means that N₁ is most likely modified by **a clause***. Since there is no *toiu* before N₁, let us assume that the clause is a noun modifier clause but not a *toiu* clause from which the *toiu* has been omitted. We will check this later.

> * If *V-ta* is used as an ADJ it can constitute a phrase by itself: *kootta ike* "a frozen pond." See also ch. 1, § 3.1.1A, for single modifiers.

5 [. . . *oshieta*] *N₁*

> "N₁ who taught . . . ," "N₁ whom someone taught . . . ," or "N₁ which someone taught."

In order to decide which of these applies here, we must see what N₁ is.

6 [. . . *oshieta*] *Sumisu-san*

> "Mr. Smith who taught . . ." or "Mr. Smith whom someone taught . . ."

The verb *oshieru* **is Vt, and so it is likely that one will find an object word. Look for the object particle** *o.*

7 [. . . *N₃ o oshieta*] *Sumisu-san*

> "Mr. Smith who taught N₃" or "Mr. Smith whom someone taught N₃."

Is there a subject word for the predicate *oshieta*? Since a topic cannot occur in a noun modifier clause, one must **look for the subject particle** *ga* **or** *no*.

8 [. . . *N₄ ga N₃ o oshieta*] *Sumisu-san*

> "Mr. Smith whom N₄ taught N₃."

➥ Is N₄ modified? Check to see what comes before N₄. If what comes before N₄ is not a modifier for N₄, it will most likely be an adverbial of TIME,

PLACE, MANNER, CONDITION, REASON, CAUSE, PURPOSE, EXTENT, or some combination of these. For adverbial clauses, see ch. 1, § 3.1.1A.

9 ➤ [*Raishū (*ADV*) N₄ ga N₃ o oshieta*] *Sumisu-san*
next week

> "Mr. Smith whom N₄ **taught** N₃ **next week**"

This doesn't make sense. The *raishū* cannot indicate the time for the predicate of this modifier clause, which is in the past tense, and so it must apply to the main predicate.

10 *Raishū* [*N₄ ga N₃ o oshieta*] *N₁ wa N₂ e kaeru.*
TIME   SUBJ OBJ PRED   TOP DRN MAIN PRED

> "N₁ whom N₄ taught N₃ **will return** to N₂ **next week**."

🖾 N₁=*Sumisu-san* N₂=*Amerika* N₃=*Nihongo* N₄=*ane* "older sister"

TRANSLATE the sentence, substituting for N₁ to N₄ the words given above:

> Mr. Smith, whom my older sister taught Japanese, will return to America next week.

√ The assumption that [*N₄ ga N₃ o oshieta*] is a modifier clause for N₁ instead of a *toiu* clause has been confirmed. See (4).

10.1 Time expressions can generate uncertainties when there is more than one element in the sentence which they could modify. Examine the two ways of construing the following sentence:

Kyonen [*ane ga nihongo o oshieta*] *Sumisu-san wa Amerika e* **kaetta.**

[**Kyonen** *ane ga nihongo o* **oshieta**] *Sumisu-san wa . . .*

Kyonen "last year" could indicate the time for the main predicate ("returned last year") or for the predicate of the modifier clause ("taught last year"). There is no way to decide which from the sentence alone; we must examine the context in which the sentence appears.

10.2 The time element may be given by a noun phrase including a modifier clause: . . . *toki (ni), mae ni, aida, uchi ni, to,* etc. (see ch. 1, § 3.1.3A).

[*Nihon e kite ichinen tatanai*] *uchi ni* [*ane ga nihongo o oshieta*] *Sumisu-san wa Amerika e kaetta.*

"Mr. Smith, whom my sister taught Japanese, went back to America within a year (= before one year passed) after he came to Japan."

11   Multiple subjects

When there is more than one subject, and, therefore, more than one *ga* in a sentence, it is usual for the closest subject and predicate to go together.

$$X \text{ (TIME) } [N_4 \text{ } ga \text{ } N_3 \text{ } o \text{ } \textbf{PRED}] \text{ } N_1 \text{ } ga \text{ } N_2 \text{ } e \text{ } \textbf{PRED}.$$

N_4 is the subject for the predicate in the modifier clause. N_1 is the subject for the main predicate and is either the subject in an immediate description or an emphasized subject. Without the context it cannot be decided which is the case here. The translation is either:

"N_1 whom N_4 taught N_3 **will return** to N_2 at time X"

or

"It is N_1 whom N_4 taught N_3 **who will return** to N_2 at time X."

---

3. . . . *SHIRABETA.*

1 . . . *shirabeta* (Vt).
   checked

The predicate consists simply of V. Since it is **Vt**, one can **predict a direct object + *o*.**

2 . . . N_1 **o** *shirabeta*. ". . . checked N_1"

➥ Is there **a topic** for this main predicate? **Look for *wa*.**

3 ... **N₄ ga** ... *N₁ o shirabeta.*

There is no topic but a subject. Can this be the subject for the main predicate? Or **is there a predicate** for it **to its right** to form a clause. The closest subject and predicate should be grouped together.

3.1 [*N₄ ga itte-iru* (Vi)]
    is going, has gone*

> * For now let us assume that the meaning of *itte-iru* is "is going." CHECK this later.

The predicate for N₄ is *itte-iru* (V-plain) which marks the end of a clause. Is this a modifier clause? **Is there a following N?**

3.2 [*N₄ ga itte-iru*] N₃

N₃ is modified by this clause: "N₃ where* N₄ is going."

> * Since N₃ is likely to be the place to which N₄ goes, "where" is appropriate, though it is also possible that N₃ is a time word. Let us assume for now that it is a place. CHECK this later.

4 There does not appear to be a topic or subject in this sentence.

Assuming that **the topic** has been **omitted**, we can take it that "I," the writer, is the topic. **The first person "I" is frequently left unmentioned** in Japanese writing, just as in speaking. We can stay with the assumption that the topic is the writer unless further information coming from the broader context renders this implausible. CHECK this later.

If N₃ is a destination one is going/coming to, it will be followed by the particle *e/ni* or *made*. If it is a departing point, it will be followed by *kara/o*. If it is a place where an action takes place, it will be followed by *de*. If it is a location where something or someone is, it will be followed by the particle *ni*. Check the particle following N₃.

5 ... [*N₄ ga itte-iru*] **N₃ ni** ...

Since *ni* can indicate either a direction for motion verbs (go/come/return, etc.) or a location for the verb of existence (*aru/iru*), we need to look at the verb to its right.

6 . . .] N_3 *ni* **aru** (V) N_2

      exists/is

Aru is in the plain form and is the predicate of a modifier clause for N_2.

➥ Where is the beginning of this clause?

7 [[N_4 *ga itte-iru*] N_3 *ni aru*] N_2

N_3 is modified by the other clause (3.2), so the beginning of the modifier clause for N_2 coincides with that of the other clause.

      "N_2 which is in/at N_3 where N_4 is going"

➥ Are there any other predicates to the right of N_2?

8 . . . N_2 *e* **itte** (*V-te*) N_1 *o shirabeta*

        go

While there are no other V-plain forms, there is a *V-te* form.

    Itte is *V-te*, which may be grouped together with other V(s) to form a multiple predicate. The V to the right of this *V-te* is the final predicate, *shirabeta*:

$$N_2 \ e \ itte \ (V_1) \ N_1 \ o \ shirabeta(V_2)$$

V_1 and V_2 constitute multiple predicates. There are three functions of *V-te*: sequence, manner, or reason (see ch. 1, § 3.2.2). Let us determine the function of V_1-*te* later when the actual words are given. For now let us translate simply as "V_1 and V_2" in sequence. CHECK this later.

      "(I*) went to N_1 and checked N_1."

      * It was assumed in (4) that the omitted topic is "I."

9 [[N_4 *ga itte-iru*] N_3 *ni aru*] N_2 *e itte* N_1 *o shirabeta.*

      "I went to N_2, which is at N_3 where N_4 is going, and checked N_1."

➥ Are there any further elements to the left of N_4?

10 . . . **kara** [[N_4 *ga* . . .

Kara is either the particle "from" after N, an element of a *V-te kara* sequence, or else "because" after a clause ending in a predicate (*V, ADJ, AN/N dearu/da*).

➥ **What comes before** *kara* **in this case?**

10.1 . . . *shirabe-takatta* (V) *kara*
  wanted to check

The word before *kara* is V-plain form, which marks the end of a clause. This must be a REASON CLAUSE: "because . . . wanted to check"

10.2 Since *shiraberu* is Vt, one would expect a direct object. However, the *-tai* ending is an ADJ. V-*tai* can take either *ga* or *o* (see Ch. 1, § 1.1): *X ga/o shirabetai* "want to check X."

Look to the left of *shirabe-takatta*.

  > N_5 *ni tsuite* ("about/regarding") *shirabe-takatta*] *kara*

There is no subject or direct object, but there is *N ni tsuite* "about N_5."

  "Because . . . wanted to check on N_5"

➥ Is there a subject in this clause?

10.3 Since there is no subject in this reason clause, we can assume that it is the same as the topic of the sentence — namely, the "I" of the writer.

  [(*watakushi ga*) N_5 *ni tsuite shirabe-takatta*] *kara*

  "Because (I) wanted to check on N_5"

11 Add (7) to (8).

  8: N_2 *e itte* N_1 *o shirabeta*. "(I) went to N_2 and checked N_1."

  7: [[N_4 *ga itte-iru*] N_3 *ni aru*] N_2 "N_2 which is at N_3 where N_4 is going."

    [[N_4 *ga itte-iru*] N_3 *ni aru*] N_2 *e itte* N_1 *o shirabeta*.

  "(I) went to N_2 which is at N_3 where N_4 is going and checked N_1."

Add (10.2):

  [N_5 *ni tsuite shirabetakatta*] *kara* "Because (I) wanted to check on N_5"

  (*Watakushi wa*) [N_5 *ni tsuite shirabetakatta*] *kara*
    OMIT-TOP   PRED   RSN
  [[N_4 *ga itte-iru*] N_3 *ni aru*] N_2 *e itte* N_1 *o shirabeta*.
    SUBJ   PRED LOCN PRED   DRN PRED   OBJ   MAIN PRED

  "Because (I) wanted to check on N_5, (I) went to N_2 which is at N_3 where N_4 is going and checked N_1."

$\sqsubseteq$ N$_1$=*sore* "that" N$_2$=*engekihakubutsukan* "performing arts museum" N$_3$= *daigaku* "college/university" N$_4$=*Hanako* N$_5$=*nōshōzoku* "Noh costume"

12 Translate the sentence, substituting for N$_1$ to N$_5$ the above words:

> Because (I) wanted to do research on Noh costumes, (I) went to the performing arts museum (that is located) at the college where Hanako is going and did it (= the research).

CHECKLIST:

√ From (3.1) and (3.2): N$_3$ (*daigaku*) is not a time word but is a place, a college where one "is going (= attending)" rather than "has gone."

√ From (8): The function of V$_1$-*te*: Is sequence appropriate in this context? Yes: neither MANNER ("I did research in the manner of going to the museum") or REASON ("I did research because I went to the museum") makes much sense.

√ From (4): For the omitted topic, is "I" appropriate for the entire sentence? Yes.

4. . . . *ITTE-ITA.*

1 . . . *itte-ita* (Vt).
    was saying

This predicate consists of the -*te* form of the verb *iu* (Vt) and *iru* to indicate an on-going action (ch. 4, § 2.5.1). But "was saying" what? **Look for** a clause followed by **the quotation particle** *to*.

2 . . . **itta** (Vi)] **to** *N$_1$ no N$_2$ ga itte-ita.*
    went (PRED)

Itta is the ending of a quotation clause: "that . . . went."

N_2 *ga* is the subject for the main predicate, *itte-ita*: "N_2 was saying that . . . went."

2.1 See above, Sentence 1, step 6, for the functions of *no* in N_1 *no* N_2. The function of *no* here will be clear when the actual words are given. For now let us take it as "N_2 of N_1": "N_2 of N_1 was saying that . . . went . . ." CHECK this later.

2.2 In a quotation clause either TOPIC + *wa* or SUBJECT + *ga* or both can occur. Since the main predicate already has a subject (N_2 *ga*), if N + *wa* appears to the left of *itta* (the predicate of the quotation clause) it is more likely to be the topic of the quotation clause rather than of the entire sentence. **Is there a *wa* or *ga* to the left of the predicate *itta*?**

3 > [N_3 (TOPIC) **wa** . . . *itta*] *to* N_1 *no* N_2 *ga itte-ita.*

There is no subject for *itta* but there is a topic (N_3). This could be the topic for the main predicate *itte-ita*, since a sentence can have both a topic and a subject — as in *X wa Y ga wakaru* "X understands Y." However, N_3 is closer to *itta*, the predicate of the clause than to *itte-ita*, the main predicate and, furthermore, a quotation clause can allow TOPIC + *wa*. So it is likely that N_3 is the topic inside the quotation clause: "N_2 of N_1 was saying that N_3 went . . ." CHECK this later.

➥ Where did N_3 go? **Look for a particle signifying direction or a terminal point:** *e* or *ni/made*.

4 [N_3 wa . . . N_8 **e** *itta*] "N_3 went to N_8"

➥ **Is N_8 modified?** Let us examine what comes before it.

4.1 . . . **yūmei na** (*AN* + *na*) N_8
famous

➥ Is this a single modifier or the predicate of a modifier clause, *AN* + *na* (=*da*)? Look farther to the left.

4.2 . . . **utsukushiku-te**(*ADJ-kute*) *yūmei na* N_8
is beautiful

The *-te* form of ADJ has the function of LISTING OUT or indicating a REASON (see ch. 1, § 3.2.2B). Let us assume here that *utsukushiku-te* is used for LISTING OUT: "beautiful and famous N_8." CHECK this later.

➥ Is N_8 modified by a clause? In other words are these *ADJ-kute* and *AN + na* predicates of a modifier clause? If so is there a subject to their left? **Look for a** *ga*.

4.3 . . . N_7 *ga utsukushikute yūmei na*] N_8 *e itta*] *to* N_1 *no* N_2 *ga itte-ita.*

N_7 is the subject for multiple predicates *utsukushikute* (PRED$_a$) and *yūmei na** (PRED$_b$), which are grouped together as predicates of the modifier clause for N_8: "N_8 the N_7 (SUBJ) of which is beautiful (PRED$_a$) and famous (PRED$_b$)"

> * *Da* has been changed to *na* after AN and before N (ch. 1, § 3.1.1).

> "N_2 of N_1 was saying that . . . went to N_8 **the N_7** of which is beautiful and famous . . ."

➥ **Is N_7 modified? Look to its left.**

4.4 . . . **motte** (Vt) N_7 *ga utsukushikute yūmei na*] N_8 *e itta*
      have/hold   PRED$_a$ PRED$_b$

Since *V-te* cannot modify N, the beginning of the modifier clause for N_8 must be just before N_7. *Motte* is the *-te* form of the verb *motsu* (Vt) "have/hold," and since such a *-te* form cannot stand by itself, it is likely to be a component in a multiple predicate.

➥ **Can we find another PRED(s) associated with** *motte* **to its right?**

Since *motsu* is **Vt, look for a DIRECT OBJECT +** *o* **to its left.**

5 N_3 *wa* . . . N_6 *o* **motte** N_7 *ga utsukushikute yūmei na*] N_8 *e* **itta**] *to*
           PRED$_1$ PRED$_a$ PRED$_b$ PRED$_2$

5.1 The predicates to its right are PRED$_a$ (ADJ) and PRED$_b$ (AN), and *itta* (V) the main predicate of the quotations clause. Since *motte* is V, it is natural to assume that it goes with another verb *itta*, although sometimes a V can be grouped with ADJ or AN/N as multiple predicates (ch. 3, § 2.1). Let us assume now that *motte* "have/hold" is PRED$_1$ and *itta* "went" is PRED$_2$, which means that the beginning of the modifier clause for N_8 is N_7:

> . . . N_6 *o motte* [N_7 *ga utsukushikute yūmei na*] N_8 *e itta.*
>   PRED$_1$ PRED$_2$

The function of *V-te* is sequence, manner, or reason. Let us assume that this *V-te* is in a sequence. CHECK this later.

5.2 "N$_3$ took N$_6$ and went to N$_8$ the N$_7$ of which is beautiful and famous."
N$_6$ is the direct object for *motte*.

➥ **Is N$_6$ modified?**

6 *N$_5$ no* **tsuite-iru** (Vi) *N$_6$*
is attached

The V-plain form *tsuite-iru* marks the end of a clause. It is the predicate of the modifier clause for the following word N$_6$.

What is the function of the *no* after N$_5$? There is not another N after N$_5$ *no* to constitute *X no Y*. If Y had been omitted, for example as in *Hanako no [da]* "(It's) Hanako's" or *Nihon no [chizu]* "(a map) of Japan," then *X no* would have to be treated as a N. If it were a N there would have to be a following particle before the V. However, *N$_5$ no* is followed immediately by the verb *tsuite-iru* (Vi) which would take a subject word: SUBJ *ga* + *tsuite-iru*. This *no* must therefore be the subject particle *no* (=*ga*) in a modifier clause.

> *N$_5$* no tsuite-iru] *N$_6$* "N$_6$ to which N$_5$ is attached."
> SUBJ   PRED

➥ **Is N$_5$ modified?** In other words, is N$_5$ the beginning of this clause?

7 *N$_4$ no* **dekiru** (V) *N$_5$ no* tsuite-iru] *N$_6$*

N$_5$ is not the beginning of the modifier clause for N$_6$. *Dekiru* is the plain form of the verb "can do, is possible," and is the predicate of a modifier clause for either of the following nouns, N$_5$ or N$_6$. Let us assume that the clause modifies the immediately following N, N$_5$. CHECK this later.

➥ **Is there a subject in this clause?**

Yes. Potential verbs or the potential form of a verb take a subject instead of a direct object. The **no** of *N$_4$ no* **is a subject particle**, so that N$_4$ is the subject for the predicate *dekiru*.

There are two possibilities for *N$_4$ no* (=*ga*) *dekiru*:

> "N$_4$ can do"   or   "N$_4$ is possible."

Let us assume that the former is the case. CHECK this later.

➥ **Is N$_4$ modified?** In other words, **is N$_4$ the beginning of this clause?**

8 *N₃ wa saikin* **katta** *N₄ no dekiru] N₅ no tsuite-iru] N₆*

Katta is the plain past form of the verb *kau* "to buy," and is the predicate of a modifier clause for N₄ (= the following N), or N₅, or N₆. Let us assume that it modifies the immediately following N, N₄. CHECK this later.

Since there doesn't appear to be a subject for the predicate *katta*, we will let X stand for the omitted subject. The beginning of this clause is right after *N₃ wa* and before *saikin*.

> [(*X ga*) *saikin katta* (PRED-V)] *N₄*   "N₄ which X bought recently"

➥ **Where is the beginning of the modifier clause for N₅?**

9 [[(*X ga*) *saikin katta*] *N₄ no dekiru] N₅*

Since the subject N₄ is modified by the preceding modifier clause, the beginning of that clause coincides with that of the modifier clause for N₅.

> [[(*X ga*) *saikin katta*] *N₄ no dekiru] N₅*

"N₅ which N₄, which X bought recently, can do" This is a bit awkward but we leave it as it is for now.

➥ **Where is the beginning of the modifier clause for N₆?**

10 [[[*(X ga) saikin katta*] *N₄ no dekiru] N₅ no tsuite-iru] N₆*

Since N₅, the subject of the modifier clause for N₆, is itself modified by a modifier clause, the beginning of the former clause is the same as that of the latter.

> [[[*(X ga) saikin katta*] *N₄ no dekiru] N₅ no tsuite-iru] N₆*

"N₆ to which N₅ is attached which N₄, which X bought recently, can do"

11 Translate the entire sentence

[N₃ (TOPIC) wa [[[(X ga) saikin katta] N₄ no dekiru] N₅ no tsuite-iru] N₆ o motte, [N₇ ga utsukushikute yūmei na] N₈ e itta (PRED)] to *N₁ no N₂ (SUBJ) ga itte-ita* (MAIN PRED).

> from (5): "N₃ took N₆ and went to N₈ the N₇ of which is beautiful and famous"

> Add (10): "N₃ took N₆ **to which** N₅ is attached which N₄, which X

bought recently, can do and went to N_8 the N_7 of which is beautiful and famous"

Put this into (4.3): "N_2 of N_1 was saying that N_3 took N_6 to which N_5 is attached which N_4, which X bought recently, can do and went to N_8 the N_7 of which is beautiful and famous."

Now here are the words:

> N_1=*Jon* "John" N_2=*tomodachi* "friend" N_3=*Jon* N_4=*torihazushi* "removing" N_5=*bōen-renzu* "telephoto lens" N_6=*kamera* "camera" N_7=*mizuumi* "lake" N_8=*Hokkaido*

CHECKLIST:

√ From (2.1): N_1 *no* N_2 = *Jon no tomodachi*
The possibilities are: N_2 **of** N_1 = "a friend of John"
N_1**'s** N_2 = "John's friend (a friend of John's)"

(APPOSITION is not possible here. "My friend, John" would be *tomodachi no Jon*.) "John's friend" The possessive *no* is better in this context.

Most of the time it is easy to tell the meaning of *X no* Y from the context, but it is a good habit always to check the other possibilities.

√ From (3): N_3 is the topic inside the quotation clause rather than the topic of the entire sentence (= for the main predicate *itte-ita*): "John's friend said that **John** went . . ."

√ From (8): Normally the omitted subject is the writer "I," or a person whose identity is given by the context. Since this sentence is about John, it is best to take him as the subject (*Jon ga katta* "which John bought").

√ From (4.2): *mizuumi ga utsukushikute yūmei na] Hokkaidō e* . . .
The possibilities are:
   a. "to Hokkaido where the lakes are beautiful and (lakes are) famous" LIST
   b. "to Hokkaido which is famous because the lakes are beautiful" REASON
   c. The difference is subtle. However, . . . *-te yūmei da* is normally used idiomatically to mean "something is famous for . . ." Therefore (b) is appropriate here.

√ From (5): *Jon wa kamera o* **motte** . . . *Hokkaidō e* **itta**. The possibilities are:
   a. "John had a camera and went to Hokkaido." SEQUENCE
   b. "John went to Hokkaido taking a camera." MANNER
   c. "Because John had a camera,* he went to Hokkaido." REASON

> * This would be more appropriately expressed as: *Jon wa kamera o motte-ita kara*.

(b) is the best. The assumption made in (5) was wrong.

√ From (7): N_4 *no dekiru*] N_5 = *torihazushi no dekiru bōen-renzu*
    The possibilities are:
    a. "N_5, which N_4 can do" = "a telephoto lens which removing can do"
    b. "N_5, the N_4 of which is possible" = "a telephoto lens the removing of
       which is possible" (meaning "detachable")

The latter is obviously the meaning.

√ From (7) and (8): (X *ga*) *saikin katta* N_4 *no dekiru* N_5 *no tsuite-iru* N_6

    = *Jon ga saikin katta torihazushi no dekiru bōen-renzu no tsuite-iru kamera*

First possibility: [[[(*Jon ga*) *saikin katta*] **torihazushi** (N_4) *no dekiru*] *bōen-renzu*
(N_5) *no tsuite-iru*] *kamera* (N_6):

Since the noun *torihazushi*, "removing," does not make sense as what is
modified by *Jon ga katta* ("the removing which John bought recently"), the clause
Jon ga saikin katta must modify either N_5 or N_6.
Second possibility: If it modifies N_5, it will read:

[[(*Jon ga*) *saikin katta*] [*torihazushi* (N_4) *no dekiru*] **bōen-renzu** (N_5)
no tsuite-iru] *kamera* (N_6):

"the camera to which the detachable telephoto lens which John bought
recently is attached"

Third possibility: If it modifies N_6, it will read:

[(*Jon ga*) *saikin katta*] [[*torihazushi* (N_4) *no dekiru*] *bōen-renzu* (N_5)
no tsuite-iru] **kamera** (N_6):

"the camera John bought recently, to which a detachable telephoto lens
is attached," meaning "the camera with a removable telephoto lens which
John bought"

The latter is more likely, since the *no tsuite-iru* suggests that the two items connected by it (lens and camera, in this case) come together "as a set."

[[Jon wa [(Jon ga) saikin katta] [[torihazushi no dekiru] bōen-renzu no tsuite-iru]
   TOP   SUBJ   TIME   PRED   SUBJ (= *ga*) PRED   SUBJ   (= *ga*) PRED

kamera o motte, [mizuumi ga utsukushikute yūmei na] Hokkaidō e itta] to
   OBJ   PRED$_1$ SUBJ   PRED$_a$ PRED$_b$ DRN PRED$_2$ QUOT

Jon no tomodachi ga itte-ita.
     SUBJ   MAIN PRED

> John's friend was saying that he (John) went to Hokkaido, which is
> famous for its beautiful lakes, taking the camera he bought recently
> which has a detachable telephoto lens.

5. . . . *TO IERU*.

1 . . . *to ieru* (V).
    One can say that . . .

Ieru is the potential form of the verb *iu* (Vt) "to say," and [. . .] *to ieru* is used to express "one/we can say that . . ." It is one of the typical sentence-ending expressions used in written texts (see ch. 4, § 13). Leaving it aside for now, since it covers the rest of the sentence, let us examine the content of what "one can say."

2 . . . *toiu* **koto** *(N)* **da**

The sentence pattern is *N wa N da*. **Look for the topic.**

    N is modified by a *toiu* clause (ch. 1, § 3.1.1B): "the N (fact/rumor/etc.) that . . ." The predicate of the clause (= the ending of the clause) comes right before *toiu*.

3 [. . .] *toiu* **koto** (N_1) **wa,** [. . .] *toiu* **koto** (N_2) **da**

Koto (N_1) is the topic for the predicate *koto* (N_2) *da*. The topic word is often followed by a comma, especially when it is separated from its predicate.
    N_1 is also modified by a *toiu* clause: "the fact (N_1) that . . . is/means the fact (N_2) that . . ."
    Check the content of the *toiu* clause for N_1.

4 > N_3 *no* N_4 *ga fueru* (Vi)] *toiu koto* (N_1)
                            increase

Fueru is V-plain form and the predicate of the *toiu* clause. N_4 is followed by *ga* and therefore is the subject for the predicate *fueru* that is Vi: N_4 *ga fueru* "N_4 increases."
    Let us assume that N_3 *no* N_4 is "N_4 of N_3" for now. CHECK later the relationship of N_3 to N_4.

N_3 is the beginning of this clause and also of the sentence.

[N_3 *no* N_4 (SUBJ) *ga fueru* (PRED-V)] *toiu koto* (N_1)

"the fact (N_1) that N_4 of N_3 increases"

Now look at the content of the *toiu* clause for N_2.

5 ... *hette-yuku**] *toiu koto* (N_2)

* *V-te yuku/iku* means "something happens gradually" or "something continues to happen." (See ch. 4, § 2.5.3.)

Hette-yuku is V-plain form and the predicate of the *toiu* clause.

➡ **Is there a subject?** Look for *ga* to its left.

N_6 *ga hette-yuku*] *toiu koto* (N_2)

N_6 is the subject of this *toiu* clause:

"the fact (N_2) that N_6 gradually decreases."

➡ **Is N_6** modified? In other words, is this the beginning of this clause? Look to its left.

6 ... *koto* (N_1) *wa*, N_5 *o uenai* (Vt) **kagiri**, N_6 *ga hette-yuku*] *toiu koto* (N_2)
                                                  not plant

The *o* of N_5 *o uenai* indicates that N_5 is the direct object of *uenai* "not plant," the plain nonpast negative form of the verb *ueru* "to plant."

Uenai is V-plain form and is a predicate. Is this the ending of a modifier clause? Look at the following word. *Kagiri* is the stem form of the verb *kagiru* "to limit." The verb stem form is used often as a variation of *V-te* form (ch. 1, § 3.2.2). However, if *kagiri* is functioning as *V-te*, it should not be preceded by V-plain form (*uenai*).

This is therefore not a case of *V-te* but rather of an adverbial construction consisting of a noun modifier clause and a following noun (ch. 1, § 3.1.1A). The V-stem *kagiri* is used as a N in the adverbial construction [...] *kagiri* "as long as ... ."

➡ Where is the beginning of this clause for *kagiri*? **Is N_5** modified?

6.1 The beginning of this clause should be right after N_1 *wa*, because N_1 is the topic for the main predicate *koto* (N_2) *da* to constitute N_1 *wa* ... *koto* (N_2) *da* and it cannot be included in this clause. There is therefore no modifier for N_5.

. . . *koto*(N₁) *wa*, [**N₅** *o uenai*] *kagiri*, "as long as . . . does not plant"

6.2 Is there a subject in this *kagiri* clause? Since there is no *ga* or *no,* we shall let X stand for the omitted subject in this clause.

[(X *ga*) N₅ (OBJ) *o uenai* (PRED-V)] *kagiri*, "as long as X doesn't plant N₅"

➥ **What does this adverbial clause modify?** What does it go with?

7 [N₃ *no* N₄ *ga fueru*] *toiu koto* (N1) (*wa*), [(X *ga*) N₅ *o uenai*] *kagiri*, N₆ *ga hette-yuku*] *toiu koto* (N₂) *da.*

7.1 If . . . *kagiri* goes with *hette-yuku*, then the beginning of this clause coincides with that of the *toiu* clause. In other words, it is an adverbial clause within the *toiu* clause:

. . . [[(X *ga*) N₅ *o uenai*] *kagiri*, N₆ *ga hette-yuku*] *toiu koto* (N₂)

"the fact that, as long as X doesn't plant N₅, N₆ gradually decreases"

7.2 If the . . . *kagiri* clause modifies N₁ *wa* N₂ *da* (the entire sentence), then it should be outside the *toiu* clause for N₂. The beginning of the *toiu* clause will then be right after *kagiri.*

[N₃ *no* N₄ *ga fueru*] *toiu koto*(N₁) *wa* [(X *ga*) N₅ *o uenai*] *kagiri*, [N₆ *ga hette-yuku*] *toiu koto* (N₂) *da.*

"as long as X doesn't plant N₅, the fact that N₄ of N₃ increases means the fact that N₆ gradually decreases"

📖 N₁=*koto*　N₂=*koto*　N₃=*kami* "paper"　N₄=*shōhi* "consumption"　N₅= *atarashii ki* "new trees"　N₆=*shinrin* "forest"

8 Translate the entire sentence, substituting for N₁ to N₆ the actual words given above.

CHECKLIST

√ From (4): "the fact (N₁) that N₄ of N₃ increases" = "the fact that the consumption of paper increases": "N₄ of N₃" is confirmed.

√ From (2): "the fact that the consumption of paper increases **means that** the forest gradually decreases . . ." In this context "means that . . ." is better than "is . . ."

√ From (7):
　a. "the fact that the consumption of paper increases means that, as long

as X doesn't plant new trees, the forest gradually decreases."
b. "as long as X doesn't plant new trees, the fact that the consumption of paper increases means that the forest gradually decreases."

There is no material difference between these two, although the Japanese structure is more accurately reflected by the second alternative, insofar as it associates the condition (as long as people don't plant new trees) more closely with the second fact (the decrease in the amount of forest).

Add (1) to the above:

"One can say that, as long as X doesn't plant new trees, the fact that the consumption of paper increases means that the forest gradually decreases."

√ From (6.2) The omitted subject in the adverbial clause is either "we" in general or "people," which is often omitted, as is "I."

> [*Kami no shōhi ga fueru*] *toiu koto wa*, [(*X ga*) *atarashii ki o uenai*] *kagiri*,
> SUBJ   PRED   TOP   SUBJ   OBJ   PRED
>
> *shinrin ga hette-yuku*] *toiu koto da*.
> SUBJ   PRED   MAIN PRED

> One can say that, as long as people don't plant new trees, the fact that the consumption of paper increases will mean that the forest will gradually decrease.

6. . . . *TO OMOWARERU.*

1 . . . *to omowareru* (V).
    It seems as if one could think that . . ."

This is another typical sentence ending expression used in written texts to show a lesser degree of commitment to the assertion and thus indirectness or humbleness (ch. 4, § 14). *Omowareru* is the **spontaneous** form of the verb *omou* "to think," which is actually the same form as the passive form. If the meaning were passive, *omowarete-iru* "it has been thought" would be used instead of *omowareru* (ch. 4, § 14). Set this phrase aside and go on to examine the content of the main sentence. Look immediately to the left.

2 . . . *kara da*

The particle *kara* is either "from" or "because" (REASON). This sentence pattern is *A wa X kara da*: "A is from X" or "A is because X."

If *kara* means "from," X could be time, place, person, etc. Check what comes before *kara*.

> *hōrikomareru* (V-PASSIVE) *kara da*
> be thrown into

Since what precedes *kara* is not a noun, this *kara* must indicate REASON: "is because . . . is thrown into . . ."

Look for the particle *wa* to find a noun for the topic.

3 . . . *no wa* . . . *kara da*

3.1 What is the function of *no*? **Look at the word preceding it.** It will be one of the following:

   a. N, constituting *N no N*, or
   b. ADJ/AN *na*/V plain + *no* (PRONOMINAL) ". . . one," or "one which . . ."
   c. V-plain (nonpast) + *no* (NOMINALIZER).

Both (b) and (c) can take a preceding V, but (c) takes only the nonpast form.

(See ch. 4, §6 for more details.)

3.2 . . . *ataeru* (Vt) *no wa*
      give

Since the verb *ataeru* "to give" is V nonpast form, *no* can be either a pronominal or a nominalizer. But since the main predicate is . . . *kara* (REASON) *da*, it is best to assume that *no* is a pronominal that has replaced the noun *riyū* "the reason." CHECK this later.

> . . . *ataeru*] **no** (TOPIC-PRONOM. = *riyū*, "reason") *wa* [. . .]**kara da**.
>
> **"The reason why** . . . gives . . . **is that . . ."**

➥ **What precedes** *ataeru*? Since *ataeru* is Vt, one expects DIR OBJ + *o*. What about a subject? Is there a *ga* or *no*?

3.3 ➤ N₁ *no* N₂ *ga* *tōtotsu* (AN) *na* N₃ o *ataeru*] *no wa*
                abrupt

N₂ is the subject. Let us suppose that *N₁ no N₂* is "N₂ of N₁." CHECK this later.

Tōtotsu na is AN, and *na* can be the end of a clause followed by N to be modified.

➥ Is N₂ the subject for *tōtotsu na* or *ataeru*?

        N₁ no N₂ *ga* **tōtotsu na** *N₃* (OBJ) o **ataeru** *no wa*
                 PRED?-AN *na* (= *da*) PRED?-V

a. If N₂ is the subject for *tōtotsu na*:

    [*N₁ no* N₂ *ga tōtotsu na*] N₃ o *ataeru*] *no wa* "the reason why . . .*
    gives N₃ the N₂ of N₁ of which is abrupt."

> * There is no subject for *ataeru*, so one can assume a subject X has been omitted. X is most likely "I" or the general "we": [(X *ga*) [*N₁ no N₂ ga tōtotsu na*] *N₃ o ataeru*] *no wa*

b. If N₂ is the subject for *ataeru*] *no wa*:

    [*N₁ no* N₂ *ga tōtotsu na N₃ o* **ataeru**] *no wa* "the reason why N₂ of N₁ gives an abrupt N₃." This makes more sense. CHECK this later.

4 What are the next closest subject and predicate to be marked as a clause to the right of the topic *no*?

4.1 . . .] *no wa* N₄ *ga deru* (Vi) *mae ni*
                come out

N₄ (SUBJ) and *deru* (PRED-V) are grouped as a clause. This is a N modifier clause which modifies the following TIME noun *mae* to constitute an adverbial construction of TIME: . . . *mae ni* "before . . ." (ch. 1, § 3.1.1A). The clause begins with N₄ because the topic *no* + *wa* goes with the main predicate, *kara da*, and so is not in this clause.

    . . . *wa* [*N₄* (SUBJ) *ga deru* (PRED-V)] *mae ni*: "before N₄ comes out"

➥ Which predicate is this TIME phrase for?

4.2 [. . .] *mae ni* (TIME) . . . **miru** (Vt) N_5 *ga* . . . **hōrikomareru** (Vt)] *kara da.*
               see/look   be thrown into

It is either for *miru* (PRED-V) or for *hōrikomareru* (PRED-V). CHECK this later.

5 Locate the next predicate (to the right) to be marked as a clause ending.

     . . .] *mae ni ikinari* (ADV) **miru** N_5
                 suddenly

Miru is V-plain form and the predicate of a modifier clause for the following N_5.

     ikinari miru (PRED-V)] N_5

     "N_5 which . . . sees suddenly" or "N_5 who sees suddenly."

➥ Is there a subject to the left of *miru*?

No; so let us assume that N_5 is the subject. CHECK this later.

    The beginning of this clause cannot be determined yet, since it depends on the answer to (4.2)—concerning which predicate the . . . *mae ni* modifies.
    Locate the next predicate.

6 . . . *miru*] N_5 *ga* . . . **hōrikomareru**] *kara da.*

N_5 is the subject since it is followed by *ga*. *Hōrikomareru* is V-plain form and the predicate for N_5:

     N_5 (SUBJ) *ga* . . . *hōrikomareru* (PRED-V)] "N_5 is thrown into . . ."

➥ Thrown into where? Look for PLACE + *ni* to the left.

6.1 N_5 *ga* N_6 *no* N_7 *ni hōrikomareru*: "N_5 is thrown into N_7 of N_6"*

       * CHECK the relation of N_7 to N_6 later.

6.2 . . . *wa* [N_4 *ga deru*] *mae ni ikinari* **miru**] N_5 *ga* N_6 *no* N_7 *ni* **hōrikomareru**]
   kara da..

Where is the beginning of the REASON clause that ends with *hōrikomareru*? In other words, does the [. . .] *mae ni* go with: (a) *miru*, or (b) *hōrikomareru*, or (c) . . . *kara da*?

There are three possibilities:

a. If it modifies *miru*:

[[[**N**₄ *ga deru* (PRED-V)**]** **mae ni** *ikinari* **miru]** *N₅ ga N₆ no N₇ ni hōrikomareru*] *kara da*.

". . . is because N₅ who sees suddenly before N₄ comes out is thrown into N₇ of N₆."

b. If it modifies *hōrikomareru*:

[[**N**₄ *ga deru*] *mae ni* [*ikinari miru*] *N₅ ga N₆ no N₇ ni* **hōrikomareru**] *kara da*

". . . is because, before N₄ comes out, N₅ who sees suddenly is thrown into N₇ of N₆"

c. If it modifies *kara da*:

. . . *no wa* [**N**₄ *ga deru*] *mae ni*, [[*ikinari* (X *ga*) *miru*] *N₅ ga N₆ no N₇ ni hōrikomareru*] **kara da**.

"Before N₄ comes out, . . . (= *no*) is because N₅ who sees suddenly is thrown into N₇ of N₆."

CHECK this later.

📝 N₁=*sono eiga* "that movie" N₂= *hajimari* "beginning" N₃=*kanji* "feeling" N₄=*taitoru* "titles" N₅=*mono* "person" N₆=*dekigoto* "events, action" N₇= *mattadanaka* "midst"

7 Translate the entire sentence, substituting for N₁ to N₇ the actual words given above.

CHECKLIST

√ From (2): It is confirmed that *kara* is the REASON particle: "The reason why . . . gives . . . is that . . . are thrown . . ."

√ From (3.3): N₁ (*eiga*) *no* N₂ (*hajimari*) = "N₂ of N₁" = "the beginning of the movie"

It is confirmed that the function of *no* is "of," and not possessive or apposition.

√ From (6.1): N₅ (*mono*) *ga* N₆ (*dekigoto*) *no* N₇ (*mattadanaka*) *ni hōrikomareru* "a person is thrown into midst of an event." It is confirmed that the function of *no* in N₆ *no* N₇ is "N₇ of N₆."

√ From (5.1): "One who sees" is better than "one which [someone] sees" in this context because "one who sees" will mean audience/viewers, since this sentence is about a film. However, "one who sees **suddenly**" sounds strange. Could the ADV *ikinari* modify something else?

The other possibility is that *ikinari* modifies *hōrikomareru*, the next verb after the immediately following verb *miru*. Thus, *miru* stands by itself as a modifier clause for *mono*. The corrected structure is:

. . . **ikinari** [*miru*] N_5(*mono*) *ga* N_6 *no* N_7 *ni* **hōrikomareta**

"The reason for . . . is because one who sees is **suddenly thrown into** the action"

This makes more sense.

√ From (3.3):

a. [(X *ga*) [N_1 *no* N_2 *ga tōtotsu na*] N_3 *o ataeru*] *no*

"the reason why X (= I/we) give a feeling the beginning of the film of which is abrupt"

b. [N_1 *no* N_2 *ga tōtotsu na* N_3 *o ataeru*] *no*

"The reason why the beginning of the movie gives an abrupt feeling"

It is confirmed that (b) is better.

√ From (6.2): . . . *wa* N_4 *ga deru*] *mae ni ikinari miru*] N_5 *ga* N_6 *no* N_7 *ni hōrikomareru*] *kara da* is modified from 4 above:

. . . *mae ni ikinari* [**miru**] N_5 *ga* . . .

a. . . . is because one [**who sees before the titles come out (= appear)**] is suddenly thrown into the midst of the action.

b. . . . is because **before the titles appear** one who sees **is suddenly thrown into** the midst of the action.

c. **before the titles appear**, . . . **is because** one who sees is suddenly thrown into the midst of the action.

Among the above, (b) makes most sense.

√ From (3.2): "The reason for . . . is because": it is confirmed that *no* is the pronominal which has replaced the noun *riyū* "reason."

Add (1): "It seems as if one could think that"

[*Sono eiga no hajimari ga tōtotsu na kanji o ataeru*] *no wa* [*taitoru ga deru*]
                          SUBJ   OBJ   PRED   TOP   SUBJ   PRED
mae ni ikinari [*miru*]*mono ga dekigoto no mattadanaka ni hōrikomareru*] *kara da*.
TIME ADV PRED SUBJ   LOCN   PRED   MAIN PRED

> It seems as if one could think that the reason why the beginning of the movie gives an abrupt feeling is that before the titles appear the viewer is suddenly thrown into the midst of the action.

$$\textit{Strategic exercise B}$$

R ead the following sentences and answer the questions. The questions are designed to guide you in decoding the structure of the sentences. After you answer each question yourself, look at the correct answer in order to confirm or revise it. Most of the nouns are represented by letters of the alphabet. Don't worry about the words they actually represent; just concentrate on analyzing the structure. The words will be given for the translation at the final stage.

Sentence 1

A に置き去りにされた B の C は驚いた。

A ni okizari ni sareta[1] *B no C wa odoroita.*[2]

> [1] Past tense of the passive form of *okizari ni suru* "leave . . . behind"
> [2] "was surprised"

1 What is **the main predicate**?

The main predicate is at the end of the sentence: . . . **odoroita** (V).

2 What is **the sentence pattern** here?

N wa V: . . . *C wa odoroita.*

3 *B no C wa odoroita* — **What is the relationship of B and C?**

The *no* of *B no C* is not the pronominal *no* because it is not immediately followed by a particle or *da* (COPULA); nor is it the EMPHASIS or SOFTENER *no* since it is not within a predicate, as in *byōki* (N) *na no da,* or *ii* (ADJ) *no da.*

The possibilities are the four functions of *no* mentioned above in connection with the first sentence of Strategic Exercise A (step 6).

Let us assume that *B no C* is "C of B" for now. CHECK this later.

4 Is there **a topic**? If so, what is it?

C is the topic because it is followed by the topic particle *wa*: . . . **C wa** *odoroita.* "C was surprised."

5 Are there **endings of noun modifier clauses**? In other words, are there any plain forms of V or ADJ, or *N/AN dearu,* or *N no* or *AN na*? If so, what are they?

Sareta is V-plain form and is the predicate of a modifier clause:

> *A ni* **okizari ni sareta** ("was left behind")] *B no C wa odoroita*

6 Where is **the beginning of this clause**? Is *A ni* inside of it? Consider the alternatives.

If *A ni* isn't part of this clause,then it belongs to the main predicate and indicates TIME or the thing C was surprised at — but in that case it would most likely be marked by a comma or else come right before the verb *odoroita*: **A ni,** . . . *C wa odoroita* or *C wa* **A ni** *odoroita.*

When used with the verbs *aru* or *iru*, *ni* can indicate a location. But in this case the verb is not the verb of existence, so it would take PLACE + *de* instead of LOCATION + *ni*.

If it belongs to the modifier clause, it probably indicates the LOCATION where something/someone was left behind. The possibilities are:

> **A ni** (TIME) [*okizari ni sareta*] *B no C wa* **odoroita**
> **"At time A**, C of B who was left behind was surprised" or

> **A ni** ("[surprised] at A") [*okizari ni sareta*] *B no C wa* **odoroita**
> "C of B who was left behind **was surprised at A**" or

> [**A ni** (LOCATION) **okizari ni sareta**] *B no C wa odoroita*
> "C of B who **was left behind at A** was surprised"

Let us assume that *A ni* is the location for the closest predicate *sareta*. CHECK this later.

7 Which does the modifier clause in (6) modify, B or C?

This cannot be determined until the actual words are given and the context understood. It is either [X]B *no C* or [X]B *no Ċ*, where X is the content of the clause. See also ch. 3, § 1.1.1 on the issue of noun modification. CHECK this later.

8 Given the words, try to resolve the problems left from (3), (6), and (7).

> *Hashira no ue* (A) *ni okizari ni sareta] meijin* (B) *no ishiya* (C) *wa odoroita.*
> on the pillar   master   stonemason

√ From (6): It is confirmed that *A ni* "on the pillar" is not TIME (for the main predicate) but LOCATION for the predicate *okizari ni sareta* "was left behind." The beginning of the sentence is therefore the beginning of the clause.

[*Hashira no ue ni* (LOCATION) *okizari ni sareta*]: "left behind on the pillar"

√ From (3): What is the relationship between B and C (*meijin no ishiya*)?

Apposition: *meijin no ishiya* "The master stonemason"

√ From (7): Which does the clause modify, B (*meijin*) or C (*ishiya*)?

B and C are in apposition where C is the main noun, so that C is modified: "the master **stonemason** who was left behind on the pillar"

> [*Hashira no ue ni*   *okizari ni sareta*]   *meijin*(B) *no* **ishiya**(C)   **wa**
> on the pillar   be left behind=V-PASS-PRED   the master APP stonemason TOP
>
> **odoroita**.
> was surprised=V-PRED

> TRANSLATE: [. . .] *BC wa odorioita* "BC [who . . .] was surprised."

Insert BC=the master stonemason and [who . . .]=[who was left behind on the pillar]

The master stonemason who was left behind on the pillar
was surprised.

This sentence appears in a story in which a boastful king ordered the best stonemason in the country to build him the tallest stone pillar in the world. When the stonemason completed the pillar the king had all the ladders and scaffolds removed while the stonemason was still on top of the pillar. Given the above context, the final translation is:

> The master stonemason was surprised at having been left behind on the pillar.

Sentence 2

A が B を得るのは、たとえて言えば、 C に D が宿るようなものである。

A ga B o eru[1]no wa, tatoete ieba[2], C ni D ga yadoru[3] yō na mono dearu.

[1] "to obtain"   [2] "allegorically speaking"   [3] "to dwell"

1 Identify **the main predicate** and its type.

. . . **mono dearu:** *N da*

2 What is the **sentence pattern**?

N wa N da.

3 What is the **topic word** for the predicate *N da*?

. . . *no* is the topic because it is followed by the topic particle *wa*:

A ga B o eru **no** *wa,* . . .

4 **What is this** *no*? Consider the various usages of *no* and determine which *no* this is.

Since it doesn't follow N, it will not be "of," possessive, apposition, or a predication reduced to *no* (ch. 4, § 6.1).

Since the *no* in this case is not followed by the copula *da* and is not in a predicate, it cannot be the EMPHASIS/SOFTENER *no* (ch. 4, § 6.4). It is followed by a particle, and so it must be some kind of noun—either a pronominal or the nominalizer (ch. 4, §§ 6.5 and 6.6).

> PRONOMINAL: "the one, the thing" as in *ii no* "a good one"

> NOMINALIZER: makes a verb into a noun, as in *kiku no* "to listen, listening, a matter of listening"

a. Suppose that *no* is a pronominal, identify its modifier clause.

A is the subject for the verb *eru* because it is followed by the subject particle *ga*. Normally the closest subject and predicate are grouped as a clause.

A ga B o **eru]** *no wa,* . .

the one (thing, person, time, place, etc.) which A obtains B

b. Suppose that *no* is a nominalizer: "for A to obtain B," or "(a matter of) A's obtaining B."

The latter is more probable, but CHECK this later.

5 Are there any other **plain forms**?

Yadoru (V-plain). This is the predicate of a clause:

> *A ga B o eru no wa, tatoete ieba, C ni D ga* **yadoru**] *yō na mono dearu.*

6 *Yadoru* is followed by *yō na*. What is *yō na*?

Yō (*da*) is a kind of AN which follows *N/AN dearu, N no, AN na, ADJ, V,* or a clause and means "like . . . , it seems (as if) . . ." Hence,

> It seems as if . . . dwells

7 Explain the function of *na* in *yō na mono*.

At the end of a modifier clause the copula *da* is changed to *na* after AN and before N (*mono*). Since *yō* functions as an AN (see ch. 4, § 4.1.1), *da* has been changed to *na* at the end of the modifier clause.

> . . . *yadoru*] *yō na* (AN + *da*, PRED)] *mono dearu*
> is something like . . . dwells

8 Is there **a subject** for the predicate *yadoru*?

Yes. D is the subject because it is followed by the subject particle *ga*:

> . . . *no wa tatoete ieba C ni* **D ga** *yadoru*] *yō na*

9 What is the *ni* of *C ni*?

The particle *ni* can indicate TIME, LOCATION, or GOAL to constitute an adverbial phrase. CHECK later which is the case here.

10 Does the adverbial phrase *C ni* belong to the clause [*D ga yadoru*] or to the main predicate *mono dearu*?

Most likely it belongs to the clause, since the verb *yadoru* "dwell" can take either TIME or LOCATION, whereas *N da* (*mono dearu* here) is unlikely to go with either. CHECK this later.

11 Does *tatoete ieba* "allegorically speaking," go with the predicate *yadoru* or with the main predicate?

> . . . **tatoete ieba,** *C ni D ga* **yadoru**] *yō na*] **mono dearu.**

a. With *yadoru*:

> . . . *no wa,* [[**tatoete ieba,** *C ni D ga* **yadoru**] *yō na*] *mono dearu*
> . . . is something like D dwells in C allegorically speaking.

b. With *mono dearu*, the main predicate:

... *no wa*, **tatoete ieba**, [[*C ni D ga yadoru*] *yō na*] **mono dearu**
... is, allegorically speaking, something like D dwells in C.

The second alternative sounds more plausible, but CHECK this later.

12 The main structure of this sentence is: *X wa Y yō na mono dearu*, where X is [*A ga B o eru*] *no* and Y is [*C ni D ga yadoru*]. Now translate the sentence.

X="a matter of A's obtaining B"
Y="D dwells in/at C (TIME/LOCATION)"

A matter of A's obtaining B is something like that D dwells in C.

13 With the words given, translate the entire sentence.

[*Hito*(A) *ga satori*(B) *o eru*] *no wa, tatoete ieba, mizu*(C) *ni tsuki*(D) *ga yadoru**] *yō na*] *mono dearu*.

A= a person, a human being   B= enlightenment   C= water
D= moon

* *Yadoru* "put up at, stay; dwell"

√ From (4): The function of *no* is the nominalizer: "For a human being to attain* enlightenment" or "the human being's attaining enlightenment."

* From the context "obtain" has been changed to "attain."

√ From (9) and (10): *C ni* is the location for the verb *yadoru*: [*mizu ni tsuki ga yadoru*] "the moon dwells in the water (= the moon is reflected in the water)"

√ From (11):

a. For a human being to obtain enlightenment is something like that the moon dwells (temporarily) in the water **allegorically speaking**.
b. For a human being to obtain enlightenment is, **allegorically speaking**, something like that the moon dwells in the water.

Of the two, b makes more sense.

[*Hito*(A) *ga*   *satori*(B) *o*   *eru*]   **no wa**   *tatoete ieba,*
a person SUBJ enlightenment OBJ   obtain=V-PRED   PRON TOP   allegorically speaking

[[*mizu*(C) *ni* *tsuki*(D) *ga*   *yadoru*]   *yō na*]   **mono**
  in the water   the moon SUBJ   dwell=V-PRED   like is=AN+COP(*da*)-PRED   something

dearu.
is=N-COP-PRED

> The human being's attaining enlightenment is, allegorically speaking, something like **the moon's being reflected** in the water (for the time being).

↪ Words in bold letters have been changed slightly from the somewhat artificial and mechanical translations of the intermediate stages.

Sentence 3

A，Bの話しによると、Cで「DのE」と言うことが言われ出したのは、Fで、Gが起こって、HとJを異にするKが強まったLだと言う。

A, B no hanashi ni yoruto[1], *C de 'D no E' to iu koto ga iware-dashita*[2] *no wa, F de, G ga okotte*[3], *H to J o koto ni suru*[4] *K ga tsuyomatta*[5]*L da to iu.*

[1] "according to what . . . says"

[2] "began to be talked about"

[3] "took place"

[4] "differ from H with respect to J." This idiom should not be confused with *V-ru koto ni suru* "decide on doing . . ."

[5] "became stronger"

1 The sentence begins with "according to . . ." **The structure** must be:

> . . . (*no hanashi*) *ni yoruto*, [. . .]   (*sō da/to no koto da/to iu*)
> According to the story/account of . . . I hear/understand that . . .

There are cases where the above sentence-ending expressions are omitted.

Look at **the ending of this sentence**:

> *A, B* no hanashi ni yoruto*, [. . .] *to iu.*

> * *A, B* are two Ns in apposition, as in *musuko Tarō* "(my) son Taro."

Let us set this aside and examine the content of what it is that is understood—namely, the content of the quotation clause.

2 [*C de 'D no E' to iu koto ga iware-dashita no wa, F de, G ga okotte, H to J o koto ni suru K ga tsuyomatta L da*]

Since the predicate of this quotation clause is *L da*, the sentence pattern here is **N wa N da.** Identify **the topic.** (*Wa* can occur in a quotation clause.)

> . . . *iware-dashita** **no** (TOP) **wa,** . . . *tsuyomatta* **L da** (PRED)
> began to be talked about   became strong

> > * *Iware* is the stem of the passive form, *iwareru*, of the verb *iu* "to say."
> > V-stem + *dasu* means "begin doing . . ."

3 What is the function of the *no* in *iwaredashita no wa*?

Since this V + *no* is followed by a particle, it is either the pronominal *no* or the nominalizer *no*. And since the **V is in the past tense** (*iware-dashita* "began to be talked about,") it must be **the pronominal** rather than the nominalizer (ch. 4, § 6.5)

What has the pronominal *no* in . . . *no wa L da* replaced?
In the construction . . . *no wa* . . . *X da*, the N which the pronominal *no* has replaced corresponds to X. In . . . *no wa* . . . *niji* ("two o'clock") *da*, for example, the pronominal *no* has replaced *toki* "the time (when)."

Let us wait until the word for L is given, and CHECK this later.

4 The pronominal *no* that is the topic of the clause in (2) may have a modifier clause.

4.1 Identify **the modifier clause for** *no*.

The V-plain form *iware-dashita* is the predicate. The N *koto* is followed by the particle *ga* and is the subject for *iware-dashita*.

> **koto** (SUBJ) *ga* **iware-dashita** (PRED)] *no wa*
> *no* which* a matter/fact . . . began to be talked about

> > * This can be "who" if *no* represents a person, "when" if *no* is a time, or "where" if it is a place or circumstance.

4.2 Is there a modifier for the subject *koto*?

Yes: **'D no E' toiu** *koto ga* . . . Let us assume that *D no E* is "E of D." CHECK this later.

> *Toiu* is a V-plain form but **not a predicate** of a clause:

> > *X toiu Y* = Y called/of X

4.3 Is there any other element in the modifier clause for *no*?

C de 'D no E' toiu koto ga iware-dashita] *no wa,* . . . *L da.*

De may be the **instrumental** *de* "by means of, " or may indicate **a place of action**, or **reason** "due to . . . ," or else is **the** -*te* **form of the copula** *da* (ch. 1, § 3.2.2). Since there is no *N* + *wa* to the left of *C de* to constitute *N₁ wa N₂ de,* . . . ("N$_1$ is N$_2$ and . . . ,") this *de* is most likely not the -*te* form of *da*. It indicates the place of an action, gives a reason, or is the instrumental *de*. Let us assume that *C de* gives the place for the closest verb *iware-dashita*. CHECK this later.

> [[*C* (PLACE) *de 'D no E' to iu koto* (SUBJ) *ga iware-dashita* (PRED)]
> the matter of E of D began to be talked about at C

5 Is L modified? What is to the left of the predicate *L da*?

Tsuyomatta is V-plain form and the predicate of a modifier clause for L.

> . . . **tsuyomatta** (PRED)] *L da*
> is L which . . . became strong

6 Is there **a subject** for *tsuyomatta*?

> **K ga** (SUBJ) *tsuyomatta* (PRED)] *L da*
> . . . *is L which K became strong*

7 Is K modified?

Suru is V-plain form and the predicate of a modifier clause for K.

> **H to J o koto ni suru** (PRED)] *K ga tsuyomatta*] *L da*
> differ from H with respect to J   became strong
>
> is L which K, which differs from H with respect to J, became strong

8 Is H modified? There is a *V-te* form to its left.

> *G ga* **okotte** (*V-te*), *H to J o koto ni suru*] *K ga tsuyomatta*] *L da*
> take place

Since *okotte* is a *V-te* form rather than a V-plain form, it is not a predicate at the end of a clause. Accordingly there is no modifier clause for H.

9 *V-te* is a component of a multiple predicate. Does *okotte* go with *(J o) koto ni suru*, or *tsuyomatta*?

> a. If *okotte* goes with *koto ni suru*:
> *G ga* **okotte** (PRED$_a$), *H to J o* **koto ni suru** (PRED$_b$)] *K ga tsuyomatta*

> b. If *okotte* goes with *tsuyomatta*, the beginning of the modifier clause for K is H:
> *G ga* **okotte** (PRED$_a$), [*H to J o koto ni suru*] *K ga* **tsuyomatta** (PRED$_b$).

When the actual words are given the context will determine which is more appropriate. CHECK this later, and also the function of *V-te*: sequence, manner, or reason.

10 Is G modified?

. . . no wa, **F de,** *G ga okotte, H to J o koto ni suru] K ga tsuyomatta] L da*

There is no modifier for G because *. . . no* is the topic for the predicate *L da*.

F de can be a place, instrumental, reason or the *-te* form of the copula *de*.

Notice the comma after *F de*. A comma is often used when *de* is the *-te* form of the copula *da*. Let us assume that *F de* is PRED$_1$, "is F," for the topic *no*.

$$. . . no \text{ (TOP) } wa, F de \text{ (PRED}_1\text{)}, [. . .] L da \text{ (PRED}_2\text{)}$$
$$\text{X is F, and is L}$$

CHECK this later.

11 With the words given, translate the entire sentence.

Kyōiku-gakusha(A), *Kaigo Muneomi shi*(B) *no hanashi ni yoruto,* [[*Nihon*(C) *de kyōiku*(D) *no chūritsu*(E) *toiu koto ga iware-dashita] no wa, Meiji jūnen-dai*(F) *de, jiyūminkenundō*(G) *ga okotte, seifu*(H) *to iken*(J) *o koto ni suru] seron*(K) *ga tsuyomatta] toki*(L) *da] to iu.*

> A= education scholar B= (name) C= Japan D= education E= neutrality
> F= second decade of Meiji G= freedom and rights movement H= government J= opinion K= public opinion L= time

√ From (1): "According to the story/account* of an education scholar, Mr. Muneomi Kaigo, I understand that . . ."

> * "Account" would be better in this context.

√ From (4.2) and (4.3): "the matter called/of* neutrality (E) of education(D) began to be talked about in Japan"

> * "of" would be better in this context.

It is confirmed that *E no D* is "D of E" "neutrality of* education"

> * "in" might be better here: "neutrality in education."

It is also confirmed that C ("Japan") is the place for *iware-dashita* "began to be talked about."

√ From (3) and (10): It is confirmed that *de* of *F de* (= *Meiji jūnendai de* "is the second decade of Meiji") is not instrumental or place but the *-te* form of *da* serving as PRED$_1$. *Toki* (L) *da* is PRED$_2$. Accordingly *no* should be the pronominal meaning "time":

. . . no wa, meiji jūnendai de, . . .   toki (L) *da . . .*

TOP   second decade of Meiji (PRED₁)   was the time when (PRED₂)

the time when . . . in Japan was the second decade of Meiji, and was the time when . . .

√ From (11.3) above *F de* is confirmed as PRED1. Thus, G is the beginning of a clause.

From (9) Supposing that PREDₐ and PREDᵦ are in SEQUENCE*:

   a. [*G ga okotte* (PREDₐ), *H to J o koto ni suru* (PREDᵦ)] *K ga tsuyomatta*

    public opinion, in which the "freedom and rights" movement **took place and differed** from the government with respect to its opinion, became stronger

   b. [*G ga okotte* (PREDₐ), [*H to J o koto ni suru*] *K ga tsuyomatta* (PREDᵦ)

    the freedom and rights movement **took place** and public opinion which differed from the government with respect to its opinion **became stronger**.

Of the two, (b) makes more sense.

> * PREDₐ could also be considered as the reason for PREDᵦ: "public opinion which differed from the government became stronger because the freedom and rights movement took place."

Combine (11.1), (11.3), (11.2) and (11.4) above.

Kyōiku gakusha,   *Kaigo Muneomi shi no hanashi ni yoruto,* [[*Nihon de*
education scholar APP Mr. Muneomi Kaigo   according to the account of   in Japan

kyōiku no chūritsu *toiu koto ga*   *iware-dashita*] **no wa,**
neutrality in education   a matter SUBJ   began to be talked=V-PRED PRON TOP

Meiji jūnendai de,   [*jiyūminken - undō ga*
second decade of Meiji is=N+COP-TE-PRED₁   freedom and rights movement SUBJ

okotte,   [*seifu to iken o koto ni suru*]
took place=V-TE-PREDₐ   from the government with respect to an opinion differ=V-PRED

seron ga   *tsuyomatta*]   **toki da**]
public opinion SUBJ became stronger=V-PREDᵦ   the time is=N+COP-PRED₂

to iu.
I understand=PRED

According to Mr. Muneomi Kaigo, an education scholar, I understand that the time when the matter of neutrality in education began to be talked about in Japan **was** the second decade of the Meiji (Period), **which was** [the time] when the "freedom and rights" movement took place and public opinion **differing** from the government's became stronger.

Sentence 4

A を、こうした思いもかけぬ B の C の D で、しかも、追われて E の F も分からずに逃げているという、思いもかけぬ G で歌うのです。

A o, kōshita[1] *omoi mo kakenu*[2] *B no C no D de, shikamo,*[3] *owarete*[4] *E no F mo wakarazuni nigete-iru*[5] *to iu, omoi mo kakenu G de utau no desu.*

[1] *Kōshita* (PreN) = *kono yō na* or *konna,* "this kind of." This should not be confused with *V-ta* as a predicate ending a modifier clause just as *kōshite* "in this way" should not be taken as a *V-te* form in a multiple predicate. (See ch. 4, § 3.6.2 on this issue.)

[2] *nu* is the equivalent of *nai*, the negative suffix. The emphasis particle *mo* is inserted after the *omoi* of *omoigakenai* (ADJ) "unexpected" (consisting of *omoi* and *kakenai*) to mean "truly/totally unexpected."

[3] "moreover"

[4] "being chased"

[5] "is running away"

1 What is **the sentence pattern?**

The predicate is *utau* (V-plain) *no* (EMPHASIS/SOFTENER) *desu*. (See ch. 4, § 6.4.) The sentence pattern is **N wa V.**

> ↪ In conversation, politeness is a concern, and so a *no* might be a softener. But since this sentence is not part of a conversation, it is unlikely to be in this case. Let us take this *no* as emphasis for the time being, and CHECK it later.

2   Where is the topic?

Since there is no *wa* or *ga*, **let us suppose that the topic word X has been omitted.** (Usually an omitted topic is the same topic as that of the previous sentence, or else stands for a person already mentioned earlier, or for "I," the writer, or else for the general "we" or "one.") CHECK this later.

3 *Utau* is Vt and takes a direct object.

3.1 Is there **a direct object particle** *o*?

A is followed by *o* and is therefore the direct object of *utau*. Since it is far from the verb, it is followed by a comma. By deviating from the usual order of *N wa* PLACE *de N* (OBJ) *o Vt*, a special effect is intended—perhaps to emphasize or highlight the direct object. The double occurrence of the word "unexpected" may also suggest a certain dramatic effect.

The sentence structure is:

(*X* (TOP) *wa*) **A** (OBJ) o, . . . *utau no* (EMPH) *desu* (PRED).
X **does** sing **A** . . .

3.2 Is there a place of action for the Vt *utau*? Look for the place particle *de* to the left of *utau no desu*.

D and G are both followed by *de*. Normally there should be only one place of action in a sentence. The second *de* is closer to the verb *utau* "sing" and probably indicates a place or is instrumental. Let us determine the first *de* later, and assume for now that G indicates the place of an action. CHECK this later.

(*X wa*) *A* o, . . . *G* (PLACE) *de utau no desu.*
X does sing A at G.

3.3 What is G modified by?

. . . *nigete-iru*] *toiu,*   **omoi mo kakenu** *G de* . . .
running away   totally unexpected

at totally unexpected G that . . .

G is modified by an ADJ, *omoi mo kakenu*, as well as a *toiu* clause.
   Nigete-iru is a V-plain form and the predicate of the *toiu* clause. Since *toiu* is followed by a comma, it does not modify the N immediately after *omoi* (literally, "thought"). In other words G is modified by a *toiu* clause, but with the ADJ *omoi mo kakenu* "totally unexpected" inserted: "totally unexpected G that . . ."

4 Analyze:

shikamo, owarete E no F mo wakarazuni nigete-iru] *toiu, omoi mo kakenu G de* . . .

4.1 What is the subject for *nigete-iru*?

Let us assume that the subject for this predicate is the same as the topic of the whole sentence:

[(*X ga*) . . . *nigete-iru*]
X is running away

CHECK this later.

4.2 *E no F mo wakarazuni.* What is *wakarazuni*?

Wakarazu is the negative V-te form of the verb *wakaru* "understand." *Wakarazu ni,* "without understanding," functions as a component of a multiple predicate. Its function is sequence, manner, or reason (ch. 1, § 3.2.2).

4.3 The verb *wakaru* is Vi. Is there a subject for *wakarazuni*?

The *mo* of *F mo* indicates emphasis—"not even F of E*"—and has replaced the subject particle *ga*:

> *E no F mo (= ga) wakarazuni*
> without even knowing F of E

> * CHECK later the relationship of E and F.

4.4 There are three verbs: *owarete* (V_1-*te*), *wakarazu ni* (V_2-Neg-*te*), and *nigete-iru* (V_3). How are they related?

It is not likely that V_1 and V_2 and V_3 are in sequence, in view of the meanings already given: "be chased," "not understand," and "be running away."

There are two other possibilities for the following segment:

> *shikamo, owarete* (V_1) *E no F mo wakarazuni* (V_2) *nigete-iru* (V_3)] *toiu, omoi mo kakenu G de*

   a. The -*te* forms are giving a REASON for $V_3 - V_3$ because V_1 and V_2:
      "(X is) running away (V_3), because being chased (V_1) and without even understanding (V_2) F of E"

   b. V_3 goes with V_1 and V_2 respectively, with the -*te* forms having more the sense of MANNER:
      "(X is) running away, being chased and not understanding F of E."

CHECK which is the case later.

5 Where is the beginning of the *toiu* clause?

> **A o**, *kōshita omoi mo kakenu B no C no D de, shikamo* ("moreover"), *owarete E no F mo wakarazuni nigete-iru*] *toiu, omoi mo kakenu* **G de utau no desu**.

What is the *de* of D *de*? What does *shikamo* connect?

We notice a parallel structure: . . . **D de** / *shikamo* . . . **G de** *utau no desu*. Since we took G as a place, let us also assume that D is a place for *utau no desu* ("sing"): "sing **at D** and moreover **at G**." CHECK this later.

Shikamo "moreover" connects the two places for *utau*, D and G. The beginning of the *toiu* clause for G should then be right after *shikamo*.

> (*X wa*) *A o, kōshita omoi mo kakenu B no C no D de, shikamo,* **[owarete E no F mo wakarazuni nigete-iru]** *toiu, omoi mo kakenu G de utau no desu*.

> X **does** sing A at D . . . and moreover at G . . .

6 Examine what is to the left of D.

6.1 Let us assume *B no C no D* is "D of C of B" for now. CHECK this later.

6.2 The ADJ *omoi mo kakenu* "totally unexpected" probably modifies D rather than B or C, since the other place word G is also modified by *omoi mo kakenu*: **omoi mo kakenu** *B no C no* **D** *de* "at a totally unexpected D of C of B."

6.3 *kōshita*, which means "this kind of," also modifies D.

> **kōshita** *omoi mo kakenu B no C no* **D** *de*
> at this kind of totally unexpected D of C of B

7 With the words given, translate the sentence.

> *Sore* ("Home Sweet Home*")(A) *o, kōshita omoi mo kakenu ikyō*(B) *no yama*(C) *no naka*(D) *de, shikamo, [owarete asu*(E) *no inochi*(F) *mo wakarazu ni nigete-iru] toiu, omoi mo kakenu kyōgū*(G) *de utau no desu.*

> * This is the name of a song mentioned earlier in the passage where this sentence appears.

A= (a song) B= a foreign land C= mountain D= in E= tomorrow F= life
G= circumstance

√ From (2) and (3.1): Since this sentence is from a passage about "we Japanese soldiers," the omitted topic X is "we": "we do sing it at G."

√ From (4.1): It is confirmed that X, the subject for *nigete-iru*, is the same as the topic "we": "we (= Japanese soldiers) are running away."

√ From (3.2): It is confirmed that the *de* of *G de* is a place particle, indicating here a circumstance: "we do sing in the circumstance."

√ From (4.3): "F of E" = the life of tomorrow (in this context it means "tomorrow's fate" — whether one will be alive or dead the next day).

√ From (4.4):

> a. (we) are retreating (V3) because we are being pursued (V1) and we don't know (V2) whether we will be alive or dead the next day.
> b. (we) are retreating (V3), being pursued (V1) and without even knowing (V3) whether we will be alive or dead the next day.

Of these, (b) makes more sense.

√ From (5) and (6.1): it is confirmed that *de* of *D de* indicates a place of action and that *B no C no D* is "D of C of B."

√ From (6.2), and (6.3): *kōshita omoi mo kakenu ikyō*(B) *no yama*(C) *no naka*(D) *de* "in this kind of totally unexpected mountains of a foreign land."

Omoi mo kakenu, "totally unexpected," modifies *C no D* rather than just D: "in the totally unexpected mountains."

√ Put (6.3), (3.3) and (7.5) above into (5):

"We do[1] sing it[2] in this kind of totally unexpected mountains of a foreign land, and moreover in the totally unexpected circumstance where we are retreating while being pursued, and without knowing whether we will be alive or dead the next day."

> [1] The entire passage is about something which happened in the past. The use of the present tense here is for dramatization (see ch. 3, § 3.2). In the final translation one should use the past tense.
>
> [2] "It" here refers to a British song "Home Sweet Home" which Japanese soldiers sang in the jungles of Burma during the Second World War.

√ From (3.1) It is confirmed that a kind of emphasis or certain dramatization is achieved by placing the direct object at the very beginning of the sentence.

(X wa) Sore o, *kōshita omoi mo kakenu ikyō no yama no naka de,*
("we"=OMIT-TOP) it OBJ this kind of totally unexpected foreign land in the mountains

shikamo, [owarete   *asu no inochi mo*
moreover , being chased=V-PASS-PRED$_1$ tomorrow's life SUBJ (= *ga*)

wakarazuni   *(X ga)*   *nigete-iru] toiu,*
not knowing=V-TE-MNR-PRED$_2$ ("we"=OMIT-SUBJ)   running away=V-ONG-PRED$_3$

omoi mo kakenu kyōgū de   **utau no desu**.
totally unexpected in the circumstances   do sing=V-EMPH-PRED

> We **did*** sing **that song** in **such unimaginable** mountains of a foreign land, and moreover, in the totally unexpected circumstance of retreating **in the face of pursuit**, without knowing whether the next day **we would live or die**.

> * From (1): It is confirmed that the *no* of *utau no desu* is used for emphasis rather than as a softener in this context.

A から帰る B で C と行き合いながら、知らずに通り過ぎた事が二度あった
そうである。

A kara kaeru B de C to iki-ai[1]*-nagara, shirazuni*[2] *tōri-sugita*[3] *koto ga nido*[4] *atta sō dearu.*

[1] "come across"

[2] "without knowing"

[3] "passed by"

[4] "twice"

1 Look at the end of the sentence. Is there **a sentence-ending expression**?

Sō dearu "I hear/understand that" is the sentence ending (ch 4. § 14). This kind of ending often takes . . . *ni yoruto*, "according to," at the beginning of the sentence, though it apparently doesn't in the present case. The structure is simply [. . .] *sō dearu*: "I hear/understand that . . ."

2 [**A kara kaeru B de C to iki-ai-nagara, shirazuni tōri-sugita koto ga nido atta**] *sō dearu.*

What is the structure of the content of what is heard?

Since the predicate of this clause is *atta* "there was," one can expect to find a **subject** + *ga* to its left.

> *koto** (SUBJ) *ga nido atta* (PRED)
> have done something twice

V-**ta** *koto ga aru* is a construction meaning "have the experience of having done . . ." It should be carefully distinguished from: V-**ru** *koto ga aru* "there are times when one does . . . (or when something happens)."

Since the verb preceding *koto* is in the past tense, it is a case of the former construction: *tōri-sugita koto ga nido atta* "have passed by twice."

3 [**A kara kaeru B de C to iki-ai-nagara, shirazuni tōri-sugita** *koto ga nido atta*] *sō dearu.*

Is there **a topic** for the clause of what is heard?

No, there is **no TOPIC** + *wa* to the left of *koto* (SUBJ). Let us have X stand for **an omitted topic**. (CHECK X later.)

> (*X wa*) . . . *tōri-sugita koto ga nido atta*
> (X) has passed by twice.

4 What or whom did X pass by? Since *tōri-sugita* is Vt, it can have **a direct object**.

Since there is no DIR OBJ + *o*, let us have Y stand for an object that has been **omitted**.

> (*X wa*) (*Y o*) *tōri-sugita koto ga nido atta*
> X has passed by Y twice.

CHECK this later.

5 *A kara kaeru B de C to iki-ai-nagara,* **shirazu ni** *tōri-sugita*

To the left of *tōri-sugita* is *shirazuni*. What is its function and meaning?

It is a negative *V-te* form meaning "without knowing," and it conveys **the manner** for *tōri-sugita*:

> (*X wa*) (*Y o*) *shirazu ni* (Vneg-*te*, MANNER) *tōri-sugita koto ga nido atta*
>
> X has passed by Y twice without knowing (it).

6 *A kara kaeru B de C to* **iki-ai nagara**, *shirazu ni*

To the left of *shirazu ni* is *iki-ai nagara*. What is its function?

Iki-ai is the stem of the verb (*hito*) *to iki-au*, "to come across (a person)."

Nagara is used for either (a) simultaneous actions, or (b) "although, even though" (ch. 4, § 2.6)

> a. *X wa C to iki-ai-nagara* (SIMULTANEOUS ACTION), . . . *Y o tōri-sugita*
>   X passed by Y . . . coming across C
>
> b. *X wa C to iki-ai-nagara* ("even though"), . . . *Y o tōri-sugita*
>   X passed by Y . . . even though coming across C

Of these (b) seems to make more sense.

7 [*A kara kaeru B de* . . .

7.1 *Kaeru* ("return") is V-plain and is therefore the predicate of a modifier clause for the following N, B. The beginning of this clause should be A, which is also the beginning of the clause for *sō dearu*:

> [*A kara kaeru*] B
> B which/who returns from A, or
> B where (someone) returns from A.

7.2 *De* is the instrumental *de*, or it indicates the place of an action, or reason, or else it is the *-te* form of the copula *da*. It is most likely that *de* here indicates a place of an action since the verbs appearing to its right are *iki-ai* "come across" and *tōri-sugita* "passed by."

For now let us assume that it indicates a place of action. If so, [*A kara kaeru*] *B de* should mean "at B where (someone) returns from A." CHECK this later.

7.3 Who returns from A?

There is **no subject** for *kaeru* so let us assume that Z returns:

> [(*Z ga*) *A kara kaeru*] *B de*
> at B where Z returns from A.

CHECK this later.

There are three possible verbs for *B de* to go with:

> [*A kara kaeru* **B de** *C to* **ikiai** (V₁)-*nagara, shirazu ni* **tōri-sugita** (V₂) *koto ga nido* **atta** (V₃)] *sō dearu.*

It may go with the closest V, *ikiai*; or with the next V, *tōri-sugita*; or with the third V, *atta*.

Let us assume that it goes with the first, *ikiai*. Since . . . *to iki-ai* means "to come across someone," the *B de* must indicate a place:

> [(*Z ga*) *A kara kaeru*] **B de** *(X wa) C to* **iki-ai**-*nagara*
> even though X comes across C at B where Z returns from A

CHECK this later.

8 With the words given, translate the sentence.

> [(*Z ga*) *daigaku*(A) *kara kaeru*] *michi*(B) *de tsuma*(C) *to iki-ai-nagara,* (*X wa*) (*Y o*) *shirazuni tōri-sugita koto ga nido atta*] *sō dearu.*

📝 A= university   B= road/way   C= wife

↪ This sentence is from a passage about a university professor recounting his experience on the day the atomic bomb was dropped on Nagasaki. The paragraph it occurs in describes his life with his wife prior to that day when he was engrossed with his research. The topic X is therefore "I," the writer. Accordingly, Z is also "I," and Y is *tsuma* "my wife." See (3), (4) and (7.2).

√ From (7.3): It is confirmed that *B de = michi de* ("on the road/way") is the place for the closest verb, *iki-ai* "to come across":

> "I had passed by my wife twice without knowing it, even though coming across my wife **on my way back from the university**."

Add (1)

> "I understand that I had twice passed by my wife without knowing it, while (=even though) coming across **her** on my way back from the university."

[[(*Z ga*) *Daigaku kara kaeru*]   *michi de tsuma to*
("I"=OMIT-SUBJ) from the university return=V-PRED   on the way (home) my wife

iki-ai-nagara,   **(X wa)**   **(Y o)**   *shirazu ni*
come across even though ("I"=OMIT-TOP) ("my wife"=OMIT-OBJ) not knowing=V$_1$-neg-TE-MNR

tōrisugita koto ga   *nido* **atta**] *sō dearu.*
have passed by=V$_2$-PRED   twice   I hear=PRED

> I understand that I had twice passed by my wife without knowing it, on my way back from the university.

Sentence 6

誰がＡに言い出したことかは知らないが、このＢで言うなら、Ｃもどこか
Ｄに似ていて、考えた後で歩き出す、といったＥに属すると言ってよいか
もしれない。

Dare ga A ni ii-dashita[1] *koto ka wa shiranai ga, kono B de iunara, C mo dokoka*[2] *D ni nite-ite*[3]*, kangaeta ato de aruki-dasu, to itta* E ni zokusuru*[4] *to itte yoi kamo shirenai.*

[1] "began to say"

[2] "somewhere/somewhat"

[3] "resemble"

[4] "belong to"

> * *... to itta* + N, "such a N as/that ..." or "a N something like ..., the kind of N that ..." is a variation of *... toiu* + N. This should not be confused with the past tense of the verb *iu*, which as a predicate would indicate the end of a clause. (See ch. 4, § 8.1.)

1 Look at **the end of the sentence.**

[. . .] *to itte yoi kamoshirenai*, "it may be all right to say that . . . " (consisting of
. . . *to* itte yoi* "is alright to say . . ." and *kamoshirenai* "maybe, perhaps, probably") is a typical sentence-ending expression qualifying the writer's commitment to the assertion. (See ch. 4, § 14.) Set this aside for the time being.

* *to* is the quotation particle attached to a quotation clause.

2 In a quotation clause followed by a sentence-ending expression one is likely
to find TOP + *wa*, but let us first ascertain **the predicate of this clause.**

> *Dare ga A ni ii-dashita koto ka wa shiranai ga, kono B de iu nara, C mo
> dokoka D ni nite-ite, kangaeta ato de aruki-dasu, to itta E ni* **zokusuru** (V-
> plain, PRED)] *to itte yoi kamoshirenai.*

Zokusuru "belong to" is V-plain and the predicate of the "that" clause. The *ni* of
E ni can indicate time, location, a goal, or else form an adverbial phrase—as in
hontō ni "truly, really" (ch. 4, § 7). Here, it is likely to indicate the location for
something to "belong to": *E ni zokusuru* "belong to E." CHECK this later.

3 [. . . *to itta E ni zokusuru*]

Is E modified?

Yes, it is modified by the *to itta* clause which has the meaning of "the kind
of E that . . ."

> *kangaeta ato de* **aruki-dasu** (V-plain, PRED)], *to itta* **E** *ni zokusuru*]
> . . . belongs to the kind of E that . . . begins to walk

4 . . . *kangaeta* **ato de** *aruki-dasu* (V-plain, PRED)], *to itta E ni zokusuru*]
What is *ato de*?

Ato de ("later, after") is an adverbial phrase of TIME for *aruki-dasu* ("begin to
walk").

Is *ato* a N? If so, is it modified?

Yes, it is a N and is modified by a clause whose predicate is *kangaeta* (V-
plain, "thought"):

> . . . **kangaeta**] *ato de*
> after . . . thought

5 . . . **C mo dokoka D ni nite-ite, kangaeta** (V-plain, PRED)] *ato de aruki-
dasu* (PRED)], *to itta E ni zokusuru*]

Is there a topic or subject for the predicate *kangaeta*?

The *mo* of *C mo* has replaced the original particle—either *ga* or *wa*. Let us assume that *mo* has replaced the subject particle *ga*. CHECK this this later.

6 . . . *C mo dokoka D ni* **nite-ite**, *kangaeta*] *ato de*

There is another V to the left of *kangaeta*. Is it **a predicate at the end of a clause?**

No, it is the *V-te* form of *N ni nite-iru*, "to resemble N." It is PRED$_1$ (V$_1$) of a multiple predicate.

7 . . . *C mo* (= *ga* SUBJ) *dokoka D ni* **nite-ite** (V$_1$-*te*), **kangaeta** (V$_2$)] *ato de* (TIME) **aruki-dasu** (V$_3$)], *to itta E ni* **zokusuru** (V$_4$)] *to itte yoi kamoshirenai.*

Which verb does *nite-iru* go with? Assuming for now that the verbs are in sequence, the possibilities are:

a. *Nite-ite* (V$_1$) goes with the closest V, *kangaeta* (V$_2$), in a modifier clause for *ato*. If it does, the *mo* can be considered to have replaced the subject *ga*, since *wa* is not possible in a modifier clause.

   C mo (= *ga*) *doko ka D ni* **nite-ite** (V$_1$), **kangaeta** (V$_2$)] *ato de aruki-dasu*], *to itta E ni zokusuru*

   . . . belongs to the kind of E that . . . begins to walk after C also somewhat resembled* D and thought

   * The tense of multiple predicates is determined by that of the final V (ch. 1, § 3.2.2). V$_2$ is in the past tense and so V$_1$ here will also be past.

b. *Nite-iru* (V$_1$) and *aruki-dasu* (V$_3$) go together. If so, *kangaeta* constitutes a clause by itself. Let us have X stand for the omitted subject of *kangaeta*.

   C mo (= *wa**/*ga*) *doko ka D ni* **nite-ite** (V$_1$), [(*X ga*) *kangaeta*] *ato de* **aruki-dasu** (V$_2$)], *to itta E ni zokusuru*

   . . . belongs to the kind of E that C also somewhat resembles D and begins to walk after X has thought

   * C could be the topic in a quotation clause which ends with *aruki-dasu.*

c. *Nite-iru* (V$_1$) and *zokusuru* (V$_4$) go together. Let us have Y stand for the topic for *aruki-dasu.*

   C mo (= *wa**/*ga*) *dokoka D ni* **nite-ite** (V$_1$), [(*Y wa*)][(*X ga*) *kangaeta*] *ato de aruki-dasu*], *to itta E ni* **zokusuru** (V$_2$)] *to itte* . . .

   C also somewhat resembles D and [it=C**] belongs to the kind of E that Y begins to walk after X has thought

We are now assuming that X is the omitted subject for *kangaeta* and Y is the topic for *aruki-dasu*.

> * C could be the topic in a quotation clause that ends with *zokusuru*.
>
> ** V$_2$ shares with V$_1$ the same topic/subject, C: *C wa/ga* V$_1$, . . . V$_2$.

CHECK which possibility fits best when the actual words are given. The context will determine the structure.

8 What is to the left of C?

. . . **ga, kono B de iu nara**, *C mo dokoka D ni nite-ite,* [(Y wa) [(X ga) kangaeta] *ato de aruki-dasu*], *to itta E ni zokusuru*

What is *iu nara*?

Iu is V-plain form and is the predicate of a conditional clause marked by *nara*.

8.1 . . . *kono* **B de** *iu*] *nara* (CONDITIONAL), . . .

What is the *de* of *B de*? It can be the instrumental *de*, the reason *de*, or else it can indicate a place of action. Let us assume for now that it indicates a place.

CHECK this later.

8.2 Is there a subject for *iu*?

Dare ga A ni ii-dashita koto ka wa shiranai **ga,** *kono B de iu*] *nara,*

Does this *ga* indicate a subject?

No. Since it follows V, it is not a particle but **the conjunction** *ga* connecting two sentences. It thus marks the end of the first sentence. In this case the beginning of the conditional clause will be *kono*: . . . [*kono B de iu*] *nara,* . . .

Let us assume that the subject of this clause has been omitted, and that the omitted subject is the writer, "I": [(*Watakushi ga*) *kono B de iu*] *nara,* "if I speak at this B." CHECK this later.

9 What does this conditional clause go with: (a) *nite-ite,* (b) *aruki-dasu,* (c) *zokusuru,* or (d) *to itte yoi kamoshirenai*?

CHECK this later.

10 Examine the first sentence: **Dare ga A ni ii-dashita koto ka wa shiranai ga,**

10.1 The closest subject *dare* and the predicate *ii-dashita* constitute a modifier clause for the following N, *koto. A ni* can indicate time, goal (as in "to A"), or else be an adverbial phrase consisting of *N + ni* (as in *hontō ni* "truly, indeed").

> [**Dare** (SUBJ) **ga** *A ni* (TIME, GOAL., or ADVERBIAL) **ii-dashita** (PRED)] *koto ka*
> a matter [of] who began to say . . .

10.2 *Koto* is followed by the question particle *ka* which marks the end of an interrogative clause: [*Dare ga A ni ii-dashita*] *koto ka*]

This interrogative clause is a case of either an indirect quotation or a N clause. (See ch. 1, § 3.1.2B.)

10.3 The sentence pattern of this interrogative clause is *N wa N (da) ka*, in which the copula *da* has been omitted because it is within an interrogative clause. Since there is no topic, let us assume an omitted topic, Z:

> [(**Z wa**) [*Dare ga A ni ii-dashita*] **koto ka**] *wa shiranai*

10.4 [(*Z wa*) [*Dare ga A ni ii-dashita*] *koto ka*] *wa* **shiranai** ("not know")

Since *shiranai* is Vt one would expect to find a direct object.

The *wa* here does not follow a N but rather a clause. This clause, then, must be a N clause as the direct object for *shiranai*, with either the topic or contrast *wa* having replaced the original *o*. Let us assume that it is the contrast *wa* in the sense of "not knowing who began to say . . . but (at least) knowing . . ."

> [(*Z wa*) [*Dare ga A ni ii-dashita*] *koto ka*] *wa* (= *o*, OBJ) *shiranai*

10.5 Is there a topic or subject for *shiranai*, the predicate of the first sentence?

There is no topic mentioned. Let us assume that the writer "I" is the omitted topic. CHECK this later.

> (**Watakushi** *wa*) [(*Z wa*) [*Dare ga A ni ii-dashita*] *koto ka*] *wa (= o)*
> **shiranai** *ga,*

> "I don't know if Z is a matter of who began to say . . . ," meaning
> "I don't know who began to say Z, but . . ."

11 With the words given, translate the entire sentence.

(*Watakushi wa*) [(*Z wa*) [*Dare ga saisho*(A) *ni ii-dashita*] *koto ka*] *wa(=o) shiranai ga,* [[(*watakushi ga*) *kono hippō*(B) *de iu nara, doitsujin*(C) *mo dokoka furansujin*(D) *ni nite-ite, kangaeta*] *ato de* (*X ga*) *aruki-dasu*], *to itta burui*(E) *ni zokusuru*] *to itte yoi kamoshirenai.*

⟨image⟩ A= first B= penmanship/style C= Germans D= Frenchmen E= a group, category

√ From (2): *E ni zokusuru* "belongs to a group." It is confirmed that E is a location something belongs to.

√ From (7):

> a. *doitsujin mo dokoka furansujin ni* **nite-ite** (V₁), **kangaeta** (V₂) *ato de aruki-dasu], to itta burui ni* **zokusuru** (V₃)
> ". . . to the kind of group that . . . begins to walk after the Germans also somewhat **resembled** the French and **thought**"

> b. *doitsujin mo dokoka furansujin ni* **nite-ite** (V₁), [(*X ga*) *kangaeta] ato de* **aruki-dasu** (V₂)] *to itta burui ni zokusuru*
> ". . . belongs to the kind of group that the Germans also somewhat **resemble** the French and **begin to walk** after X has thought"

> c. *doitsujin mo dokoka furansujin ni* **nite-ite** (V₁), [(*Y wa*) [(*X ga*) *kangaeta] ato de aruki-dasu* (V₂)], *to itta burui ni* **zokusuru**(V₃)
> "the Germans also somewhat **resemble** the French, and they (= the Germans) **belong** to the kind of group that Y begins to walk after X has thought"

Among these, (c) makes the most sense: *nite-ite* (PRED₁) and *zokusuru* (PRED₂).

Nite-ite is accompanied by an explanation of the respects in which one resembles the other, and is thus closer to the "reason" than the "sequence" type of *-te*:

> the Germans also somewhat resemble the French
> in belonging to (= insofar as they belong to) the kind of group that Y* begins
> to walk after X* has thought

> > * Y and X in this context is "(a type of) people."

√ From (8.2): (*watakushi ga*) *kono hippō de iu nara* "if I speak in (= using) this style [of writing]" or "speaking in this manner." *De* does not indicate a place but an instrument ("by means of").

From (8.2): It is confirmed that the omitted subject for *iu* "speak" is "I," the writer.

√ From (7) and (9): "if I speak in this manner" or "in speaking in this manner" (from 11.3 above) does not go with *aruki-dasu* (from 11.2 above): it goes with *to itte yoi kamoshirenai*.

> . . . **(watakushi ga) kono hippō de iu nara**, [*doitsujin mo dokoka furansujin ni nite-ite*, [(*Y wa*) [(*X ga*) *kangaeta ato de aruki-dasu*], *to itta burui ni zokusuru*] *to itte-yoi kamoshirenai*.

> **If I speak in this manner, it may be all right to say that** the Germans also somewhat resemble the French and belong to . . .

√ From (10.5) and (10.4): "(I) don't know who began to say Z first, but . . ." It is confirmed that "I" is the omitted topic.

Combine this with (11.4) above and add (1)

> "**It may be all right to say** that I don't know who began to say Z first, but . . ."

This doesn't make sense. The sentence-ending expression must cover only the second sentence (after . . . *ga,*). Let us try again.

> "I don't know who began to say Z first, but, if I speak in this manner, **it may be all right to say** that the Germans also somewhat resemble the French, in belonging to the kind of people who begin to walk after they thought."

Z seems to refer to "the speaking manner" which appears in the conditional *nara* clause as *kono hippō* "this style (of speaking)." If so, the first sentence is actually inserted or added on to the conditional clause rather than being parallel to the second sentence which begins after the conjunction *ga.*

⮑ This sentence is from a passage about characterizing nationalities in terms of their modes of thinking and acting, using the metaphor of walking for action. The French and the Germans think first, but the French then run (= act in a rush whereas the Germans then walk (= act steadily). But the French and the Germans are similar in that they think before acting.

√ From (11.4): It is confirmed that the *wa* of . . . *wa shiranai ga* is the contrast *wa* contrasting the writer's not knowing who began to speak this way with his at least knowing this way of speaking.

(*Watakushi wa*) [(Z *wa*)   [*Dare ga saisho ni ii-dashita*]
("I"=OMIT TOP)   ("this speaking manner"=OMIT-TOP)   who SUBJ first began to say=V-PRED

koto ka]   *wa   shiranai   ga,*
a matter (is)=N+(COP)-PRED-QUES OBJ (= o)-CONT don't know-V-PRED   but=CONJ

[*(watakushi ga) kono hippō de iu*]   *nara*   [**doitsujin mo**   *dokoka*
("I"=OMIT-SUBJ)   this style   INST say=V-COND-PRED Germans TOP (*wa*) ALSO somewhat

furansujin ni **nite-ite,**   [(*Y wa*)   [*(X ga*)
French resemble=V₁-STATE-TE-PRED₁   ("people"=OMIT TOP)   ("people"=OMIT SUBJ)

kangaeta]   *ato de aruki-dasu*],   *to itta*   *burui ni*
thought=V-PRED   after   begin to walk=V-PRED   something like group

zokusuru]   *to*   *itte yoi*   *kamoshirenai.*
belong=V₂-PRED₂   QUOT   may be all right to say=(*V-te ii*)   probably-PRED

> If I use this kind of **[metaphorical] language**—I don't know who **first spoke in this way**—it may be all right to say that the Germans also somewhat resemble the French **in being the kind of people who begin to "walk" [act] after having thought.**

ことに A は、 B が C をする D の E の F を歌ったもので、 G の H は、 J を聞くと、 K の幼かったころの事、 L の事、 M の事を思うのです。

Kotoni[1] *A wa, B ga C o suru D no E no F o utatta mono de, G no H wa, J o kiku to, K no osanakatta*[2] *koro no koto, L no koto, M no koto o omou no desu.*

[1] "especially"
[2] "was little/young"

1 Examine the end of the sentence.

There is no special sentence-ending expression. The predicate has *no desu,* and so it is a case of *N desu.* There are two possibilities for *no desu:* (a) N_1 *no* (N_2) *desu* in which N_2 has been omitted, or (b) V-plain *no desu.* The predicate here is *omou no desu* (V-plain + *no* + Copula). *No* in the predicate is either EMPHASIS or SOFTENER (ch. 4, § 6.4). Let us take this *no* as emphasis since this sentence is not part of a conversation. CHECK this later.

> . . . *omou no desu.*
> . . . do think.

2 Since *omou* is Vt, is there **a direct object**?

Yes: . . . *koro* ("about the time") *no koto1* (N_1), *L no koto2* (N_2) and *M no koto3* (N_3) are the objects. Three *koto*(N)s without any particle in-between are either in apposition or are being listed out (with a particle such as *to* "and," or *ya* ". . . and so on," being omitted.) CHECK this later.

> . . . *K no osanakatta koro no* **koto**₁, *L no* **koto**₂, *M no* **koto**₃ *o omou no desu*
> . . . think of *koto*₁, *koto*₂, and *koto*₃

3 Locate **the topic** for the main predicate *omou.*

Kotoni **A wa**, *B ga C o suru D no E no F o utatta mono de, G no H* **wa**, *J o kiku to,* . . .

There are two *wa*'s: *A wa* and *G no H wa.*

This may be a case of two topics (ch. 4, § 5.1.1): *A wa B wa C ga* . . . "As for A (TOP1), as for B (smaller TOP2), C (SUBJ) is/does . . ." as in *Kyō wa Jon wa atama ga itai:* "As for today, as for John, his head aches (= John has a headache today)."

Alternatively, A and H may have their respective predicates: *A wa* PRED₁, *G no H wa* PRED₂ (*omou no desu*).

If there are two predicates, the first predicate is likely to be a *-te* form. Is there a *-te* form?

> *Kotoni* **A** (TOP1) **wa**, *B ga C o suru D no E no F o utatta mono de*, **G no H** (TOP2) **wa**, *J o kiku to, K no osanakatta koro no koto, L no koto, M no koto o* **omou no desu** (PRED2).

There is no *V-te* form. However, since the *de* of *mono de* is followed by a comma, it could be the *-te* form of the copula *da* and thus be the predicate for A. CHECK this later.

> *A* (TOP1) *wa*, . . . **mono de** (PRED₁), *G no H* (TOP2) *wa*, . . .
> *omou no desu* (PRED₂)

> A is a thing . . . and H of G* does think

> * CHECK the relationship of H and G later.

4   *Kotoni A* (TOP1) *wa*, **B ga C o suru D no E no F o utatta** *mono de* (PRED₁),

Are there **any clauses** to the right of *A wa* and to the left of *mono de*, the first predicate?

Yes, B is followed by *ga* and is the subject for *suru* (V-plain), and the closest predicate *suru* marks the end of a modifier clause for the following noun, D. *Suru* has a direct object, C.

> [**B** (SUBJ) **ga** *C* (OBJ) *o* **suru** (V-plain, PRED)] **D** *no E no F*
> F of E of D* which B does C

> * Let us assume that *D no E no F* is "F of E of D." Accordingly, F (rather than D) **is modified by the clause.** CHECK these later.

5   *Kotoni A wa*, [**B ga C o suru**] *D no E no F o utatta mono de*,

Are there **any other clauses**?

Yes. F is the direct object for the predicate *utatta*, which marks the end of a modifier clause for the following N, *mono*.

> *Kotoni A wa*, [*B ga C o suru*] *D no E o* **utatta** (V-plain, PRED)]
> *mono de* (PRED₁),

6   Where is **the beginning of this modifier clause**?

The beginning of this clause is at B, since D is modified by the clause identified in (4) above and A is the topic for *mono de*.

> *Kotoni A* (TOP1) *wa*, **[** [**B ga C o suru**] **D** *no E no F o* **utatta]** *mono de* (PRED₁)
> especially A is a thing which sang F of E of D which B does C

7 . . . *mono de, G no H* (TOP2) *wa,* **J o kiku to, K no osanakatta koro** *no koto, L no koto, M no koto o omou no desu* (PRED2).

Are there any predicates to the right of H, the second topic? In other words, are there **any more clauses**?

Kiku ("to hear") is a V-plain form and a predicate. The beginning of the clause is at J, since *G no H* — as the topic for PRED₂, *omou no desu* — cannot be inside this clause.

> [J o **kiku** (PRED)]
> . . . hear J

7.1 What is J? Is there **a subject for** *kiku?*

J is followed by *o* and therefore is a direct object for *kiku*. Since there is no subject in this clause, let us let X stand for an omitted subject here:

> [(X (SUBJ) *ga*) J (OBJ) *o kiku* (PRED)]
> X hears J

7.2 Is *kiku* **the predicate of a modifier clause?**

No. It is **the predicate of an adverbial clause**, since it is followed by *to*. The functions of *to* are:

"when", "if", other adverbial constructions, such as . . . *to sugu/totsuzen* "immediately after . . . ," (see ch. 1, § 3.1.3).

The *to* in this sentence is either "when" or "if," since it is not followed by words such as *sugu* or *itsumo* to constitute an adverbial phrase. Since there is often little difference in meaning between the two, let us leave it for now and let the context determine which is best.

> [[(X *ga*) J *o kiku*] **to**
> when X hears J

8 *G no H wa,* [(X *ga*) J *o kiku*] **to, K no osanakatta**] *koro no koto, L no koto, M no koto o omou no desu.*

What is the next predicate?

Osanakatta is ADJ-plain and could be the predicate of a modifier clause for the following N *koro*, "about the time." K is followed by *no*. Since *no/ga* can indicate a subject in a modifier clause, K must be the subject for the predicate *osanakatta*.

> [K (SUBJ) *no osanakatta* (ADJ-plain, PRED)] *koro*
> about the time when K was little

9 With the words given, translate the entire sentence.

Kotoni "Hanyū no yado"(A) *wa,* [[*igirisujin*(B) *ga jiman*(C) *o suru*] *karera*(D) *no katei*(E) *no tanoshimi*(F) *o utatta*] *mono de, subete*(G) *no igirisujin*(H) *wa,* [[*X ga*) *kore*(J) *o kiku*] *to,* [*jibuntachi*(K) *no osanakatta*] *koro no koto, hahaoya*(L) *no koto, furusato*(M) *no koto o omou no desu.*

> A= "Home Sweet Home" B= the English C= brag D= their E= family and home F= joys G= all H= English J= this K= (one)self L= mother M= home-town

√ From (3.1): *G no H* is not "H of G" but "G-H": "all the English."

√ From (3.1) and (1): It is confirmed that the *de* of *mono de* is the *-te* form of *da* and is therefore the first predicate for the first topic: "'Home Sweet Home' is a thing and . . . all the English do indeed think . . ."

√ From (4): "joys of family and home* which the English are proud of**"

> * [*karera*(D) *no katei*(E)] *no tanoshimi*(F) is "F of D's E": "joys of their home."
>
> ** In this context "be proud of" is better than "to brag" or "be boastful."

√ Put (9.2) and (9.3) together with (6): "Especially 'Home Sweet Home' is a thing which sang about the joys of family and home, which the English are proud of"

√ From (7.2): [[(*X ga*) *J* ("this") *o kiku* ("to hear")] *to*: "when X hears this"

It is confirmed that *to* here means "when."

X is "the English" in this context, and "this" refers to the song "Home Sweet Home."

√ From (8) and (2): "matters concerning the time when they (themselves) were little, matters of mothers, matters of home-towns." In the final translation there is no need to retain the term "matters."

Since these three "matters" are somewhat different but all related to family and home, there is hardly any difference in meaning between taking the relationship as apposition ("matters concerning childhood — that is, mothers and home-towns") or as listing out.

Combine (9.4), (9.5) and (9.6) into (9.2).

Kotoni	**"Hanyū no Yado" wa,**	[[*Igirisujin ga*	*jiman o suru*]
especially	"Home Sweet Home" TOP1	the English SUBJ	be proud of=V-PRED

karera no katei no tanoshimi o	*utatta*]	**mono de,**
their family and home joys OBJ	sang=V-PRED	thing is=N+COP-PRED1

subete no **igirisujin wa,**	[[*X ga*)	*kore o kiku*]	*to,*
all English TOP2	("the English"=OMIT-SUBJ)	this OBJ hear	when

[*jibuntachi no   osanakatta*]   *koro no* **koto,**   *hahaoya no* **koto**

they SUBJ (= *ga*)   were little-ADJ-PRED   about the time matters (N₁)   mothers matters (N₂)

furusato no **koto**   **o**   **omou no desu.**

.home-town   matters (N₃)=OBJ   think=V-EMPH-PRED₂

"Home Sweet Home" **in particular** is a **song** [which sang] **about** the joys of family and home, in which the English **take pride**—and indeed* all the English think of **their childhoods**, their mothers, or their home-towns when they hear this song.

---

* From (1): it is confirmed that the *no* of *omou no desu* indicates EMPHA-
SIS in this context.

Sentence 8

ただちょっと見ただけではまるでAのない様なB が、 C の上からは、お互いによく似た D に見えると言う E の F に G を上げてみたのです。

Tada chotto mita dake de wa marude¹ A no nai yō na B ga, C no ue kara wa, otagaini² yoku nita³ D ni mieru toiu E no F ni G o agete-mita no desu.

¹ "entirely"

² "mutually"

³ "very much resembled"

1 Examine the end of the sentence.

The main predicate is not *N desu* but *agete* (*V-te*, "to raise/give")-*mita** (V-plain) *no* (EMPHASIS or SOFTENER) *desu*.

* *V-te* miru "try doing . . .": *agete-miru* "try raising/giving . . ."

Since this isn't a conversation, let us take the *no* as EMPHASIS.

2 Since *ageru* is Vt, one will expect **a direct object**.

G (OBJ) o *agete-mita no desu* "indeed tried raising/giving G."

3 **Tada chotto mita dake de wa marude A no nai yō na B ga, C no ue kara wa, otagai ni yoku nita D ni mieru toiu E no F ni** *G o agete-mita no desu.*

Is there a topic for the predicate *agete-mita no desu*?

Wa appears twice: . . . *tada chotto mita dake* **de wa** and *C no ue* **kara wa.** Both follow particles rather than the Ns which one would expect as topics for "raising/giving G." Therefore, these *wa*'s are not topic but CONTRAST particles.

Since there doesn't appear to be a topic mentioned, let us assume that the writer, "I," is the omitted topic. CHECK this later.

The items before each *wa*, *tada chotto mita dake* ("by just a glance") and *C no ue kara* ("from on C"), must be in contrast. CHECK this later, too.

4 *(Watakushi wa)* . . . *toiu* **E no F ni** *G o agete-mita no desu*

Let us take *E no F* as "F of E," and CHECK this later.

What is the *ni* after F?

Since the verb is *ageru* "to raise/give," this *ni* is likely to indicate a GOAL (in this case the recipient of the giving): "indeed I tried giving G **to** F of E"
CHECK this later.

5 *marude A no nai yō na B ga, C no ue kara wa, otagai ni yoku nita D ni* **mieru** *toiu* **E no F**

Be careful not to take the *iu* of *toiu* as a V-plain form and thus the predicate of a clause. The *toiu* here is either in a *N toiu N* construction, or else it marks the end of a [. . .] *toiu* clause for E.

5.1 *Tada chotto mita dake de wa marude A no nai yō na B ga, C no ue kara wa, otagai ni yoku nita D ni* **mieru]** *toiu* **E no F**

Mieru is V-plain and the predicate of the *toiu* clause. Since we took *E no F* as "F of E" in (4) above, let us assume that F rather than E is modified by the *toiu* clause: . . . **mieru]** *toiu E no* **F** "F of E that . . ."
CHECK this later.

5.2 Since *mieru* ". . . can be seen," is Vi, one will expect to find a subject. Look for N followed by *ga*.

> . . . *B* (SUBJ) *ga,* . . . *mieru* (PRED)
> B can be seen/appears . . .

⤷ Note that there is another predicate *nita* to the left of *mieru* which might require a subject word. Normally the closest subject and predicate form a clause. However, *B ga* is followed by a comma, which seems to indicate that it is distant from its predicate. Let us assume that B is the subject for *mieru*. CHECK this later.

5.3 What is to the left of *mieru*?

> *B ga, C no ue kara wa, otagai ni yoku* nita **D ni** *mieru*]
> B can be seen as D . . . / B appears to be D . . .

5.4 *B ga, C no ue kara wa, otagai ni* ("mutually") *yoku* **nita** *D ni mieru*]

Is D modified by a clause?

Yes. *Nita* (V-plain) is the predicate of a clause modifying the noun, D.

⤳ *Nita* is the past tense of *niru* "to resemble" and is used in this case as the equivalent of *nite-iru*, the STATE construction functioning as a single ADJ to describe a state as in *kowareta* (= *kowarete-iru*) *omocha* "a broken toy." (See ch. 1, §3.1.1A.)

> . . . *otagai ni yoku nita*] *D*
> Ds* that closely resemble one another

> * Because of *otagai ni* "mutually," D has to be plural.

5.5 Does the phrase *C no ue kara* ("from on C") *wa* (CONTRAST) belong to this clause, or does it go with *mieru*?

> a. *B ga,* **[C no ue kara wa,** *otagaini yoku* **nita]** *D ni mieru*
> "B can be seen to be Ds which closely resemble one another from on C"
> b. *B ga,* **C no ue kara wa,** [*otagai ni yoku nita*] **D ni mieru**
> "from on C, B can be seen to be Ds which closely resemble one another"

(b) seems more likely, insofar as the phrase gives a place or point where B appears to be Ds. Also the comma after *wa* further suggests that the place phrase, *C no ue kara wa*, is not inside the modifier clause for D. CHECK this later.

6 Tada chotto mita dake de wa marude A no nai yō na *B ga,* . . . *D ni* mieru]

Is B modified by a clause?

Yes, it is modified by a clause whose predicate is *yō da*, "it seems that . . . ," (the *da* has been changed to *na* after *yō* (AN) at the end of a modifier clause [ch. 1, § 3.1.1A]):

> . . . **yō na** (COP-PRED)] *B*:
> B which seems that . . .

(See ch. 4, § 4.1.1 and § 14 for *yō da*.)

6.1 ... marude A no nai *yō na* (= *da*)]*B*

Is there another clause involved here?

Yes. *Nai* is the negative plain form of the V *aru* "there is/exists" and the predicate of a clause modifying *yō*: ... *marude A no* **nai**] *yō na*] *B*

6.2 What is the *no* of *A no nai*?

This cannot be the *no* that connects two Ns, since there is no N following it. Nor is it a case in which the second N in N_1 *no* N_2 has been omitted. If it were, the *N no* would be followed by another particle or the copula. It is not the EMPHASIS *no* in a predicate because there is no copula following. It must therefore be the subject particle *no*. (A subject can be followed by either *ga* or *no* in a modifier clause.)

> *A* (SUBJ) *no* (= *ga*) *nai* (PRED)] *yō na* (= *da*)(PRED)] *B*
> B which seems that A doesn't exist

6.3 What is *marude*?

Marude is ADV, "entirely, as if ... ," modifying the verb *nai*.

> **marude** *A no* **nai**] *yō na*] *B*
> B which seems that there is no A at all

6.4 Tada chotto mita dake de wa *marude A no nai*] *yō na*] *B ga, C no ue*
> *kara wa, ... D ni mieru*] *toiu E no F ni ...*

What is the *de* of *chotto mita dake de wa*?

This *de* doesn't denote a place or reason, since it doesn't follow N but rather V + *dake*. And since *de wa* isn't followed by a comma, it is unlikely that the *de* is the *-te* form of *da*. **It must therefore be the instrumental** *de*.

> *Tada chotto mita dake* **de** *wa* (CONTRAST)
> with (= using) just a glance

6.5 What does this instrumental phrase go with?

From the context this phrase does not appear to go with the main predicate *agete-mita no desu*: "By just a glance indeed I tried raising/giving ..."

The possibilities are:

a. [[[*Tada chotto* **mita dake de** wa marude A no **nai**] *yō na*] *B ga,*
C no ue kara wa, ... D ni mieru] *toiu*

B which seems that, by just a glance, there is no A at all, can be seen as Ds ... from on C.

b. [*Tada chotto* **mita dake** *de wa* [[*marude A no nai*] *yō na*] *B ga, C*
no ue kara wa, ... D ni **mieru**] *toiu*

> By just a glance, B, which seems that there is no A at all, can be
> seen from on C as Ds . . .

CHECK this later. In either case the beginning of the *toiu* clause coincides with
the beginning of the sentence.

7 With the words given, translate the entire sentence.

[**Tada chotto mita dake de** *wa marude kankei*(A) *no nai*] *yō na*] *kotogara*(B) *ga,*
genri(C) no ue kara *wa,* [*otagaini yoku nita*] *mono*(D) *ni mieru*] *toiu hitotsu*(E)
no rei(F) *ni kaminari*(G) *o agete-mita no desu.*

> A= relationship B= matter/thing C= principles D= thing E= one F= ex-
> ample G=a thunderstorm

> This sentence is from a passage comparing hot water in a teacup with a thun-
> derstorm.

√ From (3): It is confirmed that **"from just a glance"** and **"from on principles (= the
point [of view] of principles)" (both in bold letters)** are in contrast.

√ From (1) and (3): **"indeed** I tried giving"

√ From (4) and (5.1): *E no F* is not "F of E" but simply "E-F": *hitotsu no rei* "one example." Accordingly, not E ("one") but F ("example") is to be modified by the *toiu*
clause.

> *hitotsu no rei* **ni** *kaminari o ageta* "raised/gave a thunderstorm **to** (= GOAL) one ex-
> ample of one" doesn't make sense. *Ni* does not indicate GOAL as in "give **to** . . ."
> From the context, "raised/gave a thunderstorm **as** one example" is the meaning
> (see ch. 4, § 7.5C).

√ Combine (7.2) and (7.3): "indeed I tried giving a thunderstorm as one example"

√ From (5.5): It is confirmed that (b) is better:

> [. . . *kotogara*(B) *ga, genri*(C) *no ue kara wa,* [*otagai ni yoku nita*]
> *mono*(D) ni mieru]
>
> from the point [of view] of principles, things can be seen to be
> things which closely resemble one another

√ From (6.3): "things which seem that there is no relationship at all" or "things
which seem to have no relationship at all"

√ From (6.5):

> a. things which seem that, **by just a glance,** there **is no relationship** at
> all (=seem to have no relationship at all from just a glance) can be

seen as things which closely resemble one another **as far as principles are concerned.***

> * This has been changed from "the point [of view] of principles" in (7.1) above.

b. **by just a glance,** things which seem to have no relationship at all **can be seen,** from the point [of view] of principles, as things that closely resemble one another as far as principles are concerned.

Since it doesn't make sense to say that things that appear to be totally unrelated can appear to be related on principle when they are glanced at, (a) is better. The modifier clause for *kotogara* begins at the beginning of the sentence which is also the beginning of the *toiu* clause:

> [[[*Tada chotto mita dake de wa marude kankei no nai*] *yō na*] *kotogara* (SUBJ) *ga, genri no ue kara wa, . . . mono ni mieru* (PRED)] *toiu hitotsu no rei.*

Combine (7.7) above and (7.4) for the final translation:

(Watakushi wa) [[[*Tada chotto mita dake de wa   marude kankei*
("I"=OMIT TOP)   only a little   saw   only   with CONT entirely   relationship

no nai]   *yō na*]   *kotogara ga,*
SUBJ (= *ga*) there is not=V-PRED seems=AN+COP(= *da*)-PRED matters SUBJ

genri no ue kara wa, [*otagaini yoku nita*]   *mono ni mieru*] *toiu*
from on principle CONT mutually well resemble=V-PRED thing   appears=V-PRED

hitotsu no rei ni **kaminari o agete-mita no desu**
as one example thunderstorm OBJ tried raising=V-EMPH-PRED

> Indeed[1] I[2] tried giving a thunderstorm as one example of things[3] which, **while seeming at first glance to be totally unrelated may** be seen **to be connected** as far as principles are concerned.

---

[1] From (1): It is confirmed that the *no* of *agete-mita no desu* is for EMPHASIS.

[2] From (3): It is confirmed that the writer "I" is the omitted topic.

[3] From (5.2): It is confirmed that this "thing (B)" is the subject for *mieru* "can be seen."

Chapter Three

Problematic Sentences

1. AMBIGUITY 126

2. MULTIPLE PREDICATES 136

3. IRREGULAR USAGES OF TENSE 148

4. COMPLEX STRUCTURES 151

5. WORD MEANING 157

6. THE ROLE OF CONTEXT 168

7. METAPHOR 179

8. LOGICALITY 183

9. CULTURE 188

Problematic Sentences

THIS CHAPTER OFFERS example phrases and sentences which include various points that often cause problems in comprehension and translation. These difficulties derive for the most part from mental processes, logic, metaphors, and so on that are peculiar to Japanese.

Japanese people's thinking tends to be more intuitive and less analytical than Western thinking, and to be far more concrete than abstract. The Japanese language allows rich nuances through its use of various auxiliaries, indirectness, and ambiguity, and to this extent its structure may appear to the Western reader to be lacking in logical rigor. Japanese did not have a writing system until around the fourth century, when Chinese writing was introduced. After the adoption of the writing system and the subsequent development of *kana* out of *kanji*, thinkers who wanted to express abstract ideas tended to use *kanbun*, a style of writing modeled on classical Chinese, while for literary works—poetry, novels, diaries and so on—the indigenous Japanese language was preferred. This had also to do with the fact that *kana* were initially used by women, who did not have access to the intellectual world of Japan at that time. To this day, most abstract concepts are expressed using Chinese compounds, many of which were created in the course of the Meiji Restoration when there was a major influx of Western ideas into Japan. The Japanese penchant for concreteness led to the development of rich systems of metaphors; at the same time, however, discourse often came to be long and complex, and thus can be difficult to understand for the Western reader who has been trained to seek clear relations among the elements in an argument.

The kinds of difficulties experienced by speakers of Indo-European languages can be further explained with reference to Japanese syntax. Syntactically, the Japanese language usually ignores such things as plurality, gender, articles, agreement according to person and number, relative pronouns, and abstract nouns. Originally, there was relatively little use of the passive voice of verbs; it was rare, for example, for an inanimate being to figure as the subject of a verb in the passive voice. The passive was used primarily for situations in which an animate subject is affected adversely by an external agent or event. And still today, in order to avoid having to specify the agent of an action, intransitive verbs are favored over transitive verbs even when the subject is an animate being, thus creating ambiguity about the agent of an action (see ch.4, § 2.2). The use of conjunctions also has a different, less tightly structured logic than in Indo-European languages.

A salient feature of Japanese culture which is reflected in the language concerns the priority of social relationships over the individual. Because of the high value placed on social harmony and membership in a social group, an elaborate honorific language was developed, which not only employs special honorific and humble forms of nouns, adjectives, and verbs, but also cultivates indirectness and ambiguity by not completing sentences and by omitting certain elements. The omission of the subject or topic in particular causes foreigners many problems in reading comprehension, insofar as they do not participate in the tight network of social relationships that allows so many things among the Japanese to be left unsaid — or unwritten.

As far as word meaning is concerned, to the extent that different peoples view the world differently in accordance with their cultural values, at least some of these differences become embodied in their respective languages. Certain English words do not therefore have exact equivalents in Japanese, and vice versa; or else the meanings of territories of words overlap only partially. A striking example is the case of the word "I" or "self." Since a definite sense of the self in opposition to the objective world is lacking in Japanese culture, several words are used, depending on the context, ranging from *watakushi* "I, secret, private," *onore* "self," *jiko* or *jibun* "one's self, oneself," *jibun (jishin)* "one(self)," and *jiga* "self, ego" — all of which are written in Chinese characters. It is interesting that there is no independent word for the first person plural: it is made by adding *-tachi*, the plural marker, to *watakushi* "I" — to mean literally "I and others." This *-tachi* can be added to any person, as in *Tanaka-san-tachi*, "Tanaka and others," where the individuality of the other persons is not specified. A number of comparable differences between Japanese and English modes of expression stem from such differing views of the individual in relation to society.

The points discussed above appear singly or in combination in the following sections. First, a problematic phrase or sentence is given without notes. Students are encouraged to analyze and translate it on their own, and then to read the notes and explanation afterward. In a few of the examples there may be alternative possible ways of analyzing the structure, but these will generally not be discussed unless they concern the feature under discussion in that section.

Many of the examples given in this chapter are taken from philosophical texts, so that the meanings of the sentences are often quite complex and ab-struse. This has the advantage of forcing the student to rely all the more heav-ily on a careful analysis of the structure, since the sense of the examples is unlikely to be evident at first glance. Unless they are intending to study Japan-ese philosophy, readers of this book will rarely encounter passages as difficult as some of the examples presented here. The point of employing such exam-ples is that they vividly exemplify the features that cause students the most difficulty in understanding written Japanese.

(In many of the examples that follow the sentence(s) will first be translated literally, and then reworked into idiomatic English. Significant changes in the final version will be marked in boldface type.)

1. Ambiguity

1.1 Noun Modification

1.1.1 MODIFIER CLAUSE + *N no N*

Since Japanese does not have relative pronouns or case declensions that serve to make syntactic and logical relationships clear, ambiguity enters easily in cases where nouns are juxtaposed, as in the Modifier + *N no N* construction. In some cases such ambiguity may serve to express subjective aspects of situations or shadings of emotion.

Although there were originally no relative pronouns, the term *tokoro no* "of a place" is sometimes used after a modifier clause to mean "which."

EXAMPLE 1

その魂は ｜ 苦悩[1] を与えた[2] ｜ ものを愛し、 困窮を

that soul TOP　　suffering OBJ　gave=V-PRED　　thing/person OBJ love-V_1-(TE)[3]-$PRED_a$,　　need OBJ

転ずる ｜ ところの魂であり、 ｜ 最も多く軽蔑する ｜

convert=V_2-$PRED_b$　　**which** soul is=N+COP_1-TE (=*deatte*)-$PRED_1$,　most much despise=V-PRED

ところにおいて最も多く愛する ｜ 魂である。

place at most much love=V-PRED　　　　soul is=N+COP_2-$PRED_2$

¹ In the original text this character was written in *kyūkanji* (= old kanji) thus: 惱 . In this book *kyūkanji* have been replaced by their modern equivalents. Students should be aware of the use of *kyūkanji* when they read texts written during the Meiji, Taishō, and Shōwa periods up to around 1945, when the government began the efforts of simplifying kanji.

² In the original this word was written 與へた . As with the old kanji, the modern equivalents of *kyūkana* (old kana) have been substituted in the present text. See Appendix § 5 for the use of *kyūkana*.

³ (TE) indicates that the alternative *-te* form (= stem form) is being used or the *-te* form has been omitted entirely.

In this chapter, clauses are marked by boxes around the kanji rather than by brackets.

TRANSLATION

That soul is a soul (PRED₁) **which** loves that which gave suffering and converts need [into something beneficial], and is a soul (PRED₂) which loves most (at the place) where it despises most.

> Such a soul loves what has caused it suffering; it converts its need, and loves most where it most despises.

See Examples 7 and 8 for other irregular modifier clause constructions.

EXAMPLE 2

世界を変えた思想家の伝記

世界を変えた	思想家の伝記

world OBJ changed=V-PRED   thinker (N₁) of biography (N₂)

The structure of this phrase is: [X*] N_1 *no* N_2

* X stands for the content of the modifier clause: "changed the world"

The possible modifying relations are:

a. X modifies N_1: [X] N_1 *no* N_2

"the biography of the **thinker** who changed the world"

b. X modifies N₂: [X] N_1 *no* N_2

"**the biography** of the thinker, which changed the world"

(a) makes more sense, although (b) is also possible in a special context. In the above example the modifier clause came right before the noun it modified, but this is not always the case. Consider the following example:

EXAMPLE 3

人が通常避ける実存の不安

人が通 常避ける

実存の不安

person SUBJ generally avoid＝V-PRED   existence (N₁) of anxiety (N₂)

The possibilities are:

a. X* modifies N₁: [X] N_1 *no* N_2

"the anxiety of the **existence** that people generally avoid"

> * X stands for the content of the modifier clause: "people generally avoid"

b. X modifies N₂: [X] N_1 *no* N_2

"the **anxiety** of existence, which people generally avoid"

(b) is obviously the meaning here, since it is impossible for people to avoid existence, whereas they may well have an interest in avoiding *Angst*. Note that in this case the clause modifies the noun farther away from it.

EXAMPLE 4

原罪及びそれに根差す有限性と死

原罪及び   それに根差す

有限性と死

original sin and*   in it is rooted＝V-PRED   finitude (N₁) and death (N₂)

> * *Oyobi* is a literary word meaning "and."

The structure is: N and [X] N_1 and N_2.

The possibilities are:

a. X modifies N_1: N *oyobi* [X] N_1 *to* N_2

"original sin and **the finitude** that is rooted in it and death"

b. X modifies both N_1 and N_2: N *oyobi* [X] N_1 *to* N_2

"original sin, and **the finitude** and **death** that are rooted in it"

(b) makes more sense. The usual particle for "and," *to*, tends to connect the closest Ns (N_1 and N_2), while the more literary and formal *oyobi* tends to connect larger units (N with **N_1 and N_2**).

1.1.2 *ADJ + N no N*

EXAMPLE 5

新しい町の地図

新しい　　町　　の　地図
new＝ADJ　town (N_1)　of　map (N_2)

The structure is: *ADJ N_1 no N_2*.

This phrase is ambiguous, in that either:

a. ADJ modifies N_1: ADJ N_1 *no* N_2

"a map of the new town"

or:

b. ADJ modifies N_2: ADJ N_1 *no* N_2

"a new map of the town."

Sometimes the punctuation gives a clue, insofar as "a new map of the town" can be written: *atarashii, machi no chizu*. Otherwise one has to depend on the context.

1.1.3 *AN na + N no N*

EXAMPLE 6

急激な物価の上昇

急激な　物価　の　上昇
rapid＝AN　prices (N₁)　of　increase (N₂)

The possibilities are:

a. AN modifies N₁: **AN** *na* **N₁** *no N₂* "an increase of rapid **prices**"

b. AN modifies N₂: **AN** *na N₁ no* **N₂** "a rapid **increase** in prices"

(b) obviously makes more sense. However, the AN can just as easily modify the first noun in a *N no N* sequence:

> **kyūgeki na henka** *no eikyō*
> "the influence of **rapid change**."

1.1.4 Irregular Modifier Clauses

EXAMPLE 7

これは、言うまでもなく、熱い水蒸気が冷えて、小さなしずくになったのが無数に群がっているので、丁度雲や霧と同じ様なものです。

これは、　言うまでもなく、　熱い水蒸気が冷えて、　小さなしずくに

this TOP,　　　needless to say　　hot vapor SUBJ cooled down＝V₁-TE-PRED₁,　small droplets

なった　　のが無数に群がっている　ので、　丁度雲や

became＝V₂-PRED₂ PRON SUBJ countlessly crowded＝V-STATE-PRED RSN,　exactly cloud or

きり　おな　よう
霧と同じ 様な | | ものです。

mist is the same as seems=AN+COP(=*da*)-PRED　thing is=N+COP-PRED

In this sentence, the modified N (hot vapor) that is the subject of the modifier clause still remains in the clause. This is an example of archaic irregular modifier clause, which occasionally occurs in modern Japanese.

[(**hito** *ga*)*　*Tōkyō e itta*]　　**hito**
person SUBJ　　Tokyo to went-PRED　person

　　a person who went to Tokyo

　　　* The subject is omitted in a regular modifier clause.

The modified N (hot vapor) is also represented by the pronominal *no* which appears in the normal position of a modified noun as a head noun — namely, right after the modifier clause. This construction shows the original sequence of events, and has not been completely rearranged as a modifier clause.

The sentence structure is: **N wa**, [X-REASON] *node*, [Y] **N desu**.

The reason clause is inserted after the topic. In this clause the subject *no* is modified by a modifier clause which contains a multiple predicate, V_1 and V_2. The noun in the final predicate is also modified by a modifier clause, Y.

TRANSLATION

　　This is, needless to say, just like clouds or mist, because hot vapor that
　　has cooled down and become small droplets is crowded countlessly.

This literal translation sounds awkward and is not clear. A more natural and clearer English rendering would be:

It is just like clouds or mist, because the hot vapor has cooled and become innumerable small droplets.

EXAMPLE 8

フォイエルバッハによれば、神々とは、未開人の満たされざる幸福衝動がその
構想力を動かして、彼等の願望を自然のうちへ投射せしめ、その願望を対象化
したものであり、．．．

フォイエルバッハによれば、神々と ¹は、	未開人の	満たされざる ²

according to Feuerbach, what are called gods TOP, primitive humanity's unfulfilled=V-PASS-PRED

幸福衝動³が	その構想力を動かして、	彼等の願望を

impulse for happiness SUBJ   its imaginative power OBJ move=V₁-TE-PRED₁,   their desires OBJ

自然のうちへ投射せしめ、 ⁴	その願望を対象化した

nature into make project=V₂-CAUSE-(TE)-PRED₂,   that desire OBJ objectified=V₃-PRED₃

ものであり ...

thing is=N+COP-(TE=*deatte*)-PRED1

[1] *iu no* has been omitted here. The *iu no* in *X to iu no* **wa** . . . "what is called X is . . ." is often left out.

[2] The *zaru* of *mitasarezaru* is the noun-following form of *nu* which is the classical equivalent of the negative form *nai* and is sometimes used in literary style.

[3] In the above archaic irregular modifier clause, the modified N (the impulse for happiness of primitive humanity) that is the subject of the clause has not been deleted, but remains in the clause while being represented simultaneously by the noun *mono*. In a normal modifier clause the modified N is omitted from the clause because it is represented by the head noun (the modified N) right after the clause.

[4] *-shimeru* is the alternative form of the causative suffix *-(s)aseru*. Since its classical equivalent *-shimu* was used mainly in *kanbun* (Chinese style writing), *-shimeru* is used in highly literary style. Consonant verbs take *-ashimeru* as in *iw-ashimeru* "make one say." *Suru* with *shimeru* is changed to *se-shimeru*. This *-shimeru* type causative can occasionally appear in the classical construction *X wa Y* **o shite** *kak-ashimeru* "X makes Y write" instead of the modern equivalent: *X wa Y* **ni** *kak-aseru*.

TRANSLATION

According to Feuerbach, gods are the unfulfilled impulses for happiness of primitive humanity, using its imaginative powers, causing its desires to be projected on to nature and objectifying them . . .

The sense of the irregular modifier clause is conveyed by the final translation:

According to Feuerbach, gods **are created by** the unfulfilled impulse for happiness of primitive humanity, who by using its imaginative powers projects its desires on to nature and objectifies them . . .

1.2 Plurality of the Noun

Japanese nouns do not normally have an indication of number. Although there is a way to indicate plurality, it is limited to the case of human beings, where one adds *-tachi* or *-ra* to a noun.

EXAMPLE 9

之に反して、地表の世界に生きる所謂ノルマルな人間、「直情径行的な活動」の人間は、自分のうちに何か或る固い底をもっている。

之に反して、[1] 地表の世界に生きる　　　　所謂ノルマルな人間 (A)、
In contrast to this,　the above the ground world in live=V-PRED　so-called normal humans,

「直情径行的な活動」の人間 (B) は、　　自分のうちになにか或る[2] 固い
"straightforward activity" human beings TOP　oneself of inside something certain hard

底をもっている。
bottom OBJ have=V-STATE-PRED

[1] . . . *ni hanshite* "in contrast to . . ." should not be mistaken for a V-*te* form functioning as a component of a multiple predicate.

[2] *Aru* is a preN meaning "a, a certain" and should not be confused with the V-plain form of *aru* marking the end of a clause.

Since nouns A and B are in apposition, the structure of the sentence is:

N (A,B) *wa* OBJ *o Vt.*

The topic *ningen* is "human being(s), humankind." From the context it is obvious that it does not mean humankind, but it is not clear whether it refers to a human being or human beings. If we look at the next sentence, **Karera** *o sasaeru* . . . " . . . support **them**" we can tell that it must be plural. The number of the noun often has to be ascertained from the context in this way.

TRANSLATION

> In contrast, so-called normal **humans** who live above ground, **human beings** of "straightforward activity," have some kind of solid ground within them.

See also the case of *hito* "person/people/human being" in ch. 2, sentence 2.

EXAMPLE 10

（レヴィット）氏自身、現在の学生について、彼等がそのヨーロッパ研究から「自分たち自身の日本的な自我 を肥やすべき何等の結果をも引き出さない」と言っているが、 . . .

（レヴィット）氏自身、	現在の学生について、	彼等がその [1] ヨーロッパ
(Löwith) Mr. himself (OMIT-TOP),	students of today regarding,	they SUBJ their European

研究から	「自分たち自身 [2] の日本的な自我を肥やすべき [3]	何等の結果
studies from	their own Japanese ego OBJ should enrich=V-*beki*-PRED	anything result

をも [4] 引き出さない」	と言っているが、 . . .
EMPH(= *o*) do not extract=V-PRED	QUOT is saying=V-ONG-PRED CONJ, . . .

[1] *Sono* means "the" or "its" but in this context it refers to "students of today" so that it is plural, "their."

[2] *Jibun* "self" is often confusing because it is used for any person and there is no clue except for the context. In this case it does not refer to the author's general "we" but to "students of today."

[3] *Beki* is a the noun-following form of the classical auxiliary *beshi* "must, should." It now follows the affirmative plain forms of verbs and is also followed by the copula: *kaku beki da* "should write" or *kakubeki de wa nai* "should not write." Its classical negative form is *bekarazu* "should not do . . ." which is still used — but only idiomatically in notices of warning, as in *Rakugaki surubekarazu:* "No graffiti."

[4] In highly literary style the original particle *o*, which is normally replaced by *mo*, can be retained.

TRANSLATION

> Mr. Löwith himself says of contemporary students that from their study of Europe "they no longer extract anything to enrich their own Japanese selves."

2. Multiple predicates

In order to determine where a clause begins and ends, it is important to mark -*te* forms (including V-stem forms often followed by a comma—see ch. 1, § 3.2.2) because these signal that there are multiple predicates and that the clause still continues, as well as the forms that signal the existence of predicates (the ends of clauses) within a sentence and various subordinate clauses.

This practice of marking the ends of clauses allows one to see the ways in which subordinate clauses in a sentence are "nested" one within another.

The following section presents some problems relating to -*te* forms.

2.1 Variations and Irregular Cases

The most common sequences are: V_1-*te*, V_2, ADJ_1-*kute*, ADJ_2, and N_1 *de*, N_2 *da*. However, multiple predicates do not necessarily occur within the same parts of speech. Various combinations are possible:

> *V-te, N/AN da*
> *N/AN de, V*
> *ADJ-kute, V* . . . and so on.

⇨ Special attention must be given to Consonant Verbs whose roots end in -*m*, -*n*, or -*b*, and whose -*te* forms are therefore -*de* (*yonde* "read," *nonde* "drink," and *tonde* "fly"). The -*de* here should not be confused with the particle *de*.

| **2.1.1** *N de, V* |

| **EXAMPLE 11** |

もちろん、それらのシステムは、さきに出した私の「タテ」の理論につながる、あるいは組み合わされているもので、日本社会の構造をいっそう立体的に提示する作用をもっている。

| もちろん、それらのシステムは、 | さきに出した | 私の「タテ」の理論 |

Of course, those systems TOP,　("I"-OMIT SUBJ) earlier published=V-PRED my *Theory of Verticality*

| につながる、 | あるいは組み合わされている | もので、 |

are connected to=Va-PRED,　or are combined=Vb-PASS-STATE-PRED　thing is=N+COP-TE-PRED$_1$,

| 日本社会の構造をいっそう立体的に提示する | 作用を |

Japanese society structure OBJ further three-dimensionally* present=V-PRED　function OBJ

もっている。
have=V-STATE-PRED$_2$

> * "more three-dimensionally" is an architectural metaphor. In this con-
> text "more concretely" is the meaning, since the sentence concerns a the-
> ory concerning the structure of Japanese society.

Va and Vb are connected by *aruiwa*, "or," and since they both have more or less the same meaning they are basically treated as one verb constituting the predicate of the modifier clause for *mono*. PRED$_1$, *mono de*, is the predicate for the topic *sorera no shisutemu* "those systems."

The same topic is shared by another predicate *motte-iru* "have," thus forming the multiple predicate: . . . *wa N de, V* ". . . is N and (does) V." This verb is transitive, taking the object *sayō*, "function," modified by a clause.

TRANSLATION

> Of course, those systems are (the ones that are) connected to or combined with my *Theory of Verticality* which I published earlier, and have the function of presenting more concretely the structure of Japanese society.

2.1.2 *AN de, V*

EXAMPLE 12

マスコミの取材攻勢は一番苦手で、出来るだけ奥に引込んでいたい。

マスコミの取材攻勢は
mass media news gathering aggressiveness SUBJ(= *ga**)-TOP

一番 苦手で、   出来るだけ奥に
most poor at is=AN+COP-TE-PRED$_1$-RSN,   ("I"-OMIT TOP) as much as possible way behind

引っ込んでいたい。
want to stay withdrawn=V-STATE+*tai*-PRED$_2$

> * The original subject particle *ga* of *N ga nigate*(AN) *da* has been replaced by the topic *wa*.

The omitted topic for PRED$_2$ is "I," which is also shared by PRED$_1$. *Nigate* is an AN followed by the *-te* form of the copula *da*, thus constituting PRED$_1$. Its function is to give the reason for PRED$_2$. Since *de* can also be an instrumental or reason particle, or can denote the place of an activity, students tend to overlook the possibility of its representing a predicate.

TRANSLATION

> (As for myself) as for the aggressiveness in news gathering by mass media, I am most poor at it, so I want to stay withdrawn as much as possible.

> Being very poor at handling the aggressiveness of mass media reporting, I want to stay **in the background** as much as possible.

2.2 Grouping Multiple Predicates

EXAMPLE 13

ニイチェとドストエフスキイの二人は、二十歳の自分の魂にも決定的な刻印を与え、その時の戦慄は爾来たえず自分の心底を撼かすものとなっている。

ニイチェとドストエフスキイの二人は、　二十歳の自分の魂にも

Nietzsche and Dostoevsky of the two TOP1,　　　twenty years old my soul to ALSO

決定的な刻印を与え、　　　　　　　　その時の戦慄は爾来　│　たえず

critical impression OBJ give=V_1-(TE)-$PRED_1$-RSN,　that time tremors TOP2 since then　constantly

自分の心底を撼かす　　　　　ものとなっている。

my depth of heart OBJ tremble=V_2-PRED　　thing has become=V_3-STATE-$PRED_2$.

V_2 marks the ending of the modifier clause for *mono*. Therefore, the question is whether V_1 goes with V_2 or with V_3. In other words, is V_1 within the clause or not?

Since there are two quite separate topics and there is no quotation particle, and therefore no quotation clause that can contain TOP + *wa*, it is natural to regard this sentence as consisting of two sentences, the first topic being the topic for V_1 and the second the topic for V_3.

V_2 is in the plain form, which indicates that it is the ending of a clause. TOP2 cannot be within this clause because it is not a quotation clause. Therefore, V_2 cannot be the predicate for TOP2 but is a predicate in the modifier clause for *mono*. The beginning of the clause is right after *jirai*, the time adverb for V_3, and so V_1 is not in the clause. V_1 represents the first predicate for the first topic (TOP1). In comparing V_1 and V_3, it is clear that V_1-*te* gives a reason for V_3.

TRANSLATION

> The two figures of Nietzsche and Dostoevsky burned a definitive impression on to my twenty-year-old soul, and the tremors I experienced at that time have [become something which] continued to make the depths of my heart tremble ever since.

| | EXAMPLE 14 |

自己資本比率は、自己資本を総資産で割って計算され、分母の総資産が小さい
程自己資本比率が上昇、目標達成に近付くが、．．．

自己資本比率は、　　自己資本を総資産で割って
net worth ratio TOP,　　net worth OBJ total assets by divide=V_1-TE-PRED$_1$-MNR

計算され、　　　　　　　　分母の総資産が小さい　程[1]
calculated=V_2-PASS-(TE)-PRED$_2$-RSN,　denominator APP total assets SUBJ the smaller

自己資本比率が上昇（して）、[2]　　目標達成に近付く
of net worth ratio SUBJ increase=V_3-(TE)-PRED$_3$,　goal attainment approaches=V_4-PRED$_4$

が、．．．
but=CONJ, . . .

[1] *Hodo* itself means "the degree/extent," but it is used idiomatically as follows: . . . *ga* (. . . *-ba*), . . . *hodo* "the (. . .-er), the more . . ." See Appendix, § 1.

[2] *Jōshō* "rise, increase" is a verbal noun used as a verb with *suru*. The *-te* form of *suru* functioning as a component of a multiple predicate can often be omitted, as in this case.

There are four verbs in this sentence but they are not parallel. V_1 and V_2 are predicates for the topic "ratio of net worth" and are grouped together. V_1 is **the manner** for V_2: "As for the ratio of net worth, it is calculated **by dividing** the net worth by the total assets," and thus constitutes the reason for V_3 and V_4. V_3 and V_4 are the predicates for the subject "net worth" and are **in sequence**: "the ratio of net worth increases **and** approaches the attainment of the goal."

TRANSLATION

As for the ratio of net worth, it is calculated by dividing the net worth by the total assets; and so the smaller the denominator, the total assets; the more the ratio of net worth increases and approaches the attainment of the goal.

EXAMPLE 15

言語が異なるばかりか、風俗、習慣の違いは生活全般に渡ってさまざまな面に顔を出し、この違いを乗りこえて、ともに仕事をしたり、友情をもつということは、なみたいていのことではない。

言語が異なる	ばかりか、 [1] 風俗、習慣の違いは
languages SUBJ differ=V-PRED	not only, manners, customs differences SUBJ(=*ga*)-CONT

生活全般にわたって [2] さまざまな面に顔を出し、[3]

life entire throughout various aspects into face OBJ show=V_1-(TE)-$PRED_1$-RSN,

この違いを乗りこえて、	ともに仕事を
("people"=OMIT-SUBJ) this difference OBJ overcome=V_2-TE-$PRED_2$-MNR,	together job OBJ

したり、 [4] 友情をもつ	ということは、 なみたいてい [5] のことではない。
do=V_3-*tari*, friendship OBJ have=V_4-PRED	matter TOP ordinary matter is not=N+COP-PRED

[1] A *bakari ka* B (= A *bakari denaku* B) "not only A but also B" (see the end of ch. 1, § 3.2.2).

[2] *. . . ni watatte* is an idiom: "extending over, throughout" (not to be taken as a component in a multiple predicate). (See Appendix for more V-*te* phrases like this.)

[3] *Kao o dasu* literally means "show a face" or "show up," but in this context "[the difference] appears/reveals/manifests itself" is the meaning.

[4] V_1-stem-*tari* V_2-stem-*tari suru* "do things like V_1, V_2 and so on" (see the end of ch. 1, § 3.2.2).

[5] *Namitaitei no koto dewanai* is an idiom: "is extremely hard/difficult (= is not an ordinary matter)." We need to determine which two items are connected by *bakari ka*. It is preceded by a clause, "Languages differ," which is item A, and this would lead us to expect that item B is also a clause. We would thus have a case of multiple predicates involving V-plain forms rather than V-*te* forms. There is no subject particle to mark the subject of a clause, although there is a particle *wa* after *chigai*—in fact, there are two *wa*'s in this sentence.

Koto is the topic for the final predicate to constitute N (= *koto*) *wa* N (= *koto*) *da*. The *wa* after *chigai* would then be the contrast marker contrasting manners and customs with languages. It has replaced the original subject particle *ga*. Since there is no plain form to signal the ending of a clause before V_1-*te*, it is a good idea to examine the clause for the other topic, *koto*, first.

This clause has multiple predicates. V_3 and V_4 are grouped together: "do things like working together or having a friendship." The function of V_2-*te*, then, is to express **the manner** for V_3 and V_4; "**overcoming** these difference (differences in languages and in manners and customs)." The subject in this clause is not "the difference in manners and customs" but the omitted *hitobito* "people." This means that the predicate for *chigai*, the subject whose particle *ga* was replaced by the contrast *wa*, is V_1-*te* although it does not end the clause, and that the beginning of the clause for TOP, *koto*, comes after V_1-*te* and before *kono chigai*.

Item B is "[that] the difference in manners and customs appears in various aspects throughout life in general." The function of V_1-*te* is to give the reason for the final predicate: in other words, items A and B are the reasons for it. This is an unusual case of multiple predicates using V_1-plain *bakaride ka* V_2-plain where V_2 is a *V-te* form. Hence the overall structure of this sentence is:

{ A[SUBJ1 V] *bakari ka* B[SUBJ2 V] }-TE (RSN), [(OMIT-SUBJ) OBJ V_2-TE (MNR),

V_3-*tari* OBJ V_4] *koto wa . . . koto dewanai.*

TRANSLATION

> Since not only do languages differ, but also differences in manners and customs manifest themselves throughout various aspects of life as a whole, it is an extremely difficult thing for people to work together or have a friendship while overcoming such differences.

2.3 Tense, Aspect, etc. and Final Predicate

In the case of multiple predicates, the tense (past or nonpast) of the final predicate determines the tense of preceding predicates (-*te* forms). As for aspect (ongoing action, state, etc.), and the suffixes and other auxiliaries that may modify the main predicate, these normally determine previous predicates—but not always, so one must exercise care in these cases.

The case of tense is relatively easy to understand as shown below.

EXAMPLE 16

私は祝福する者となり、然りを言う者となった。

私は	祝福する	者となり、		然りを言う	者と
"I" TOP	bless=V-PRED	person become=V_1-(TE)-$PRED_1$,	yes OBJ	say=V-PRED	person

なった。]
became=V_2-$PRED_2$

Because V_2 is in the past tense, V_1 should also be in the past tense: "I have become a person who blesses and have become a person who says yes." The polished translation: "I have become one who blesses and says yes."

The cases of aspect, mood, and other auxiliaries work the same way, but they often tend to be overlooked by readers. One should therefore pay special attention to such cases.

EXAMPLE 17

どっちがいいか、分からないから、女の子は、ここに待っていて、初めて自転車の来た方へ曲がろう、と、決めました。

どっちがいいか、[1]	分からない	から、	女の子は、
Which SUBJ is good=ADJ-PRED-QUES (OMIT-SUBJ-*ga*)[1]	don't know=V-PRED	RSN	a little girl TOP,

ここに待っていて、	初めて自転車の [2] 来た	方へ
here be waiting=V_1-STATE-TE,	first bicycle SUBJ(=*ga*) came=V-PRED	to the direction

曲がろう、	と、	決めました。
turn=V_2-*ō*-PRED,	QUOT,	decided=V_3-PRED.

[1] The interrogative clause *docchi ga ii ka* is a N clause serving as the subject for *wakaranai*. The subject particle *ga* has been omitted.

[2] This *no* functions as the subject particle in the modifier clause for *hō*.

The situation is that of a little girl waiting at a fork in the road. *Kita* "came" is the predicate of the modifier clause for *hō*, "direction": *hajimete jitensha ga kita hō* "the direction (from which) a bicycle came first (=the first bicycle came)." The question is whether to take V_1 together with V_2 or V_3. In other words, does the quotation clause contain multiple predicates? If so, the volitional must cover V_1 as well. This has to be decided from the context.

Compare the following:

    a. The girl **was waiting** here **and decided** to turn in whichever direction a bicycle came from first.

    b. The girl **decided to wait** here and **to turn** in whichever direction a bicycle came from first.

(b) is better in that the girl surely decided to wait until she saw a bicycle come before deciding which direction to take.

TRANSLATION

> Since the little girl did not know which direction to take, she **decided to wait** and **go** in whichever direction a bicycle came from first.

V_1 and V_2 are in sequence and the volitional covers both V_1 and V_2: "will be waiting and will turn."

EXAMPLE 18

現代の無神論は、マルキシズムも実存主義も、そういう伝統された場を否定し、人間に人間性と自由を回復しようとするという点に於て、軸を一つにしている。

げんだい むしんろん じつぞんしゅぎ
現代の無神論は、マルキシズムも実存主義も、 [1]　　　そういう

Modern atheism TOP,　both Marxism (N_1) and Existentialism (N_2),　that kind of

伝統された	場を否定し、	人間に人間性と

inherited V=PASS-PRED place OBJ negate=V_1-(TE)-$PRED_1$ to human beings humanity and

自由を回復しようとする²	という点に於て、

freedom OBJ try hard to restore=V_2-ō to suru-$PRED_2$ point at,

軸を一つにしている。

sharing a common axis=V-STATE-PRED

[1] The *mo*'s in N_1 *mo* N_2 *mo* have replaced the original topic particles *wa*: N_1 *to* N_2 *wa*. N_1 and N_2 are sub-topics for the main topic, "modern atheism."

[2] V-*ō to suru*, "try hard to do something." This affects both V_1 and V_2 in this context: "try hard to negate and to restore."

TRANSLATION

As for modern atheism, both Marxism and existentialism share a common axis, in that they **try (hard) to negate** this kind of place which has been inherited **and to restore** to human beings their humanity and freedom.

As forms of modern atheism, Marxism and existentialism have in common that they **try to negate** this kind of inherited locus* and **to restore** to human beings their humanity and freedom.

---

* This particular term is suggested by the context.

EXAMPLE 19

本書は、その様な異なった文化に適応する時の困難さについて、それを社会人類学の立場から分析して、その原因を追及しようとするものである。

本書は、	その様な	異なった	文化に適応する

This book TOP, ("one"=OMIT SUBJ) that kind of differed=V-PRED   culture adapt to=V-PRED

時の困難さ * について、　それを社会人類学の立場から

at the time difficulties regarding,　it OBJ social anthropology standpoint from

分析して、　　　その原因を追求しようとする　　　　ものである。

analyze=V_1-TE-PRED$_1$, its cause OBJ try hard to pursue=V_2-ō to suru-PRED$_2$　thing is=N+COP-PRED

* The -*sa* is attached to ADJs and ANs to make a N, although *konnan* can
also be used as N to mean "difficulty."

The structure of this sentence is: *TOP wa* [Modifier Clause] *mono dearu. Toki* is modified by a modifier clause, "the time when . . ." (see ch. 1, 3.1.1A). There is an omitted subject, *hitobito* "people," in this clause. *Sore* refers to "the difficulty." This redundant expression *X ni tsuite sore o/wa* is often used when X is long, and is often found in legal documents. It is similar to the topicalization, *X wa* "as for X." In fact the topic particle *wa* often follows *X ni tsuite*, "as for, regarding X." Thus, X is somewhat emphasized by being repeated. The -*ō to suru* is attached to both V_1 and V_2 which are in sequence: "tries hard to analyze and to pursue."

TRANSLATION

> This book (is something that) **tries to analyze** from the social-anthropological standpoint the difficulties (experienced) when one has to adapt to such a different culture and **to pursue** their causes.

EXAMPLE 20

日本の歴史でもっとも大きな特色は、非常に早くから一つの同じ民族による統一国家が出来上がって、それ以後現在まで国が二つに分かれて、二つの国家が出来たりなどすることもなく今日まで続いていることです。

日本の歴史でもっとも大きな特色は、　非常に早くから一つの同じ民族による [1]

Japanese history in most big feature TOP,　　　extremely early from　one　same race by

とういつこっか 統一国家が出来上がって、	いごげんざい それ以後現在まで	くに ふた 国が二つに

unified nation SUBJ formed=V_1-TE-$PRED_1$, since then until present   country SUBJ into two

わ 分かれて、	二つの国家が出来たりなどする [2]		こともなく [3]

divided=Va-TE-PRED$_a$, two nations SUBJ form and something like that=Vb-PRED$_b$ without

こんにち つづ 今日まで続いている	ことです。

today until has continued=V_2-$PRED_2$ (OMIT-*toiu*)   fact is=N+COP-PRED

[1] . . . *ni yoru* is an idiomatic phrase to indicate an agent: "by . . ." This should not be taken as V-plain form marking the end of a clause.

[2] *Nado* is inserted into V-*tari suru* to mean "do things like V." Since Va does not take -*tari*, the meaning of Va-*te* . . . Vb-*tari nado suru* is "do things like **Va and Vb** (in sequence)" rather than "do things like Va, Vb, and so on."

[3] . . . *koto ga aru* "there are times when" The emphasis *mo* has replaced the original subject particle *ga*.

V_1 and V_2 are grouped together to mean "has formed and (has) continued."

TRANSLATION

The greatest characteristic in Japanese history is (the fact) that a unified country by one same race has been formed from extremely early on and has continued until the present day without the country's having been split into two and (as a result) two nations having emerged (since then until the present*) or things like that.

* This is redundant.

> The most salient feature of the history of Japan is the fact that a unitary nation has been constituted by one and the same race from very early on and right up to the present day, without the country's being split into two and two nations emerging—or some similar development.

3. Irregular usages of tense

In conversation the past tense is used in place of the non-past tense when the speaker is confirming something:

> A: *Miitingu wa ashita* **deshita** *ne*. "The meeting **is** tomorrow, isn't it?"

> B: *Ee, sō desu*. "Yes, that's right."

The past tense here presumably comes from something like "according to my recollection, it was . . ." or ". . . was what we decided, wasn't it?"

A similar thing happens in writing when the author is confirming something or summarizing a passage. In such cases the past tense is not to be translated literally.

EXAMPLE 21

運命に身を委せるということは、とりもなおさず彼自身の最も内奥なる本性に還るということであった。

運命に身¹を委せる	ということは、	とりもなおさず	彼自身の最も内奥
To fate body OBJ submit=V-PRED	matter(N₁)TOP,	in itself	he himself most deep inside

なる [2]	ほんせい かえ 本性に還る	ということであった。[3]

there is=V-PRED   essence return=V-PRED   matter(N₂) is=N+COP-PRED

[1] *Mi*, which means "body," is used in this and similar contexts to mean "(one's) self."

[2] *Naru* is the N-following form of the classical auxiliary *nari* meaning "is (= copula)" or "there is" representing in this case the predicate *ni aru* "there is."

[3] The past tense here is used to confirm a previously mentioned idea. It carries the meaning of "as mentioned before," or "as you remember, it was that . . ." This sentence appears in a paragraph where the author is reminding the reader of the idea of "love of fate" which had been discussed earlier. The sentence is followed by two more sentences in the past tense, after which the final sentence of the paragraph reverts to the non-past tense as a way of coming back to the current discussion.

The structure is: N_1 *wa* N_2 *deatta*, in which each N is modified by a *toiu* clause.

TRANSLATION

That (one) submits oneself to fate **was** in itself a matter of returning to one's innermost nature.

> The very act of submitting to fate **is** a returning to one's own innermost nature.

3.2 Non-Past Tense

The non-past tense is used in place of the past in story-telling, in order to describe vividly what was happening or how things were. The switch from the regular past tense to non-past tense in the middle of a paragraph gives the effect of drawing listeners or readers directly into the scene of the action.

| | EXAMPLE 22 |

歌の声にひかれて、この村の人が大勢集まって来ました。村人たちは我々の歌を、まるで儀式の時の様に真面目に聞いていました。老人がしきいにすわっています。子供たちが窓に腕を重ねて、その上にあごをのせてのぞいています。家の前の広場のやしの木の下にも、赤んぼうをおぶった女がしゃがんでいます。いずれもこの国の人々のくせで、やせた手足を深く折り曲げて、じっと動かずにすわっているのです。

TRANSLATION

> Drawn by our singing voices, many villagers **began to gather**. The villagers were listening to our singing as if they were attending a ceremony. The old men **are** sitting on the thresholds. . . . Under the palm trees in the open area in front of the house, women with babies on their backs **are** squatting on the ground. Every one of them **is** sitting motionless, as is the custom of the people of this country, with their slender legs and arms tightly folded.

Even though this paragraph begins with a sentence in the past tense, as the description goes on, the author switches to the non-past tense (in the third sentence above). The effect is rather like that of a camera zooming into a scene, so as to make the audience forget that they are viewing a film and draw them right into the action as if they were seeing it with their own eyes.

Although this device is used in English prose, too, for dramatic effect, it is rare in academic writing in English, which tends to aim at a more objective tone. It is especially unusual in English prose to switch tenses like this in mid-paragraph. The freer use of tenses in Japanese may derive from its oral tradition, in which numerous folktales were handed down over the centuries. (See ch. 4, § 2.4 for the nature of Japanese tense.)

4. Complex structures

Japanese sentences are often long and complex, especially in academic writing. In such cases it is all the more crucial to analyze the sentence structure and determine accurately the modifying relations between multiple modifier clauses and the nouns to be modified.

EXAMPLE 23

満州国においては、色々な民族の行動の社会慣習的型が、互いに著しく異なることに驚異の目を見張ったのであったが、米国においては、その様な型こそ民族により大いに異なり得るが、その基底を成す人間性とでも言うべきものは諸民族を通じてほぼ同一であるらしい事、並びに、ある民族の目には他の民族の習慣的行動が自分たちのとは違うことがただ断片的に映り、その複雑さが把握し難い様に見えることが少くないけれども、一般に民族の社会習慣的行動はきわめて単純な原理に支配されているものらしい事に、確信をいだき始める様になった。

満州国においては、　　1 ｜ 色々な民族の行動の

In Manchuria＝PLACE1 CONT,　("I"＝OMIT TOP) various peoples' of behavior

社会慣習的型が、　　互いに著しく異なる ｜ 1　　ことに

social customary patterns SUBJ,　mutually remarkably differ＝V-PRED　(*toiu*-OMIT) fact at

驚異の目を見張った [a] のであったが、　　　　米国においては、

was astonished＝V_1-EMPH-PRED $CONJ_1$ (connecting SENT1 to SENT2),　in the U.S.＝PLACE2 CONT,

2 | その様（よう）な型こそ民族により [b] 　　大（おお）いに異（こと）なり得（う）る [c] が、

("I"=TOP) such patterns SUBJ(=*ga*)-EMPH people depending on 　greatly can differ=V-PRED CONJ[2],

3 | その基底（きてい）を成（な）す | 3 　　人間性（にんげんせい）とでも言（い）うべき [d] 　　　ものは

its basis OBJ form=V-PRED 　humanity or something like that should call 　thing TOP-CONT

諸民族（しょみんぞく）を通（つう）じて [e] 　　ほぼ同一（どういつ）であるらしい | 2

various people throughout 　roughly identical seems to be=N+COP+*rashii*-PRED (*toiu*-OMIT)

事（こと）、並（なら）びに、4 | 7 | 6 | ある民族（みんぞく）の目（め）には | 5 | 他（た）の民族の習慣的行動（しゅうかんてきこうどう）が

fact(N[1]), and also 　　to certain people's eyes CONT 　other people's customary behavior SUBJ

自分（じぶん）たちのとは違（ちが）う | 5 　　　　ことが 　ただ断片的（だんぺんてき）に

their own-PRON from CONT differ=V-PRED 　(*toiu*-OMIT) fact-B SUBJ 　merely fragmentarily

映（うつ）り、 　　　　8 | その複雑（ふくざつ）さが把握（はあく）し難（がた）い [f] | 8 | 様（よう）に

is reflected=V[a]-(TE)-PRED[a]-RSN, 　its complexity SUBJ hard to grasp=V-PRED 　　　seems to

見（み）える | 6 　　　ことが少（すく）なくない | 7 　　　けれども、

appear=V[b]-PRED[b] 　(*toiu*-OMIT) fact-A SUBJ is not a few=ADJ-PRED 　although=CONJ[3],

一般（いっぱん）に民族の社会習慣的行動は 　　　9 | きわめて単純（たんじゅん）な原理（げんり）に

generally people's social customary behavior TOP 　extremely simple principles by

支配（しはい）されている | 9 　　もの [g] らしい | 4

is being controlled=V-PASS-PRED thing seems=N+(*dearu*=OMIT-COP)+*rashii*-PRED (OMIT-*toiu*)

事に　　　　確信を抱き始める様になった。
<ruby>確<rt>かく</rt></ruby><ruby>信<rt>しん</rt></ruby>を<ruby>抱<rt>いだ</rt></ruby>き<ruby>始<rt>はじ</rt></ruby>める様になった。

in the fact (N$_2$),　conviction OBJ came to begin to hold=V$_2$-PRED

[a] . . . *ni kyōi no me o miharu* is an idiom: "be shocked/astonished at."

[b] *ni yori/yotte* "depending on" or "according to" (not to be treated as *V-te*).

[c] V stem + *uru/eru* "can do . . ." *Uru* is a verb meaning "to gain/obtain."

[d] *X toiu mono* "a thing called X" or "what is called X." *Demo* after *to* gives the meaning of "or something like that." *Beki* after *iu* has the meaning of "must, should."

[e] *X o tsūjite* is an idiom meaning "through(out) X" (not to be taken as a component of a multiple predicate).

[f] V-*stem-gatai* "hard/difficult to do . . .": *haaku shigatai* "hard to grasp."

[g] V-Plain + *mono da* expresses general expectation/understanding: "It is normally expected that . . ." (See ch. 4, § 9.)

This sentence consists of two sentences connected by CONJ$_1$, *ga* (but). Each of them begins with a place noun in contrast (Manchuria as opposed to the United States), and has the same omitted topic, "I," with predicates V$_1$ (was astonished) and V$_2$ (came to have the conviction). The overall structure is: *[watakushi wa]* PLACE1 V$_1$, but PLACE2 V$_2$. The second sentence includes two nouns, N$_1$ (fact 1) and N$_2$ (fact 2) of which the author "began to be convinced." Both nouns are preceded by *toiu* clauses (CL$_2$ and CL$_4$).

The first half of CLAUSE2 up to *ga* (CONJ$_2$), is actually an inserted sentence because the conjunction *ga* "but" normally connects two sentences. Within a subordinate clause, *keredomo* "although" is normally used instead of *ga*. The subject of this inserted sentence is a N (such patterns) that is emphasized by the particle *koso* which has replaced the subject particle *ga*, and which has the V (can differ) as its predicate. The second half of CL$_2$ is the main clause consisting of the topic N (thing) modified by CL$_3$ (which forms their basis) and the predicate *N dearu rashii* (seems to be identical).

The second *toiu* clause, CLAUSE4, also consists of two parts, connected by the conjunction *keredomo* (although). The subject of the ALTHOUGH clause (CL$_7$) is *koto* (fact-A), and the predicate is *sukunakunai* (are numerous). This subject *koto* is modified by a *toiu* clause (CL$_6$) whose subject is *koto* (fact-B), which is in turn modified by another *toiu* clause (CL$_5$) and takes multiple predicates: Va (is reflected) functioning as RSN, and Vb (seems to appear) following CL$_8$ (its complexity is hard to grasp). CL₅ has a subject (other people's customary behavior) and a predicate (V, differ).

The second portion, the main part of CLAUSE₄ for N₂(the fact 2), has a topic (people's customary social behavior) and predicate (seem to be the thing), with the noun's being modified by CL₉ (governed by extremely simple principles).

> In Manchuria I was astonished by how remarkably different the customary social patterns of the behaviors of various peoples can be. However, in the United States I became convinced of two things: (1) that such patterns can differ greatly depending on the people, but that what one calls humanity, or whatever forms their basis, seems to be more or less the same across peoples; and (2) that although there are many cases where the differences between other people's customs and one's own are [only] partially reflected to one's eyes, and such complexity seems to be difficult to grasp, people's social customs appear to be governed by extremely simple principles.

| EXAMPLE 24 |

そこに、そのヨーロッパのニヒリズムといわれるものが、他の諸々のニヒリズム、すなわちいわば直接的な、人間の生存からじかに生じて来得るようなニヒリズムとは違って、寧ろそういうニヒリズムの克服である筈のもの（すなわちキリスト教のモラル）の破綻を通して現われて来た、いわば高次のニヒリズムであることが知られ るであろう。

そこに、	そのヨーロッパのニヒリズムといわれる	ものが、	他の諸々の

There-PLACE, that European nihilism is called=V-PASS-PRED　　thing(A) SUBJ, other various

ニヒリズム、すなわちいわば	直接的な、人間の生存からじかに

nihilisms-B, that is to say so to speak　direct, human being's survival from immediately

生じて来得る	ような	ニヒリズムとは違って、

gradually can arise=V-PRED　seems=AN+COP-PRED　nihilism(B') from CONT differ=V₁-TE-PRED₁,

COMPLEX STRUCTURES • 155

寧ろ	そういうニヒリズムの克服である筈の [1]

rather   such nihilism an overcoming is supposed to be=N+COP+*hazu*-COP(=*da*)-PRED

もの	（すなわち	キリスト教のモラル）の破綻を通し [2]	現われて来た、

something(C), namely   Christian morality breakdown through   came to appear=V-PRED,

いわば高次のニヒリズムである		ことが

so to speak higher-level nihilism(C') is=N+COP-PRED₂ (OMIT-*toiu*)   fact SUBJ

so to speak higher-level nihilism(C') is=N+COP-PRED$_2$ (OMIT-*toiu*) fact SUBJ

知られるであろう。

be known=V-PASS-probably-PRED.

[1] The copula *da/dearu* has been changed to *no* at the end of the modifier clause. The *dearu* before *hazu* is the equivalent of *no*, constituting N (*kokufuku*) *no hazu da* "is supposed to be N (overcoming)."

[2] *X o tōshite* is an idiom meaning "through X" (not to be taken as a component of a multiple predicate).

The main predicate of the sentence consists of *shirareru*, "be known," which is V-passive, and *dearō*, "probably is," an ending that conveys a sense of uncertainty or indirectness. In this kind of academic writing the element of uncertainty is minimal, but the habit of indirectness or uncommittedness of the speaker is being carried over from the spoken language. This kind of predicate can be rendered as "One can understand/see that . . ." *Koto* is the subject for the main predicate.

There is another subject, *mono* (A), which is apparently the subject of a clause, and so we need to determine the predicate for this subject. The word *sunawachi* "that is to say," connects two nouns in this case: *moromoro no nihirizumu* (B) "various nihilisms," and . . . *nihirizumu* (B') "nihilism that is . . ." B' is modified by a modifier clause ending with the predicate . . . *yō na* (the *na* of which derives from the copula *da*) which contains a clause ending with *ki-uru*. The beginning of this clause is after *iwaba*, constituting the clause "which can arise from the immediate survival, so to speak, of the human being." *Chigatte* (V₁) is therefore the first predicate of A.

There is another *sunawachi* which again connects two nouns: *mono* (C) "thing" and *kōji no nihirizumu* (C') "higher-level nihilism." *C' dearu* is another predicate for the subject, A, thus completing a rather long clause for *koto*. The predicate of the modifier clause for C is *hazu no* (the *no* of which derives from the copula *da*).

Since there is no verb of existence it is rather difficult to determine which predicate is to be modified by the location *soko ni*, "there." However, in this context *soko* refers to the fact mentioned in the preceding sentence: "the fact that it was precisely European nihilism that emerged when the logical consequence of Christian morality itself, which was the counter-measure against nihilism, was pursued psychologically to its extreme." This location word thus applies to the final predicate: "The fact . . . will be known/understood in the fact [referred to in the preceding sentence]."

TRANSLATION

There one can see that what is called "European nihilism" is different from the kinds of nihilism that can arise immediately from human life, and is a so to speak "higher" nihilism which appeared as a result of the breakdown of the institution—Christian morality—which was supposed to overcome such (so-called "immediate") nihilisms.

Hence this "European nihilism" is different from the kind of nihilism that arises immediately from human life. It is, so to speak, a "higher" nihilism that appeared as a result of the breakdown of the very institution—Christian morality—that was supposed to overcome "immediate" nihilism.

5. Word meaning

It is always difficult to establish equivalence between two languages from different language-families, and this difficulty is compounded when—as in the case of English and Japanese—the languages have grown out of such different cultures as the European and the East-Asian.

One of the basic tasks of translation concerns finding equivalents between words that share similar meanings. Each word has a certain "meaning-territory," and the meaning of the same word can vary considerably according to the context. Indeed every word lives only within a context of actual uses of it. Words that are not in use in actual discourse are more stable but, in a sense, "dead" carriers of meaning. Since word meanings are conditioned by their contexts, the same word may need to be translated by different words in differing contexts.

5.1 *Hitei*

EXAMPLE 25

併し、そのような立場の違いにも拘わらず、神の否定によってのみ人間が自ら人間性を取戻し得るという根本の主張に於ては、両者は軸を一つにしている。

併し、そのような立場の違いにも拘わらず、[1] 神の否定に [2] よってのみ

However, that kind of standpoint difference in spite of,   God negation   through only

人間が自ら人間性を取戻し得る

という根本の主張に於ては、

humanity SUBJ himself humanity OBJ able to regain=V-PRED   basic assertion in CONT,

両者は軸を一つにしている。

both TOP, are sharing a common axis=V-STATE-PRED.

[1] *nimokakawarazu* "in spite of . . ." should not be confused with negative *V-te* form in place of *V-naide* functioning as part of a multiple predicate.

[2] *Hitei* has the meaning of "negation," "denial," or "rejection," depending on the context. "Negation" is the most general, and has the deeper meaning of "making the other into nothing," while "denial" and "rejection" are more circumscribed. "Denial" has to do with discourse: one denies what has been said previously; "rejection" means, literally, "throwing back." In this context "denial" is best, in the sense that one denies what one previously said or believed concerning God. The topic and the predicate are preceded by two adverbial phrases: . . . *nimo kakawarazu* and . . . *ni oite*. The contrast expressed in these two adverbial phrases is also structurally reflected in the use of the CONT particle *wa* after *shuchō ni oite*.

TRANSLATION

> However, in spite of the difference between these standpoints, they share the basic assertion that it is only through denying God that the human being can regain his/her own humanity.

EXAMPLE 26

従って虚無は、存在するものに対する否定ではない。

従って虚無は、 存在する もの[1] に対する否定[2] ではない。

Therefore nihility TOP   exist thing regarding negating is not=N+COP-PRED.

[1] [*sonzai suru*] *mono*, is a philosophical term meaning "beings" (things that exist).

[2] *hitei* here does not mean denial, since the subject of denying is "nihility," which is not the kind of thing that could "deny" anything. However

the topic, *kyomu* (nihility), is "something" antithetical to everything that exists, and so does in a sense "negate" things.

TRANSLATION

> Therefore, nihility does not mean the negating of beings.

5.2 *ni taishite*: "regarding" or "opposing"

In the example just given above, . . . *ni taisuru* follows the word that is the object of the negating:

そんざい
存在するものに対する否定
たい　　ひ てい

"negating with respect to beings" (= negating of beings)

Consider the following sentence:

EXAMPLE 27

この妻の労苦に対して私の報いたのは、ただ雑誌に載った私の論文を見せることだけ、それだけであった。

この妻の労苦に対して* 私の報いた	のは、ただ

This wife's hardship for   I SUBJ(= *ga*) rewarded=V-PRED thing-PRON TOP, only

雑誌に載った	私の論文を見せる	ことだけ、

in a journal appeared=V-PRED my paper OBJ show=V-PRED (*to iu*-OMIT) matter only,

それだけであった。

that's all-EMPH was=N+*dake*+COP-PRED

    * In this context *ni taishite* does not mean "opposing," but rather "in return for": "what I gave in return for this hardship of (my) wife's . . ." Do not take this *V-te* form as a component of a multiple predicate.

TRANSLATION

> The only thing I did for my wife in recompense **for** her hardship was merely to show her a paper of mine which had appeared in a journal (and that was all).

| **EXAMPLE 28** |

アフリカ大陸のナイル河では、海に出て来る水は、流域に降った降水量のわずか三％程度である。これに対し、日本の河川は短く、降った雨の七〇ないし八〇パーセントがそのまま川となって海に出るので、利用の仕方によっては効率は良いわけである。

アフリカ大陸のナイル河では、　　　海に出て来る　　　水は、

African Continent at the Nile CONT,　to the sea comes out=V-PRED　water TOP,

流域に降った　　　降水量のわずか三％程度である。

along the basin fell=V-PRED　precipitation only three percent about is=N+COP-PRED.

これに対し（て）、*　　日本の河川は短く　　　　　　　降った

In contrast to this, Japanese rivers SUBJ(=*ga*)-CONT are short=ADJ-(TE)-PRED$_1$-RSN, fell=V-PRED

雨の七〇ないし八〇パーセントがそのまま川となって海に出る　ので、

rain 70 to 80% SUBJ as is river become=V$_1$-TE-PRED$_2$-MNR to the sea comes out=V$_2$-PRED$_3$ RSN,

利用の仕方によっては効率は良いわけである。

depending on how to use CONT efficiency rate SUBJ(=*ga*)-CONT is good=ADJ-EMPH-PRED

> * *Kore* contrasts the Nile with Japanese rivers. Thus *ni taishi(te)* means "opposing this." Remember that *kore ni taishite(te)* can also mean "regarding": *Kore ni taishi(te) dō omoimasu ka.* "What do you think **about** this?"

V$_1$ (*natte*) is the manner for V$_2$ (*deru*): "comes out to the sea becoming a river." *ADJ-te* (*mijikakute*) is the reason for V$_1$ and V$_2$: "because Japanese rivers are short . . ."

TRANSLATION

> In the case of the Nile on the African Continent, the water that reaches the sea is only about 3% of the (entire) precipitation along the river. In contrast to this, since Japanese rivers are short, and so 70% to 80% of the rain falling along the rivers comes out to the sea as rivers [without being lost on the way], they can be very 'efficient' if used well.

5.3   -*ka*: "transformation"

The word *ka* meaning "change, transformation" (as in *kagaku*, "chemistry," the study of transformations) can be added as a suffix to a variety of words in order to express the idea of a change of state with respect to the thing denoted by the original word. The resulting compound has to be translated in a variety of ways, according to the original meaning.

EXAMPLE 29

また憤怒が起こっても、その憤怒も意識の惰力化と共に「化学分解的に」霧散して了う。

また憤怒が起こっても、* その憤怒も意識の惰力化

Again anger SUBJ even though arises   that anger TOP(=*wa*)-ALSO of consciousness inertia-*ka*

と共に「化学分解的に」霧散して了う。

at the same time "like a chemical solution" dissipate completely=V+*teshimau*-PRED

* *V-te mo* "even though . . ." (See ch. 1, § 3.2.1.)

TRANSLATION

> Even when anger wells up again, it ends up dissipating completely "like a chemical solution" together with the **becoming**-inert of consciousness.

| **EXAMPLE 30** |

彼が反対せざるを得なかった根本は、それが魂の死、魂の機械化に導く方向であり、また人間の内的な畜群化、真の自由の剝奪に導く方向であるからであった。

| 彼が反対せざるを得なかった [1] | 根本は、 | それが | 魂の死、 |

He SUBJ couldn't help opposing=V-PRED basis TOP, it SUBJ of soul death

| 魂の機械化に導く | 方向であり、また [2] |

of soul mechan**ization** lead=V-PRED direction is=N+COP1-(TE)-PRED$_1$, again

| 人間の内的な畜群化、真の自由の剝奪に導く |

the human being's internal herd-animal-*ka*, deprivation true freedom to lead=V-PRED

| 方向である | からであった。

direction is=N+COP2-PRED$_2$ was because=*kara*(RSN)+COP-PRED

[1] *V-zaru o enai* is an idiom meaning "cannot help V-ing" (see Appendix, § 1).

[2] The *mata* in this context means "also" rather than "again."

The overall structure is: [ ]N *wa* [ ]*kara de atta* "N . . . was because . . ."

TRANSLATION

> He [Dostoevsky] had to oppose [it] because he saw it leading in the direction of the death of the soul and its mechan**ization**, as well as to the internal **transformation** of human beings into herd animals and the deprivation of true freedom.

5.4 *tettei(teki)*: "through, exhaustive"

EXAMPLE 31

彼（ドストエフスキー）の天才はそういう根本的なものをいち早く把え、然も
その帰結するところを徹底的に追求したのである。

彼（ドストエフスキー）の天才はそういう根本的なものをいち早く把え、
His (Dostoevsky's) genius TOP that kind of fundamental thing OBJ quickly grasp-V_1-(TE)-PRED$_1$,

然も ┃その帰結する┃ところを徹底的に追求したのである。
moreover it concludes=V-PRED place OBJ thoroughly pursued=V_2-EMPH-PRED2

The adverb *tetteiteki ni* means "thoroughly," but to say that someone pursued
. . . thoroughly" sounds odd in English. An idiomatic translation would be:

TRANSLATION

> It was his genius to grasp the core issue immediately and pursue it
> **through to its ultimate conclusions."**

EXAMPLE 32

そこからスティルナーは、これらすべての立場の徹底的な否定として、エゴイ
ズムというものを標榜したのである。

そこからスティルナーは、　これらすべての立場の　徹底的な否定として、
From there Stirner TOP,　　these all standpoints　　*tetteiteki* negation as,

エゴイズムというものを標榜したのである。
what is called egoism OBJ advocated=V-EMPH-PRED

Tetteiteki actually has a range of meanings, covering "thorough, exhaustive, thoroughgoing, complete, perfect, out and out, straight-out, final, drastic, radical." In this context perhaps the word "utter" goes best with *hitei*, "negation."

TRANSLATION

> From there Stirner goes on to advocate egoism as the **utter** negation of all such standpoints.

EXAMPLE 33

さきにマルキシズムや実存主義に関して語ったことは、それらがなお「人間」の立場に立つ限り、却って人間の現実存在に本当に徹底することは出来ないのではないかということである。

さきにマルキシズムや実存主義に関して語った

Earlier regarding Marxism, existentialism, etc. regarding ("I"-OMIT-SUBJ) mentioned＝V-PRED

ことは、　それらが¹ なお「人間」の立場に立つ　限り、

thing(N_1) TOP, they SUBJ still "the human" at standpoint stand＝V-PRED so long as,

---

却って人間の現実存在に本当に徹底することは²

on the contrary in man's real being truly do *tettei* matter SUBJ(＝*ga*)-CONT

出来ないのではないか、³　ということである。

cannot＋isn't it＝V-POT＋SOFT-PRED-QUES thing(N_2) is＝N＋COP-PRED

¹· *Sorera* "they (inanimate)" is the plural of *sore*. However, normally plurality is not expressed in Japanese and *sore* can mean both "it" and "they."

² The *ga* of V-plain + *koto ga dekiru* ("can do . . .") has been replaced by the CONTRAST *wa*.

³ . . . *no dewa nai ka* is a sentence-ending expression (see ch. 4, § 14) which is often added to a negative statement in order to make it somewhat vague or to "soften" it. In the present example it transforms ". . . they cannot . . ." into something like "Isn't it that they can't . . . ?"

The topic *koto* is modified by a clause in which there is an omitted subject "I," the author: "the thing/matter which (I) mentioned concerning Marxism, existentialism, etc." The predicate is *koto dearu* (*N da*), thus showing the overall structure, N_1 *wa* N_2 *da*.

N_2 has a *toiu* clause which contains an adverbial clause conditioned by *kagiri* within it: "so long as they stand on the standpoint of 'the human'." The subject in the *toiu* clause is the same as that of the adverbial clause: namely, *sorera* "they," which refers to "Marxism, existentialism, etc." in the modifier clause for N_1.

In this case, knowledge of the context is necessary in order to appreciate the force of the *kaette*: the argument so far has been that an understanding of the human standpoint is not in itself sufficient for giving a full account of "actual human being." Thus something like "contrary to expectation" would be a better translation than "on the contrary."

(*X ni*) *tettei suru* means "be thorough, be complete, be exhaustive, come home to one's heart, be driven home, be consistent (with respect to X)." *Shigoto ni tettei suru* means "to be immersed in (one's) work"; while *saishokushugi ni tettei suru* means "to be a strict vegetarian." It is often an even more difficult expression to find a satisfactory translation for than the related *tetteiteki*. In this example, something like "engage fully," or even "do justice to," would be good choices in the context of "actual human being."

TRANSLATION

> I suggested earlier (= what I have suggested earlier was) that as long as Marxism and existentialism still hold to the standpoint of "the human," they will not be able (contrary to expectation) fully to engage actual human being.

EXAMPLE 34

併しながら、それらの立場で現実存在というものが本当に徹底されていると言えるであろうか。

併しながら、それらの立場で	現実存在というものが本当に
However, those standpoints by-INST	"actual being" called thing SUBJ truly

徹底されている	と言えるであろうか。
be made *tettei*=V-PASS-STATE-PRED QUOT	("one"-OMIT-TOP) can say+probably=V-POT+*dearō*-PRED-QUES

The omitted topic of this sentence is "one" or "we" in a general sense. There is a quotation clause for . . . *to ieru*. This sentence is a rhetorical question, "Can one possibly say . . ." with the strong implication that the answer is "no: one can't really say that . . ." The *sare* of *tettei sareteiru* is the passive form and *-teiru* gives the meaning of a present state: ". . . has been done." (See ch. 4, § 2.5.1 for *V-te-iru*.)

TRANSLATION

> But can we (really) say that what is called actual being is fully engaged by these standpoints?

EXAMPLE 35

スティルナーも、ニヒリズムという言葉こそ使わなかったけれども、やはり従来の諸々の理想や価値が、自らを徹底させようとするその努力自身によって、自らを掘り上げて無に崩落するということを論理的に証明しようとした。

スティルナーも、 ニヒリズムという言葉こそ使わなかった けれども、

Stirner TOP(= *wa*)-ALSO, nihilism word called OBJ(=*o*)-EMPH did not use=V-PRED although-CONJ,

やはり従来の諸々の理想や価値が、 自らを

(Stirner-OMIT TOP) after all up to now various ideals values etc. SUBJ, them(selves) OBJ

徹底させようとする その努力自身によって、自らを

try hard to make *tettei*=V-*Ō to suru*-PRED that effort itself through, themselves OBJ

掘り上げて無に崩落する ということを論理的に

dig up=V$_1$-TE-PRED$_1$-MNR into nothing fall=V$_2$-PRED$_2$ matter/fact OBJ logically

証明しようとした。

tried hard to prove=V-*Ō to suru*-PRED

The overall structure is:

Although-Clause + Omitted Topic (= Stirner) *wa* OBJ *o* Vt.

The OBJ, *koto*, has a *toiu* clause in which V_1 gives the manner for V_2: ". . . fall into nothing by digging themselves up." This clause includes a phrase, "through effort itself" which is modified by a clause, "that tries to make them thorough." In this context *tettei suru* might best be translated something like "make them exhaustive/complete/consummate."

TRANSLATION

Though he did not use the word "nihilism," Stirner tried to demonstrate logically that previous ideals and values undermine themselves and collapse into nothing, precisely as a result of the effort to make them exhaustive (absolute).

6. The role of context

As we have seen, the part played by context is extremely important in Japanese, where things tend not to be expressed directly. Not only are elements of a sentence often omitted, but also the relationship between a demonstrative and what it refers to can sometimes be quite vague.

6.1 Omitted Elements

Elements of sentences are often omitted in Japanese when they are obvious, or sometimes when one wants to show politeness by being indirect or somewhat ambiguous. The most common things to be omitted are the topic, subject, or object of a sentence, which are generally the most important elements of the sentence in Indo-European languages.

This kind of omission has its roots in the great value the Japanese place on human relationships, on one's belonging to social groups, rather than on individual uniqueness. Since the primary goal is a harmonious social atmosphere, actions tend not to be attributed to a specific agent, who is often merely implied in a context. This does not cause much of a problem for persons who participate the same social group and share similar experiences, but in the case of formal writing which requires more objectivity, the omission of the subject or topic can often cause great difficulty in comprehension.

THE ROLE OF CONTEXT • 169

6.1.1 Topic Omission

十月末のある朝のことである。私は家の裏口へ出て、深い秋雨のために色づいた
かきの葉が面白い様に地へ落ちるのを見た。肉の厚いかきの葉は、霜のために
枯れたり、ちぢれたりはしないが、朝日が当たって来て霜のゆるむころには、
重さにたえないで、もろく落ちる。しばらく私はそこに立って、ぼう然となが
めていた位だ。

1 ＞　　十月末のある朝のことである。　　　　　　**2 ＞**　私は家の裏口へ

(X-OMIT-TOP) October end one morning a matter is=N+COP-PRED.　I TOP house back door to

出て、　深い秋雨のために ^{1} 色づいた　かきの葉が

went out=V$_1$-TE-PRED$_1$, dense autumn drizzle due to colored=V-PRED　persimmon leaves SUBJ

面白い様に地へ落ちる　のを、見た。

in an interesting way, to the ground fall=V-PRED NOM OBJ saw=V$_2$-PRED$_2$.

3 ＞ 肉の厚い　かきの葉は、霜のために枯れたり、

Meat SUBJ(=*ga*) is thick-ADJ-PRED persimmon leaves TOP, frost due to wither-V$_1$,

ちぢれたりはしないが、朝日が当たって来て ^{4}

curl up-V$_2$-*tari* CONT do not=V-PRED but-CONJ, morning sun SUBJ begins to shine=V1-TE-PRED$_1$

霜のゆるむ　ころには、重さにたえないで、^{5}

frost SUBJ(=*ga*) loosens=V$_2$-PRED$_2$ about the time CONT, weight not withstand=V$_1$-TE-PRED$_1$-MNR,

もろく落ちる。　**4 ＞** しばらく私はそこに立って、ぼう然と

easily fall=V$_2$-PRED$_2$. (Y-OMIT-TOP) for a while I TOP there stand=V$_1$-TE-PRED$_1$, blankly

ながめていた　位だ。

was gazing=V$_2$-PRED$_2$ to the extent is=N+COP-PRED.

[1] Note that . . . *no tame ni* can mean "owing to, due to" as well as "for the sake of," depending on the context.

[2] [*Niku* ("meat/flesh") *no*(=*ga*) *atsui* ("is thick")] is a modifier clause for *kaki no ha*: "persimmon leaves the meat of which is thick" or "thick persimmon leaves."

[3] V_1-*tari* V_2-*tari suru* "do things like V_1, V_2 and so on."

[4] *V-te-kuru* "something takes place gradually or begins to do . . ." (See ch.4, § 2.5.3 for other meanings.)

[5] The *taenaide* — alternative: *taezu(ni)* — is the negative -*te* form of *taeru*.

SENTENCE 1. "This sentence consists only of the predicate: . . . *koto dearu*, "X is a matter of . . ." In other words, an X, the topic is missing. This is a typical beginning of a story or an essay in which something like *sore wa* has been omitted."

TRANSLATION

> **It** was a morning at the end of October.

SENTENCE 2. *Ie no uraguchi e dete* (V_1-*te*) does not mean that the author went out of the back door (which would be *uraguchi o dete*) but rather that he went out **to** the area around the back door. V_1 and V_2 indicate sequence: "I went out . . . and saw . . ." The *no* of *ochiru no* is the nominalizer: "I saw the persimmon leaves **falling**."

As for *fukai shūu no tame ni*, "owing to a dense autumn drizzle," it modifies either *irozuita* "colored" or *ochiru* "fall." From the point of view of structure (proximity) the meaning would appear to be "persimmon leaves colored by the dense autumn drizzle." The overall sense would seem to suggest that the color of the leaves had been changed by prolonged explosure to drizzle.

Note that *omoshiroi yō ni* "in an interesting/amusing way" can have the connotation of "easily and a lot," as in *Sakana ga omoshiroi yō ni (takusan) toreta* "We were able to catch **many fish easily**."

TRANSLATION

> I went outside around the back door and saw persimmon leaves [that had been] colored by the dense autumn drizzle falling to the ground in an interesting (and abundant) way.

SENTENCE 3. The first part of the third sentence is: "Although thick persimmon leaves do not wither or curl up due to frost." As for the V_1 *omosa ni taenaide*, "not withstanding the weight," what is not withstanding whose weight? From the context it would seem that it must be their own weight that the leaves aren't able to withstand. V_1-*te* would then convey the manner for V_2.

TRANSLATION

> Although thick persimmon leaves do not wither or curl up because of the dense autumn drizzle, by the time the morning sun begins to shine and the frost loosens up they [the leaves] fall easily, being unable to withstand their own weight.

SENTENCE 4. This sentence consists only of the predicate: [*Shibaraku . . .*] *kurai da*, "(It) was to the extent that I stood up there and was gazing blankly for a while." We must figure out *what* (= Y) was to that extent, and can do so by going back to the second sentence. What was "to such an extent" was the interesting way in which such a quantity of colored leaves was falling so easily to the ground.

TRANSLATION

> It was so interesting (to watch the colored leaves fall to the ground so easily and in such quantities) that I stood there for a while and gazed [at the scene] blankly.

6.1.2 Subject Omission

EXAMPLE 37

急に私の後ろからげたの音がして来たかと思うと、ばったり立ち止まって、向こうの石がきの上の方に向いて呼びかける子供の声がした。

| 急に私の後ろからげたの音がして来た ¹ か | と |

Suddenly me behind from clogs sound SUBJ began to sound=V-PRED-QUES QUOT

| 思う | と、² ばったり立ち止まって、 | 向こうの石がきの |

(X-OMIT-SUBJ) thought V-PRED WHEN, abruptly came to a halt=V₁-TE-PRED₁, over there stone wall

> 上の方に向いて呼びかける ｜ 子供の声がした。

above toward face＝V₂-TE-PRED_a-MNR call out＝V₃-PRED_b child's voice SUBJ sounded＝V₄-PRED₂

> [1] *V-te kita* in this case means "gradually something happened, began to happen" as well as "spatially (the sound) approached the speaker/writer."
>
> [2] *. . . ka to omou to* "at the moment I thought (something happened)."

What is X, the subject for V₁ *tachidomatte*? One would expect it to be the sound of the clogs which stops, but the verb *tachidomaru* "to come to a halt" is used only of animate beings. One has to assume, therefore, that it is the person wearing the clogs who came to a halt. Here we can observe a shift in the subject. V₂ and V₃ go together as a multiple predicate with V₂ as manner for V₃. The calling out seems to be done by someone facing in the direction of the top of the wall.

The next question concerns where the modifier clause begins for the noun *kodomo no koe*. If V₁ is included, the clause would mean: "a child's voice which came to a halt abruptly and called out [facing toward] above the stone wall." V₁ should not be included in the clause because the assumed subject, the person wearing the clogs, is not identifiable with the noun to be modified, the child's voice. V₁ has thus to be taken as the first predicate of the main sentence. In other words, V₁ and V₄ are grouped together as multiple predicates: "the person wearing the clogs came to a halt abruptly and a child's voice . . . was heard."

TRANSLATION

> Just at the moment I thought I suddenly heard the sound of clogs approaching from behind, the person (wearing the clogs) abruptly came to a halt and a child's voice was heard calling out toward above the stone wall.

6.1.3 Omission of Indirect Object

EXAMPLE 38

The passage just discussed continues:

子供はお茶のはいったことを知らせに来たのだ。

子供は │ お茶のはいった │ ことを知らせに来たのだ。

child TOP tea SUBJ(=*ga*) is poured=V-PRED fact OBJ inform PURPOSE came=V-EMPH-PRED

Since the child called out toward the stone wall, the people he came to tell that the tea was ready are (we can tell from the later context) farmers working in the paddy above the wall and not the author, since the next sentence says "I, too, have become thirsty." Here the indirect object (= farmers who are working in the paddy above the wall) has been omitted.

TRANSLATION

> [It turned out that] the child had come to tell (the people working above the stone wall) that the tea was ready.

6.1.4 Omission of *V-te*

EXAMPLE 39

自己資本比率の数字を達成し得ない銀行に対して、大蔵省は「新規の海外支店新設などを認めないこともある。」と厳しく対処することにしている。

│ 自己資本比率の数字を達成し得ない │ ¹ 銀行に対して、² 大蔵省は

net worth ratio figure OBJ not able to achieve=V-PRED banks regarding, Ministry of Finance TOP

│ 「新規の海外支店新設などを認めない

"newly regulated overseas branches new establishment etc. OBJ not approve=V-PRED

│ こともある。」³ と厳しく

(OMIT-*toiu*) matter SUBJ(=*ga*)-EMPH there is=V-PRED" QUOT (*itte*-OMIT-V₁*te*-MNR) strictly

対処することにしている。 ⁴

deal with has decided=V₂-STATE-PRED

[1] V-stem + *eru/uru* "able to do . . ." or "possible to do . . ."

[2] . . . *ni taishite* "regarding . . ." (not to be confused with *V-te* as a component of a multiple predicate).

[3] The emphasis *mo* "even" in *koto mo aru* has replaced the subject particle *ga*. *V-(r)u koto ga aru* is a grammatical construction meaning "there are times when" — not to be confused with *V-ta koto ga aru* "to have [the experience of having] V-ed" (see ch. 4, § 3.4).

[4] V-plain *koto ni suru* "decide to do . . ."

After the quotation particle *to*, a *V-te* (*itte*, "say") has been omitted. (*V-te* is quite often omitted, especially in newspaper articles and news reports.) It is grouped with the next verb *taisho suru* to constitute multiple predicates, V₁ and V₂ *koto ni shite-iru* "have decided to do V₁ and V₂." V₁ (*itte*) is the **manner** for V₂ (*taisho suru*); "deal with . . . strictly **saying** that . . ."

The quotation clause includes another clause for *koto*; "there are times when the Ministry of Finance (the omitted subject) does not approve of things like the establishment of new overseas branches." The overall structure is:

> . . . *ni taishite*, TOP *wa* V₁, V₂ *koto ni shite-iru*.

TRANSLATION

> As for banks which cannot achieve the figure of the ratio of net worth, the Ministry of Finance has decided to deal with them strictly, saying that there are even cases when it will not approve the establishment of new overseas branches and the like.

(See above, Example 14, for omission of *shi-te* from a verbal noun.)

6.1.5 Predicate reduced to *no*

EXAMPLE 40

この国際統一基準の決定を受けて、大蔵省は、実施に当たっての細目を詰めて来た。

<ruby>国際統一<rt>こくさいとういつ</rt></ruby> <ruby>基準<rt>きじゅん</rt></ruby> <ruby>決定<rt>けってい</rt></ruby> <ruby>受<rt>う</rt></ruby> <ruby>大蔵省<rt>おおくらしょう</rt></ruby>
この国際統一基準の決定を受けて、大蔵 省は、

This international unified standard decision OBJ receive=V₁-TE-PRED, Ministry of Finance TOP

実施に当たっての¹ 細目を詰めて来た。²

enforcement upon details OBJ worked on continuously up to now=V₂-PRED₂

[1] The *no* derives from the copula *da* and represents the original predicate, perhaps something like *hitsuyō na* "is necessary" (see ch. 4, § 6.1.3B).

[2] *V-te-kita* here means "(one) has continued . . . up to the present."

TRANSLATION

> Receiving (Having considered) this decision concerning a unified international standard, the Ministry of Finance has been working on the details (that it will be necessary to address) upon enforcement (of it).

6.1.6 Omission of *da/dearu*

EXAMPLE 41

明治維新以後西洋の文明文化が日本に入って来た時、国内にあまり混乱が起こらなかったのは、一つには鎖国時代から少しずつながら、西洋の文明文化が長崎を通して日本に入って来ていたからとも言えよう。

| 明治維新以後西洋の文明文化¹ が日本に入って来た² |

Meiji Restoration after Western civilization-culture SUBJ to Japan began to come in=V-PRED

| 時、³国内にあまり混乱が起こらなかった | のは、 |

time (OMIT-*ni* "at"), in the country much confusion SUBJ did not take place=V-PRED PRON TOP,

一つには | 鎖国時代から少しずつながら、⁴ 西洋の文明文化 |

for one thing CONT isolation period since little by little although, Western civilization-culture

| が長崎を通して⁵ 日本に入って来ていた | から とも |

SUBJ through Nagasaki to Japan had gradually come in=V-STATE-PRED RSN (OMIT-COP)-PRED QUOT ALSO

言えよう。 [6]

("one"-OMIT-TOP) can say=V-POT-*Ō*-probably-PRED.

[1] *Bunmei-bunka* literally means "civilization and culture" and refers to "things and culture."

[2] *V-te-kuru* means "(things) begin to (come into Japan)."

[3] *Toki* is N and is modified by a modifier clause to mean "at the time when . . ."

[4] *sukoshi zutsu nagara* means "(al)though little by little." (See ch. 4, § 2.6.2 for *nagara*.)

[5] *. . . o tōshite* "through . . ." (not to be confused with a component of a multiple predicate). The particle *o* here does not indicate the direct object, but marks the place within which the motion of going, walking, running, crossing, climbing, etc. takes place.

[6] *ieyō* is the *-ō* form of the potential form of the verb *iu* and is the equivalent of *ieru dearō*. It does not have volitional meaning here but means "probably be able to say."

From the beginning of the sentence to *kara* is a quotation clause that is the content of what "one" or "we" can probably say. The topic inside this quotation clause is the pronominal *no* modified by a modifier clause, and *kara (da/dearu)* "is because" is the predicate in which the copula *da/dearu* has been omitted. The pronominal *no* refers to "the reason (why . . .)," giving the overall sentence structure:

[X] *no wa* [Y] *kara da.* "The reason for X is Y."

TRANSLATION

> One may also be able to say that the reason why there was not much confusion within the country when Western things and culture came in after the Meiji Restoration was that, for one thing, Western things and culture had gradually been coming in to Japan through Nagasaki, albeit little by little, since the period of (national) isolation.

6.2 Specification of Antecedents

It is often difficult to determine the antecedents for demonstrative pronouns such as *sore* and *kore*. Careful attention to the context is necessary in order to ascertain which previously mentioned thing(s) or event(s) are being referred to.

EXAMPLE 42

しかし、原住民の中で日本兵に好意を示してくれる種族もあるので、それをたよりに、山また山を一つずつ越えて行きました。

しかし、	原住民の中で	日本兵に好意を示してくれる	種族

However, natives among Japanese soldiers to good will OBJ show for us=V-PRED tribes

も *ある

ので、それをたよりに、山また

SUBJ(= *ga*)-ALSO exist=V-PRED RSN, that OBJ counting on, ("we"-OMIT-TOP) mountain after

山を一つずつ越えて行きました。

mountain one by one kept on going over=V-PRED.

> * This *mo* suggests that there are tribes who are friendly as well as ones who are not.

After *shikashi* there is a reason clause which includes a modifier clause for *shuzoku*. The omitted topic is "we Japanese soldiers."

> However, since among the natives there are tribes who show good will toward Japanese soldiers, counting on **that** we kept on going over one mountain after another.

The situation is that some Japanese soldiers are in retreat from the British in the mountains of Burma where they are not familiar with the natives. What keeps them going is the chance that there are occasionally friendly tribes who would be willing to help them out rather than betray their presence to the British. It may be tempting to take the *sore* as referring to *shuzoku* ("tribes") because of its proximity, but it actually refers to *the fact that* there are occasionally tribes who are friendly toward Japanese soldiers.

TRANSLATION

> However, since among the natives there are tribes who show good will toward Japanese soldiers, counting on **this fact** (that there are some friendly tribes) we kept on going over one mountain after another.

EXAMPLE 43

誰もまだ自殺者自身の心理をありのままに書いた者はない。それは自殺者の自尊心や或いは彼自身に対する心理的興味の不足によるものであろう。

誰も ¹ まだ │ 自殺者 ² 自身の心理をありのまま ³ に書いた │ 者は

No one EMPH not yet suicide himself psychology OBJ as it is wrote=V-PRED one SUBJ(=*ga*) CONT

ない。それは自殺者の自尊心や或いは彼自身に対する　心理的 興味の

there is not=V-PRED. it TOP suicide's pride etc. or himself regarding psychological interest

不足による ⁴ もの ⁵ であろう。

lack is probably due to=V+EMPH+*dearō*-PRED

¹ *dare mo . . . mono/hito wa inai* "there is no one who . . ."
² *jisatsusha* "a (person who commits) suicide"
³ *ari no mama* "as truthfully as possible, as it is, plainly"
⁴ *. . . ni yoru* "be based on, depend on, be due to, be caused by"
⁵ *mono* is for EMPHASIS. (See ch. 4, § 9.)

TRANSLATION

> No one has ever presented the true psychology of the person who commits suicide. **This** is probably due to a lack of psychological interest in the self-respect of the suicide or in the person himself.

"This" refers to the fact that no one has ever presented the true psychology of the suicide. While indeterminacy with respect to the antecedent is not considered bad style in Japanese, such vagueness is impermissible in good English prose. A careful translation will specify the antecedents of such demonstratives as clearly as possible. In this case: "This lack [of a true account of the suicide] is . . ."

7. Metaphor

Metaphors are important insofar as they grant access to broader and deeper realms of understanding, but many parts of any metaphoric system are more or less language-specific. The Japanese metaphoric system is rich and elaborate. While there are many metaphors in Japanese which can work well in English, some of them may sound strange when translated directly. They may also reveal important differences in conceptions of the self's relation to the world on the part of Westerners and Japanese. Consider the following example from a novel by Mishima.

EXAMPLE 44

母子は次第に洛陽丸に近づいて、船は見る見る、巨大な音楽のようにふくれ上がった。

母子は 次第に 洛陽丸に 近づいて、 船は

The mother and the son TOP1 gradually the Rakuyō approach＝V_1-TE-$PRED_1$, the ship TOP2

見る見る、巨大な音楽のようにふくれ上がった。

rapidly, like gigantic music swelled up＝V_2-$PRED_2$.

The function of V_1-*te* is neither sequence or reason. It indicates manner, but the precise sense here is more like "as . . . happens."

At this point in the story, the anticipations of the mother and her son are running parallel: the boy is excited at the prospect of going on board a large and impressive ship, and the mother is experiencing obscure premonitions of a potentially fatal affair about to happen. The main predicate is a compound of *fukureru* and *agaru* and means "swelled up (as if about to burst)." But the author likens the rapid looming up of the volume of the huge ship as they draw closer to it to something immaterial — the swelling of volume characteristic of orchestral music.

The emphasis of the metaphor is — as so often in Japanese literature — on the psychological states of the protagonists: it is their rising expectations that are building like a crescendo as the ship looms before them. "Mixing" metaphors in this way is considered poor style in English writing; but it is acceptable in Japanese, which does not make such rigid distinctions between "objective" states of affairs and "subjective" reactions to them.

With a fine writer like Mishima, it will often be impossible to capture all the aspects of his metaphorical structures in a corresponding English construction, and the best one can do is to try to convey as many of them as one can without laboring the imagery unduly. The following translation retains the metaphor, but it sounds somewhat strange in English, and it might be preferable to resort to some kind of simile instead.

TRANSLATION

> As the mother and son approached the *Rakuyo*, the bulk of the ship loomed up before them, swelling to an enormous crescendo.

EXAMPLE 45

彼女は女であることの柔らかさで、まわりの空気までも浸蝕してしまう存在だった。

The acidic/metallic metaphor in the following passage is more jarring in English than in the original:

彼女は│ 女である │ことの柔らかさで、まわりの空気までも

she TOP woman is＝N＋COP-PRED fact softness INST, surrounding air even OBJ(＝*o*)-EMPH

浸蝕してしまう │ 存在だった。

corrode completely＝V＋*teshimau*-PRED being was＝N＋COP-PRED

TRANSLATION

> She was a being that would even corrode the surrounding air with her softness as a woman.

This metaphor is rather jarring in English, owing to the sharp contradiction between softness and a potential for acid-like corrosion. It is presumably based on the idea of a feminine softness that is capable of melting a man's heart. While the image of melting a heart works well in English too, the idea of a softness capable of corroding anything is a little too paradoxical. (One of the reasons Mishima can make a metaphor like this work might be that the Japanese reader may have more tolerance for paradoxical formulations than the Western counterpart—in part, at least, as a result of the influence of Zen Buddhism on Japanese literary arts.)

A natural sounding English translation might have to moderate the image somewhat:

TRANSLATION

> She was a being whose softness as a woman could even melt the air around her.

However, this does not convey the somewhat disturbing feeling that the metaphor of corrosion produces. To get this across one would have to say "corrode" instead of "melt."

EXAMPLE 46

例えばニイチェは社会主義を近代的ニヒリズムの一つと考える。ただそれは自らの足元に潜んでいる虚無を自覚しないだけである。然るにかの実存主義的な人々は、歴史の根底に潜むニヒリズムを自己自身の内面へ誘い出し、主体的にそれを生き、それを克服する。

例えばニイチェは 社会主義を近代的ニヒリズムの一つと考える。

For example Nietzsche TOP socialism OBJ modern nihilism one of consider=V-PRED.

ただそれは │ 自らの足元に潜んでいる │ [1] 虚無を

Simply it TOP oneself at the foot is lurking=V-STATE-PRED *nihility* OBJ

自覚しないだけである。 然るにかの [2] 実存主義的な人々は、 │ 歴史の

not be aware of merely=V-EMPH-PRED. However, those existential people CONT, history

根底に潜む [1] ニヒリズムを 自己自身の内面へ 誘い出し、

at the bottom lurks=V-PRED nihilism OBJ of oneself to the inner aspect lure=V_1-(TE)-PRED$_1$,

主体的に それを生き、それを克服する。

subjectively it OBJ live=V_2-(TE)-PRED$_2$, it OBJ overcome=V_3-PRED$_3$.

[1] The metaphors used here, *hisomu* "to hide or conceal oneself, to lurk in " and *sasoidasu* "to lure," connote an animal hiding or lurking in such a way that it has to be lured out. This figuration of nihility or nihilism is too exaggerated and odd in English: "However, those existentialist thinkers lure the nihilism lurking in the foundations of history out into the interior of the self . . ." It is better in this case not to try to retain the vividness of this metaphor and to use something more neutral.

[2] *kano* is the classical Japanese equivalent of *ano* "that."

TRANSLATION

> For example, Nietzsche considers socialism a kind of modern nihilism, though it is unaware of the nihility concealed in its ground. However, these existentialist thinkers **bring out** the nihilism **concealed** in the foundations of history into the interior of the self, live it subjectively, and overcome it.

8. Logicality

Each language has its own characteristic way of structuring information, which both reflects the way its native speakers perceive the world and also structures their ideas about it. A sense of this kind of structuring of a text affords predictability in comprehension. When two languages are informed by different structuring patterns, the system of expectations in perceiving relationships among ideas breaks down, thus causing difficulty in comprehension.

One of the major differences between Japanese and English with respect to such broad syntactical patterns comes from the fact that Japanese relies far more on sentence initial connectives than does English. In Japanese the proposition of a sentence is determined by the predicate, the ending of the sentence, while the nature of the connections between sentences is made apparent at the beginning. Japanese favors the smooth flow of sentences and cohesion on the surface, while English sets more of a premium on clear logical relations with less reliance on connectives between them. The more frequent use of sentence initial connectives in Japanese may derive to some extent from the long period during which the Japanese language remained at the level of oral transmission. In fact, the etymology of some of the connectors derive from oral narrative: *nazeka to iu to* "why" (lit. "if I tell you why"), *itte mireba* "in other words" (lit. "if I try saying it"), and so on.

Japanese employs a variety of narrative expressions to signal a juncture in the discourse, such as *sate* "well," *tokorode* "by the way," *dewa koko de* "well, now," and these tend to be used even in formal writing. The fondness for presenting ideas in a narrative way means that the writer will frequently rephrase what has been said (*sunawachi/tsumari* "in other words," a favorite phrase of Japanese writers), sum up (*yōsuruni* "in short"), or even suggest a dismissal of previously advanced propositions through the use of *tonikaku* "in any case, at any rate."

Another reason for the extensive use of sentence initial connectives is that Japanese sees indirectness or implicitness as an integral feature of elegant style. This is due to the heavy social value placed on consensus rather than differences in Japanese society, as well as on humility and politeness. Japanese written discourse thus calls for a gradual and often lengthy introduction of ideas or points instead of the more straightforward introduction favored by English.

The differences between the two forms of rhetoric is most evident in the organization of scholarly papers. Japanese authors tend not to want to state the main point too directly at the outset, and are much inclined to use certain "apologetic" expressions—even in formal writing—which would sound strange in the corresponding kind of discourse in English. If a Japanese author writes, for example, *Mochiron korede subete setsumei dekirui toiu wake dewa nai ga, sono ikutsuka o nobeta ni suginai* ("Of course, I do not claim, by any means, to explain everything with this, but I merely offered several explanations"), this does not suggest to the Japanese reader—as it would to someone accustomed to academic writing in the West—that the author lacks confidence in what he is saying. Many of these circumlocutions are simply part of the rhetoric of the genre, and for the most part they can be omitted in translation.

Academic papers in Japanese tend to be structured differently from their counterparts in the West. In contrast to our three-part system of introduction-argument-conclusion, they often have a four-part structure that comes from Chinese poetry and is more like a dramatic narrative: *ki* (introduction), *-shō* (development), *-ten* (turn), *-ketsu* (conclusion).

It is sometimes said that sentence connectives in Japanese are not used logically. For example, *shitagatte* can mean either "subsequently" or "consequently," leaving undetermined whether the second event was a result of the first or simply happened to follow it. The conjunction *ga* has a superficially adversative meaning—"but"—but it can also simply connect two sentences—"S_1 and S_2"—depending on the context. (The explanation lies in the term's historical development: the original possessive *ga*, the equivalent of modern *no*, developed into the subjective case and finally into a conjunction where the subject word after a modifier clause dropped out entirely, further diminishing the sense of contrast in the connecting function.)

The reader is advised when reading a text to go through the entire paragraph, carefully decoding each sentence. It is better not to rely too much on the signals given by connectives, but simply to try to understand the implicit structural relations among the ideas. When translating into English, one often ends up simply omitting many of the initial connectives. It is important not to be irritated by what might at first seem a lack of logicality in Japanese prose, and to cultivate an openness for a somewhat different way of expressing ideas in written discourse. The following section consists of a few examples which should give students a sense of some of the differences in logicality and rhetorical strategies.

EXAMPLE 47

宗教に於けるこのような「自己疎外」に於ては、自然も人間も空虚で実質の
ない非本質的なものでしかないが、無神論はまさしくこの非本質性の否定で
ある。

<ruby>宗<rt>しゅうきょう</rt></ruby> 教に於ける¹ このような「<ruby>自己疎外<rt>じ こ そ がい</rt></ruby>」に於いては、² <ruby>自然<rt>し ぜん</rt></ruby>も<ruby>人間<rt>にんげん</rt></ruby>も ³
Religion in this kind of self-alienation in TOP, both nature and humanity (N_1 N_2)TOP(= *wa*)

<ruby>空虚<rt>くうきょ</rt></ruby>で<ruby>実質<rt>じつしつ</rt></ruby>のない	<ruby>非本質的<rt>ひ ほんしつてき</rt></ruby>なもの

void is=N+COP-TE-PRED₁ substance SUBJ(=*ga*) there is not=V-PRED₂ unessential thing

でしかないが、 <ruby>無神論<rt>む しんろん</rt></ruby>は まさしくこの非本質<ruby>性<rt>せい</rt></ruby>の
merely is=N+COP-EMPH-PRED but-CONJ, atheism TOP certainly of this non-essentiality

<ruby>否定<rt>ひ てい</rt></ruby>である。
negation is=N+COP-PRED

¹ *X ni okeru* Y "Y in/at X"

² *jiko-sogai ni oite* is the larger topic while *shizen* and *ningen* are smaller topics (with *wa* having been changed to *mo*): "As for this kind of self-alienation in religion, both nature and humanity are . . ." In a case of multiple topics like this, the larger topic often denotes the place or time or area of discourse within which the smaller topics are to be discussed. In this example the meaning is "In (or for) this kind of self-alienation in religion . . ."

³ Special attention must be given to the interpretation of *mo* since there is always a possibility of its having replaced *ga* or *o*, or even the topic *wa* (see ch. 4, § 5). In this example the first *mo* has replaced *to* and the second *mo* has replaced *wa* (TOPIC): *A mo B mo* "both A and B" derived from *A to B wa*.

This sentence consists of two sentences connected by the conjunction *ga*. Both sentences have the equation-sentence structure, *N wa N dearu*. Taking the first topic as PLACE, the topics of the first sentence are N_1 and N_2 and the predicate is *N de shika nai*, in which the N (*mono*) is modified by a modifier clause which in turn contains two predicates (N+COP and V). The second sentence has the simple structure of *N wa N dearu*.

This example shows that the conjunction *ga* has a broader meaning than the English "but." It is often used — as here — simply to connect two sentences, without implying any particular contrast or difference, and is thus simply translated as "and." To translate it as "but" in this context would actually be to distort the meaning of the passage.

TRANSLATION

> In this kind of "self-alienation" in religion, both nature and humanity are something unessential—void and without substance—**and** atheism is precisely the negation of this non-essentiality.

EXAMPLE 48

しかしこのハワイ島の西北にあるマウイ島、更にその西北にあるオアフ島へと進むと、火山活動は段々おとろえ、その一方で島が沈降する傾向がはっきりと現われる。

しかし │ このハワイ島の 西北にある │ マウイ島、更に

However this island of Hawaii northwest exists=V-PRED island of Maui, furthermore

その西北にある │ オアフ島へと ² 進む │ と、³

to its northwest exists=V-PRED island of Oahu to MNR ("we"-OMIT-SUBJ) proceed=V-PRED COND

火山活動は 段々おとろえ、 その一方で │ 島が

volcanic activity TOP gradually decline=V1-(TE)-PRED₁, on the other hand island SUBJ

沈降する │ 傾向が はっきりと現われる。

sink=V-PRED tendency SUBJ clearly MNR appear=V₂-PRED2.

¹ *Sarani* "further, furthermore" is an ADV which modifies the verb *susumu* and not the phrase immediately following: *sono seihoku* "its northwest."

² The *to* of *Oahutō e to* is a MANNER *to*, as in *surasura to yomu* "read fluently." It is usually omitted and does not have to be translated.

[3] The *to* of *susumu to* is the CONDITION or TIME WHEN *to*. (See ch. 4, § 8).

The pattern of this sentence is:

> CONDITION clause + TOP *wa* V_1, SUBJ *ga* V_2.

In the conditional clause there is an omitted subject "we" or "one."

TRANSLATION

> However, if (we) proceed to the island of Maui which is located to the northwest of this island of Hawaii, and further to the island of Oahu which is to the northwest of it, volcanic activity gradually declines and, **on the other hand***, the tendency of the islands to sink (under water) clearly manifests itself.

> > * *Sono ippō* "on the other hand" is used in this context to mean "in another aspect" to highlight two aspects regarding the movement of the plate under the Pacific Ocean. What has been discussed in the paragraph is that this huge plate is gradually sliding from the southeast down to the northwest, finally to be swallowed into the deep trough located at the east of the Japanese archipelago. These two facts — that volcanic activity becomes less but that we tend to find more submerged islands the farther northwest the islands are located — together constitute evidence for the sliding of the plate. Therefore, *sono ippō de* should actually be translated as "at the same time," rather than "on the other hand."

TRANSLATION

> However, if we proceed to the island of Maui which is to the northwest of this island and further to the island of Oahu which is to its northwest, the volcanic activity becomes less and, **at the same time**, we can clearly see that more islands are submerged under water.

9. Culture

Understanding a language ultimately means understanding the culture in which it developed. Even though, for example, politeness in one's relationships with others may be universal, its manifestation in social customs and its degree of linguistic formalization differ greatly from language to language. Many concepts that are deeply rooted in cultural practices will simply not have equivalents in the other language.

Since *miso* refers to "bean paste made from fermented salted soy-beans, indispensable flavoring in Japanese cuisine," we simply use the same word in English. But what about *temae-miso* which literally means "homemade miso," but by extension "the act of self-praise"? The meaning given in the dictionary for *giri* is "justice, (a sense of) duty, obligation, a debt of gratitude"; yet since it is explained as "the concept of obligation in human relations peculiar to Japanese society," then *giri-gatai*, "the meticulous observing of *giri*," is going to be impossible to translate concisely.

In cases like this we have to know the relevant features of Japanese culture in order to know what the word means, and if we are translating we may simply have to use the original word with some kind of note. Similar problems are posed by many other words and expressions that have to do with life style, social customs, and the values that underlie them. This is also an area where the study of idioms is especially important for reading comprehension.

9.1 Sociological

EXAMPLE 49

私が結婚したのは、大学を出て三年目で、当時助手として月給四十円であった。満州事変のころで、物価は安かったが、それにしても、一個月四十円で一家のやりくりをつけることは、苦しかったであろう。

私が結婚した	のは、	大学を出て [1]

I SUBJ got married=V-PRED PRON(=the time)(N₁) TOP, college from graduated=PRED ("since"-OMIT)

三年目で、当時助手として月給 [2]

third year was=N+COP1-TE-PRED₁, at that time assistant as monthly salary(N₂) (OMIT-TOP=*wa*)

四十円であった。満州事変のころ

forty yen was=N+COP2-PRED₂. ("it-OMIT-TOP") the Manchurian Incident around the time

			一個月
で、物価は安かったが、		それにしても、	

was=N+COP-PRED₁, prices TOP were cheap=ADJ-PRED₂ but-CONJ, even so, per month

四十円で 一家のやりくりをつける [3]   ことは、

forty yen INST the entire family manage=V-PRED a matter TOP,

苦しかったであろう。

was probably hard=ADJ+*dearō*-PRED

[1] *Dete* is not functioning as a component of a multiple predicate for the topic *no* (N₁) but is a part of the *V-te kara* "since . . ." construction constituting an adverbial clause for the predicate *sannenme de*. The *kara* in V-*te kara* construction is often omitted in this way.

[2] The topic particle *wa* after N₂ has been omitted—which is quite unusual.

[3] *X no yarikuri o tsukeru* is an idiom meaning "to manage (finances)."

The first sentence has multiple predicates COP1 and COP2 for the respective topics N$_1$, the pronoun *no* (= the time) which is modified by a modifier clause, and N$_2$ (= monthly salary). The second sentence also consists of two sentences, which are connected by the conjunction *ga*. *Koto*, the topic of the second sentence is modified by a clause.

TRANSLATION

> The time I got married was three years after I graduated from college and my monthly salary was forty yen as an assistant. It was around the time of the Manchurian Incident and so prices were cheap; but even so, to manage a household on forty yen a month was probably* difficult.

* It might strike the English-speaking reader as strange that the author should say "probably" here, since one would expect him to *know* whether or not it was difficult. In fact the omitted subject in a modifier clause for *koto* in the second part of sentence 2 is *tsuma* "my wife" who is in charge of managing the household. However, one must bear in mind that Japanese husbands traditionally hand over all or most of their salaries to their wives and let them manage the financial affairs of the household while they engage themselves in their work outside. Unless one is aware of this custom, one is likely to overlook the *dearō* (or think it a mistake) and thereby mistranslate the sentence.

EXAMPLE 50

夜、開け放した窓からは、しばしば汽笛が夢魔のように入って来た。母親がやさしかった夜は、彼はあれを見ないで眠ることができた。その代わりあれは夢の中に現われた。

夜、　|開け放した|　窓からは、　　しばしば汽笛が

At night left-wide-open=V-PRED window through TOP, frequently ship's horns SUBJ

夢魔のように入って来た。　|母親がやさしかった|　夜は、¹

like a nightmare gradually came in=V-PRED. Mother SUBJ was gentle=ADJ-PRED night CONT,

彼は¹ あれ²を見ないで　眠ることができた。

he TOP that OBJ without looking=V$_1$-TE-PRED1-MNR could sleep=V$_2$-POT-PRED$_2$.

その代<ruby>か</ruby>わりあれ² は夢<ruby>ゆめ</ruby>の中<ruby>なか</ruby>に現<ruby>あら</ruby>われた。
Instead that TOP in a dream appeared=V-PRED

¹ This is another case of a double topic, with the first setting the time or place for the second.

² The ordinary meaning of *are* is "that over there," referring to an object farthest from the speaker, the distance being relative to each situation. All *a*-demonstratives have this kind of meaning: *ano* (+N) (that over there), *asoko* (over there), etc. The special use of the *a*-series demonstratives indicates that the thing mentioned is known to both the speaker/writer and the listener/reader. (See ch. 4, § 3.6.2.) For example, if both the speaker and the listener have read the same book, they might say:

> *Ano hon wa omoshirokatta desu ne.*
> That book was interesting, wasn't it?

> *Ee, are wa jitsu ni subarashii desu.*
> Yes. It is indeed wonderful.

The *a*-series demonstratives are therefore seldom used in objective writing, since the author will not know the extent of the reader's acquaintance with what he is writing about.

For this reason the use of *are* in the above passage from Mishima is very unusual and is intended to call explicit attention to itself. *Are* refers to the sight of the boy's mother alone in her room, naked, as seen through a peephole which he has accidentally found in a built-in drawer in his room. If the author were making a straightforward reference to the previously mentioned sight he would use *sore* (it). The deliberate use of *are* presumes the reader's involvement by setting up a common ground between author and reader, and thereby evokes more strongly the voyeuristic aspect of the episode. (It is common for the *a*-series demonstrative to be used to refer to something of this sort that one is reluctant to name explicitly.)

TRANSLATION

> At night through the wide open windows the ships' horns screeched in like a nightmare. On nights when his mother had been gentle, he was able to go to sleep without looking (at it). But *it* would then appear in his dreams instead.

9.2 Indirectness in Writing Style

Insofar as it reflects social mores, Japanese writing style is in many ways indirect. It strives to avoid bluntness, with the result that introductions tend to be lengthy. The ending of the sentence is a typical place to show the writer's degree of commitment to his or her statement. The most frequently used ending is . . . *to omou* "(I) think that . . ." The spontaneous forms of verbs such as *omou* "think," *kangaeru* "think," or *mitomeru* "approve, recognize, see" are also used frequently. Since the spontaneous form is identical with the passive form, it is often mistaken as passive and translated accordingly (as "it is thought" for *omowareru*). In fact in this context both forms mean more or less the same: "It seems that . . ." The passive form is normally used in *-teiru* form: . . . *to omowareteiru* "It has been thought/considered."

The spontaneous form (as its name suggests) is intended to convey in this context that the ideas being presented did not come as a result of the writer's deliberate cogitation but rather arose spontaneously and without conscious effort. The use of the spontaneous form is an extension of the use of intransitive verbs such as *kowareru* "(something) breaks," *taoreru* "(something) falls down" in cases where the writer does not wish to specify an agent for the occurrence. This ambiguity or indirectness could be interpreted either as a lack of willingness to make a commitment or assume responsibility on the part of the author, or as a manifestation of his honesty and humility in not claiming the entire credit for a statement when it is not exactly his or when he is not quite certain about it—or even when he is quite confident.

The use of the spontaneous form is an important feature of elegant Japanese prose style—as are negative rhetorical questions and idiomatic phrases intended to convey the "humble" stance adopted by the author. What might be regarded in English writing as an unnecessary amount of qualification or "hedging" is the norm in Japanese discourse, where presenting a logically coherent argument is a lesser concern than being correct about the facts presented.

EXAMPLE 51

和歌は依然としてひろくつくられていたに違いなく、仮名の使用も次第にすすんでいたと思われるのであって、つぎの時代における仮名文芸の展開は、すでにこの時代にその準備を終っていたとみとめられる。

和歌 [1] は依然としてひろくつくられていた | に違いなく、 [2]

Waka[1] TOP still widely being made＝V-PASS-ONG-PRED is certain＝ADJ-(TE)-PRED_a-RSN,

仮名の使用も 次第にすすんでいた | と

the use of *kana* TOP(＝*wa*)-ALSO gradually was progressing＝V-ONG-PRED_b QUOT

思われるのであって、 [3] | つぎの時代における仮名文芸の展開は、

it seems＝V₁-SPON-EMPH-TE-PRED₁, next period in *kana* literature development TOP,

すでにこの時代にその準備を終っていた [4]

already in this period its preparation OBJ? had finished＝V-STATE-PRED

とみとめられる。

QUOT is considered＝V₂-SPON-PRED₂

[1] *Waka* or *tanka* is a 31-syllable Japanese poem.

[2] *ni chigainai* ("it is certain that, it must be that") is taking the -*te* form here, but with the -*te* omitted. It gives the reason for *susunde-ita*.

[3] The modification of "it is certain" by an emphasized spontaneous form of the verb "to think" may seem to the English-speaking reader to generate unnecessarily complex tensions between certainty and uncertainty. In this case, as in some similar cases to be considered shortly, there is no doubt that the author is certain, but the conventional rhetoric of the genre obliges him to soften his stance. The more outspoken or hard-hitting the author's assertions or crticisms are, the more likely they are to be enveloped in several layers of sentence-ending qualifications in order not to give a negative impression.

[4] *owaru* "be over, finish" is Vi and so does not take an object word. One would therefore expect either *N ga owaru* (Vi) or *N o oeru* (Vt), although *N o owaru* (Vi) is used occasionally. In this case *junbi* (SUBJ) *ga owaru* (Vi), "the preparation is finished," makes more sense.

TRANSLATION

> It does seem that waka were certainly being composed widely and, accordingly, that the use of *kana* was gradually progressing; and so, as for the development of *kana* literature in the subsequent period, it seems that the preparation had already been completed in this period.

EXAMPLE 52

これは、やはり日本文化史上画期的なできごとであったといえよう。

これは、やはり日本文化史 上 [1] 画期的な

This TOP, after all in Japanese cultural history epoch-making

できごとであった といえよう。 [2]

was an event=N+COP-PRED QUOT ("one"-OMIT-TOP) can probably say=V-POT-ō-PRED

[1] This use of -*jō* (lit. "above") is the equivalent of the expression *X no ue de*, meaning simply "in X."

[2] The -*ō* form (= volitional form) here is used to mean "probably."

TRANSLATION

> One may be able to say that this was after all an epoch-making event in the cultural history of Japan.

EXAMPLE 53

大森彦七のような猿楽者の存在を、観阿弥の親たちにかさねあわせて想像することは許されていいのではあるまいか。

おおもりひこしち　　　　さるがくしゃ　そんざい　　　　かんあみ
大森彦七のような　猿楽者の存在を、　観阿弥の

("we"-OMIT-SUBJ) Ōmori Hikoshichi like performer of Sarugaku existence OBJ, Kan'ami's

おや　　　　　　　　　　　　　　　そうぞう
親たちに　かさねあわせて　想像する　｜　ことは

parents and others overlap＝V₁-TE-PRED₁-MNR imagine＝V₂-PRED₂ (OMIT-*to iu*) matter TOP

ゆる
許されていい ¹ のではあるまい ² か。

isn't it all right to be allowed probably＝V-PASS＋*te(mo)ii*＋SOFT-PRED-QUES

¹ *V-te(mo) ii* "it is all right to do" or "(One) may do . . ."

² *-mai* here means negative tentative "probably not" (see Appendix, § 1).
Together with a question marker . . . *de wa arumai ka* (= . . . *de wa nai dearō
ka*) it constitutes a rhetorical question with the much "softened" meaning:
"Isn't it probably all right to . . . ? (= it is all right . . .)" When combined with
yurusareru "be allowed," the passive form of *yurusu*, it further intensifies the
tentative nature of the imagining (V₂).

TRANSLATION

> It is probably permissible to imagine the existence (= life span) of a
> Sarugaku performer such as Hikoshichi Ōmori overlapping with
> those of Kan'ami's parents and others.

EXAMPLE 54

おおよそのことは、まちがいなくあてはまるといっていいであろう。

． ． ．　おおよそのことは、　まちがいなくあてはまる　｜　と

. . . roughly all the matters TOP without fail apply＝V-PRED QUOT

いっていいであろう。

is all right to say probably＝V＋*te(mo)ii*＋*dearō*-PRED

"More or less" is an approximation and "probably" is indirect, while a contrasting "without fail" is used concurrently. This is another good example of the complex tensions of qualification that so often characterize Japanese writing.

TRANSLATION

> It may be all right to say that almost **everything would apply without fail**.

| **EXAMPLE 55** |

わたしが以下にこころみようとするのも、不充分ながら欧米語と日本語の論理と思考をめぐっての従来の論点を整理し、あらためて多少とも問題の所在をあきらかにしてみようという以上のことをねらいとするものではない。

わたしが以下にこころみようとする[1]　の[2]も、　不充分

I SUBJ below try hard to attempt=V-*ō to suru*-PRED PRON(N₁) TOP(=*wa*)-ALSO, insufficient

ながら 欧米語と日本語の 論理と思考をめぐって[3]の 従来の[4]

though of Western languages and Japanese logic and thinking regarding up to now

論点を 整理し、　あらためて多少とも 問題の所在を

argument-points OBJ straighten up=V₁-(TE)-PRED₁, newly even if a little problem locus OBJ

あきらかにしてみよう　という以上のことを ねらいとする

clear will try hard making=V₂-*te miru-ō*-PRED₂ more than a matter aim at=V-PRED

ものではない。

thing(N₂) is not=N+COP-PRED

> [1] *V-yō to suru* means "to try hard to V." To say that one "tries to attempt" sounds odd in English: the sense here is more like "I will try to . . ."

[2] This *no* is a pronoun that has replaced *koto* or *mono* "matter."

[3] *Megutte* is the V-*te* form of *meguru* "to go round" but is an idiom: *X o megutte* "concerning X."

[4] This *no* is a substitute for the predicate *da*, representing in this case something like *jūrai iwarete-kita* "the points that **have been made** up to now."

The pronoun *no* modified by a modifier clause is the topic of this sentence, the predicate being *mono dewanai*: N_1 *mo*(= *wa*) N_2 *dewanai*. N_2 is modified by a long modifier clause which includes a modifier clause for *koto*. In this clause there are two predicates, V_1 and V_2. The auxiliary -*te miyō* "will try to" modifies both V_1 and V_2.

TRANSLATION

> What I will attempt below is also not something that aims at doing anything more — though it may not be enough — than trying to straighten up the points of the arguments made up to now regarding the logic and thinking of Western languages and Japanese, and to reclarify — if only a little — the locus of the problem.

In translating into English one would tend to simply ignore the qualifications between the dashes in the above example, since someone of this writer's stature in the West would not make such qualifications.

| EXAMPLE 56 |

欧米語あるいは日本語の＜論理＞の問題を考えるにあたって、いまさら伝統的な形式論理学をさしあたってにもせよ考察の基軸として持ち出すことは、論理学の現在の発展の情況からして時代おくれもはなはだしい、といった類の批判がありうることをわたしも知らぬではない。

欧米語あるいは日本語の＜論理＞の問題を 考える　にあたって、

Western languages or Japanese "logic" problem OBJ think＝V-PRED upon,

いまさら 伝統的な形式論理学を さしあたってにもせよ 考察の

at this belated time traditional formal logic OBJ even if just for the time being examination

基軸として持ち出す ことは、論理学の現在の発展の情 況

basis as bring out=V-PRED matter TOP, the study of logic present development circumstance

からして 時代おくれも はなはだしい、 といった類の批判 が

not to mention behind time SUBJ-(=*ga*)-EMPH is extreme.=ADJ-PRED,   this sort of criticism SUBJ

ありうる ことを わたしも 知らぬ [1]

can exist=V-PRED fact OBJ I TOP(=*wa*)-ALSO do not know=V-PRED

ではない。 [2]

is not necessarily=(OMIT-*toiu wake*)+COP-PRED

[1] *shiranu = shiranai*

[2] . . . *(to iu wake) dewanai* "It doesn't necessarily mean that . . ."

TRANSLATION

> It does not necessarily mean that I don't know that such a criticism could be made to the effect that it is extremely anachronistic, especially considering the present state of development of the study of logic, to bring out at this late date traditional formal logic even temporarily as the basis of examination upon which to investigate the problem of the logic of Western and Japanese languages.

Again an English translation might well omit some of the qualifications in order to convey the author's feeling confident that, in spite of possible criticism, something valuable is to be gained by examining the problem from the basis of traditional formal logic.

Chapter Four

Grammar Guide

1. PARTS OF SPEECH 202

2. VERBS 207

3. NOUNS 232

4. ADJECTIVAL NOUNS 239

5. THE USES OF *WA, GA,* AND *MO* 242

6. THE USES OF *NO* 255

7. THE PARTICLE *NI* 260

8. THE PARTICLE *TO* 270

9. THE USE OF *MONO* 277

10. THE USE OF *TOKORO* 280

11. THE USE OF *WAKE* 284

12. EMPHATIC PARTICLES 287

13. *-TE MO* AND *-TE WA* 293

14. SENTENCE-ENDING EXPRESSIONS 295

Grammar Guide

This chapter presents some basic points of grammar selected with a view to aiding reading comprehension. The items included here are less structural in nature and more idiomatic than the features dealt with in Chapter One. They are arranged in such a way that they can be referred to easily by someone coming across a puzzling grammatical element while reading a text in Japanese. They are explained in terms of what they signal, and thus of what the reader should expect or not expect in a given context in the process of understanding. Some of them are important grammatical concepts that are unique to Japanese and not found in English.

Since each reader's background is different, it is recommended that one build up and strengthen one's grammar by studying here and there where weak spots are found, rather than going through the entire grammar guide from start to finish. However, when such a weak spot is discovered, it may be a good idea to study the section or sections immediately before and after the one where the relevant information has been found—as a way of strengthening one's grasp of grammatical structure in general.

Indeed, enough of the basic structure of the Japanese language is contained in this chapter for students who study it well to be able to enhance their *production* of the language as well, whether spoken or written. Even people whose Japanese is quite fluent, and whose intuitive grasp of grammatical structures is firm, may find that the explanations of certain points articulate principles in such a way as to further enhance their understanding of the language.

It should be noted that the English translations given in the examples that follow have been kept—for the purposes of structural understanding—on the literal side, and thus they rarely represent good, idiomatic English.

1. Parts of speech

Parts of speech are words with different grammatical functions. It is important to know which part of speech each word in a text is, since such information helps one predict the co-occurrence of certain elements within the sentence, thus making the process of comprehension more efficient.

1.1 Verbals

Verbals have their own inflections and can stand as predicates by themselves.

a. VERB, *dōshi* 動詞 : *aruk-u* "walk," *ar-u* "exist." See the sections below on verb forms (2), sentence-ending expressions (14), and also the appendix (§§ 2, 3, and 5).

b. ADJECTIVE (STATIVE or DESCRIPTIVE VERB), *keiyōshi* 形容詞 : *taka-i* "high," *utsukushi-i* "beautiful" Some Adjectives in English are ADJECTIVAL NOUNS in Japanese.

⟿ The ADJ-*ku* form (the final *i* replaced by *ku*) is used as an adverb: *utsukushiku* "beautifully."

⟿ Historically *onaji* was ADJ but it now functions as N: *onaji da, onaji dewa nai, onaji datta, onaji dewa nakatta*. However, its adverbial form *onajiku*, "similarly," is still used.

1.2 Nonverbals

Nonverbals do not inflect, and thus they do not stand as predicates by themselves. They need the help of the copula *da/dearu* to constitute a predicate.

a. Noun (N), *meishi* 名詞 : *hon* "book(s)," *kore* "this." There is no article ("a" or "the") in Japanese, nor is number (singular/plural) marked. N may be followed by one of several particles. At the

end of a sentence or a quotation clause N is followed by the copula *da/dearu*; at the end of a modifier clause it is followed by the
copula *no/dearu*.

↪ Sentences may occasionally end with N, in articles in newspapers and magazines, for example.

b. Adjectival Noun, *keiyōdōshi* 形容動詞 : *kirei(na)* "beautiful,
clean," *suki(na)* ". . . that I like," *shizuka(na)* "quiet." *Suki/kirai*
"like/dislike" are verbs in English, whereas other ANs are adjectives in English but function like Ns. They take *na* before N,
while N takes *no* before N. Like Ns, ANs are followed by the
copula *da/dearu* at the end of a sentence or a quotation clause,
and at the end of a modifier clause they are usually followed by
na.

↪ *AN + ni* makes ADV. See § 4.1 for special ANs.

1.3 Copula, *keiji* 繋辞

The standard form of the copula is *da/dearu*, meaning "is, equals" as in "A is B."
The copula is attached to nonverbals (N or AN) to constitute the predicate of a
sentence. The copula in Japanese is not a verb and cannot mean "exist" as the
English "is" can. (The verbs *aru* or *iru* are used to mean "exist, there is.")

Dearu derives from the classical form of *ni te aru*, whose meaning is something like "exist in the form of." The copula *da* is not used at the end of a
modifier clause, but is replaced by *no* after N and *na* after AN respectively. **De,
the -*te* form of the copula should not be confused with the particle *de***, which
indicates the place of an action for transitive verbs, the instrument by which
something is done, or else gives a reason.

Conditional: *N dewa* "if it is N," *N deatte mo/datte* "even if it is N," *N
na(=da)raba* "if it is N."

The copula is a component in some sentence-initial conjunctions: *dakara*
"therefore," *dakeredomo* "although," *dattara* "if . . . ," *datte* "because," *dewa* "if
so, well then," *nara* "if so, then."

It can also be used as an interjection in certain kinds of male speech:

Wareware wa, da, kono mondai ni tsuite, saikentō o, da, subeki toki ga kita no da.	We have come to the stage where we must reconsider this issue.

1.4 Prenoun, *rentaishi* 連体詞

Prenouns (PreN) are bound forms that always appear with a following N.

kono +N "this N," *konna +N* "this kind of N," *dono +N* "which N?" *donna +N* "what kind of N?" *aru* +N* "a [certain] N," *iwayuru* +N* "so-called N."

↪ While the pronoun *kore* can appear by itself, *kono* cannot. We can say:

Watakushi no wa **kono hon** *da*	Mine is this book

or:

Watakushi no wa **kore** *da*	Mine is this [one]

but NOT:

Watakushi no wa **kono** *da*

* *Aru* and *iwayuru* in these constructions are not to be taken as plain forms functioning as predicates of clauses.

1.5 Adverb, *fukushi* 副詞

Adverbs precede and modify verbs, adjectives, adjectival nouns, and other adverbs.

hayaku[1] "quickly": *hayaku kaku* (V) "write quickly"
totemo "very": *totemo ii* (ADJ) "is very good," *totemo yoku* (ADV) "very well"
kirei ni[2] "beautifully, cleanly": *kirei ni kaku* (V) "write beautifully"
noronoro[3] "(in a desultory manner)": *noronoro (to) aruku* "walk idly"

[1] ADVs derived from ADJ.

[2] ADVs formed with AN and the particle *ni*.

[3] Manner adverbials (+ *to*).

Some Adverbs are *V-te* forms used to express MANNER: *isoide aruku* "walk in a hurry"

Japanese employs numerous "counters" which are attached to numbers to show the quantity of items according to the shape or nature of the thing being counted: *ichi-mai* "one flat object," *i-ppon* "one long cylindrical object," *ni-hai* "two cups," *ni-satsu* "two books," *yon-tō* "four (larger) animals," *yon-hiki* "four insects, fishes, reptiles, or small/medium-size animals," *roku-dai* "six machines/cars," *nana-ki* "seven airplanes," *ha-ssō* "eight boats," *nan-kyaku* "how many chairs?".

These counters are normally used as ADVs, as in *Hon o issatsu kau* "I buy one book." However, they may also function as Ns when used as a noun modifier with the particle *no* before a noun: ***ippon no*** *bō* "***one*** stick." See § 3.4.

1.6 Particle, *joshi* 助詞

Japanese is a post-positional language, in that the particles *follow* Ns. The particles are sometimes called "relationals" because they show the relation of the preceding noun to the other words in the sentence, and especially to the predicate.

WA for a TOPIC, AFOREMENTIONED, or CONTRAST.

GA for a SUBJECT and SUBJECT EMPHASIS. *Ga* was also used as the possessive particle in classical Japanese. The reminiscence of this case appears in literary Japanese: *wa(=ware/watakushi) ga kuni* "our country," *ta(=dare) ga tame ni* "for whom."

O for a DIRECT OBJECT of a verb and also for a place where movement such as walking, running, climbing, crossing, or passing through takes place: *Ōsaka o tōru* "pass through Osaka."

MO for "ALSO," or for EMPHASIS.

KA for a QUESTION marker at the end of a sentence or an interrogative clause, or for indefiniteness when attached to an interrogative word, as in *nani ka* "something" or *dare ka* "someone."

DE
1. for a PLACE of action for action verbs: *Resutoran de taberu* "I eat at a restaurant."
2. for a PLACE regarding which a general statement is made (usually with the following *wa*): *Nihon de (= ni oite) wa shintō no keishiki de kekkon suru hito ga ōi.* "In Japan there are many people who get married in Shinto style."
3. for a LOCATION where an event takes place that is indicated by a noun with the verb *aru*, as in *Koko de miitiingu ga aru* "There will be a meeting here."
4. INSTRUMENTAL "by means of."
5. REASON "due to"

The particle *de* must be distiguished from the *-te* form of the copula *da*.

NI for a LOCATION of existence, TIME, DIRECTION, or GOAL.

NO for "OF," POSSESSIVE, APPOSITION, or a SUBJECT in a subordinate clause. These are to be distinguished from the pronominal *no* "the one" and the nominalizer *no*.

TO for "AND" to connect nouns, and also for MANNER, TIME, PROVISION.

For *kara* "since, because," see ch. 1, § 3.1.3.

1.7 Conjunction, *setsuzokushi* 接続詞

Conjunctions join sentences or parts of sentences: *shikashi* "however," *aruiwa* "or," *keredomo* "although," *demo* "although" (at the beginning of a sentence), *ga* "but" (at the end of a sentence).

⤷ The conjunction *ga* is much weaker than the English "but" and is often used just to connect two sentences, in which case it is simply translated as "and."

Ashita kaigi ga aru ga, kayōbi ni mo aru.	There is a meeting tomorrow and (there is one) on Tuesday, too.

Ga may appear at the end of a sentence, often with *no* in the predicate, in order to convey INDIRECTNESS or to "soften" the statement leaving the sentence uncompleted:

Ashita wa tsugō ga warui no desu ga, . . .	I am afraid it's rather inconvenient tomorrow.

1.8 Interjection, *kantōshi* 間投詞

Examples: *aa* "Ah!"; *maa* "Oh, my!" (in the informal *female* speech style) or "well . . . , I think . . ." or "Oh, dear!"; *oya* "Oh! Good heavens!" (in the formal speech style); *hora* "Look!"; and so on.

2. Verbs

2.1 Conjugation (Verb Forms)

Verbs are conjugated by adding various endings to the "root" of the verb.

2.1.1 Consonant Verbs

These are verbs whose roots end in a consonant: *kak*- "write." The suffixes begin with one of the five vowels *a, i, u, e, o*, arranged as in the Hiragana syllabary.

A-row: *ka, ga, sa, ta, na, ba, ma, ra, wa* for **negative**, **passive/spontaneous**, **causative**, and **causative/passive** forms:

ROOT	MEANING	SUFFIX	FORM
kak-	to write		
oyog-	to swim		
hanas-	to speak		
mat-	to wait	-*anai*/*azu* (-*anu* / -*azaru*)[1]	Negative
shin-	to die	-*areru*	Passive/Spontaneous[2]
yob-	to call out	-*aseru* / -*asu*[3]	Causative ("make someone do . . .")
yom-	to read	-*aserareru* / -*asareru*	Causative-Passive ("be made to do . . .")
tor-	to take		
iw-	to say		

[1] The negative -*te* form of -*anai* is -*anaide*. -*azu* is the negative suffix in the classical language, and -*anu* and -*azaru* are its noun-following forms.

These forms may be used in modern Japanese, especially *-azu(ni)* as the alternative negative *-te* form.

² The Japanese passive is different from that of Western languages: see § 2.3.1 for details. See also § 2.3.2 for the spontaneous form, which has the same form as the passive. Passive forms can be used as honorifics.

³ The causative suffix *-asu* is actually the classical equivalent of *-aseru*. It can also be used for the causative-passive: *-asareru* in place of *-aserareru*. See ch. 3, § 1.1.4, example 8 (note 4) for *-shimeru*, the alternative causative form in literary style.

The verb *ar-u* "to exist, to be" (for inanimate objects) is a consonant verb, while the equivalent for animate beings is the vowel verb *i-ru*. The negative form of *a-ru* is simply *nai*, which is adjectival (*-nakunai, -nakute, -nakatta, -naku-nakatta*) and also serves as a negative suffix for V, ADJ, and the copula.

I-row: *ki, gi, shi, chi, ni, bi, mi, ri, i* for the **formal nonpast** form:

kak-	*kak-*	
oyog-	*oyog-*	
hanas-	*hanaSH-*	
mat-	*maCH-*	
shin-	*shin-*	*imasu*
yob-	*yob-*	
yom-	*yom-*	
tor-	*tor-*	
iw-	*i◊-**	

* ◊ indicates that the sound (in this case *w*) is dropped.

⇨ Note the sound changes: *w* is dropped, *s* becomes *sh*, and *t* becomes *ch*.

The *-te* form and the plain past tense, *-ta* form, involve more sound changes.

ka◊-	*ite/ita*
oyo◊-	*ide/ida*
hanaSH-	*ite/ita*
mat-	*◊te/ta*

shiN-	◊ *de/da*
yoN-	◊ *de/da*
yoN-	◊ *de/da*
toT-	◊ *te/ta*
iT-	◊ *te/ta*

↪ Exception: the verb *ik-* "to go" takes *itta* instead of *iita* (unlike other verbs whose roots end in *k*).

U-row: *ku, gu, su, TSu, nu, bu, mu, ru,* ◊ for the **nonpast affirmative**:

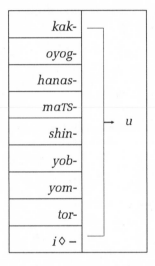

↪ Note the sound changes: *w* drops and *t* becomes *ts*.

This form is also called the DICTIONARY FORM since it is the form found in dicitonary entries.

E-row: *ke, ge, se, te, ne, be, me, re,* ◊ for **imperative**, **provisional**, and **potential** forms:

kak-		
oyog-	**e**	Imperative[1]
hanas-	→ **eba**	Provisional[2]
mat-	**eru**	Potential[3]

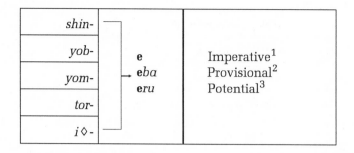

[1] The negative imperative form is formed by attaching -*na* to the plain form: *oyogu-na*.

[2] "If . . . happens" or "If someone does . . . "

[3] "can do . . ."

O-row: *ko, go, so, to, no, bo, mo, ro,* ◊ for the *-ō* form — Volitional ("I will," "let us do,") or Tentative ("probably will"):

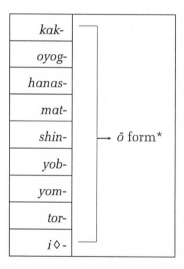

* The tentative use of this form, "probably," is highly literary and is found less frequently in modern Japanese than the volitional:

Sono koto ni tsuite wa hihan mo arō.	There may also be a criticism with regard to this matter.

See Appendix for *-mai*, which expresses negative volitional ("I will not") and negative tentative ("probably will not").

Consonant Verbs Chart:

ka	ga	sa	ta	na	ba	ma	ra	wa	-*nai* (formal: V-stem + *masen*)* -*reru* (-*remasu*) -*s(er)u* (-*semasu*) -*s(er)areru* (-*seraremasu*)
ki	*gi*	*shi*	*chi*	*ni*	*bi*	*mi*	*ri*	*i*	-*masu*
ku	*gu*	*su*	*tsu*	*nu*	*bu*	*mu*	*ru*	*u*	Formal Nonpast (Dictionary Forms)
ke	*ge*	*se*	*te*	*ne*	*be*	*me*	*re*	*e*	Imperative (V-stem + *nasai*) -*ba* (V-stem + *masureba*) -*ru* (-*emasu*)
ko	*go*	*so*	*to*	*no*	*bo*	*mo*	*ro*	*o*	-*ō* (V-stem + -*mashō*)
ite	*ide*	*shite*	*tte*	*nde*	*nde*	*nde*	*tte*	*tte*	-*TE* (V-stem + *mashite*)
ita	*ida*	*shita*	*tta*	*nda*	*nda*	*nda*	*tta*	*tta*	Past (V-stem + *mashita*)

* The forms in parentheses are the formal -*masu* form equivalents.

2.1.2 Vowel Verbs

These are verbs whose roots end with a vowel: *tabe-* "eat"

The Suffixes for vowel verbs are as follows:

	nai/zu (nu/zaru)[1]	Negative
	rareru	Passive / Spontaneous[2]
	saseru / sasu	Causative
	saserareru / sasareru	Causative-Passive
tabe- ←	*masu*	Formal Nonpast
	te/ta	Past
	ru	Nonpast Affirmative
	reba	Provisional

tabe-	*rareru*	Potential
	ro	Imperative
	yō	*-ō* form

[1] See note 1 on first Consonant Verb table above, § 2.1.1.

[2] See § 2.3.2.

The roots of the majority of Vowel Verbs end in *-e*, though there are some which end in *-i*: *tabe-ru* "to eat," *mi-ru* "to see."

In modern Japanese grammar *-iru* verbs are called *kami-ichidan* verbs and *-eru* verbs *shimo-ichidan* verbs because *i* is one above (or before) *u*, and *e* is one below (or after) *u*, in the *a-i-u-e-o* order.

For a partial list of *-i*-Verbs, see Appendix § 4.2.

⮡ *Kir-u*, "to cut," is a consonant verb, while *ki-ru*, "to wear," is a vowel verb. Thus their respective negative forms, for example, are *kir-anai* and *ki-nai*.

⮡ Some verbs ending in *-iru* or *-eru* are consonant verbs. For example:

chir-u	scatter, fall off
hair-u	enter
her-u	decrease
hashir-u	run
ir-u	be necessary
kaer-u	return
kagir-u	limit
ker-u	kick
kes-u	erase
kir-u	cut
nigir-u	grab
ser-u	compete, bid
shin-u	die

shir-u	know
ter-u	shine (of the sun)

2.1.3 Irregular Verbs

Suru "to do" and *kuru* "to come"

Negative	*shi-nai*	*ko-nai*
	se-zu (-nu/zaru)[1]	
Passive	*sa-reru*	*ko-rareru*
Causative	*sa-seru/su*	*ko-saseru/sasu*
Causative-passive	*sa-serareru*	*ko-sas(er)areru*
Formal nonpast	*shi-masu*	*ki-masu*
Past/TE	*shi-ta/te*	*ki-ta/te*
Nonpast affirmative	*su-ru*	*ku-ru*
Provisional	*su-reba*	*ku-reba*
Potential	*dekiru*	*ko-rareru*
Imperative	*shi-ro/seyo*[2]	*ko-i*
-ō form	*shi-yō*	*ko-yō*

[1] See note 1 on first Consonant Verb table above, § 2.1.1.

[2] *seyo* is the classical equivalent of *shiro* and is used in the literary style.

2.1.4 Negative Forms of Suffixes

	CV	*VV*	*Irregular Vs*	
Negative	*iw-anakunai*	*tabe-nakunai*	*shi-nakunai*	*ko-nakunai*
Passive	*iw-arenai*	*tabe-rarenai*	*sarenai*	*ko-rarenai*
Causative	*iw-asenai*	*tabe-sasenai*	*sasenai*	*ko-sasenai*
Caus-Passive	*iw-aserarenai*	*tabe-saserarenai*	*saserarenai*	*ko-saserarenai*

	CV	*VV*	*Irregular Vs*	
Provisional	*iw-anakereba*	*tabe-nakereba*	*shi-nakereba*	*ko-nakereba*
Potential	*iw-enai*	*tabe-rarenai*	*dekinai*	*ko-rarenai*
Imperative	*i(w)-u-na*	*tabe-ru-na*	*suru-na*	*kuru-na*

2.1.5 Conjugation of Passive, Causative, and Potential Forms

They all follow the conjugation of Vowel Verbs.

SUFFIXES	PASSIVE	CAUSATIVE	POTENTIAL	SUFFIXES
Negative	*kak-are-*	*kak-ase-*	*kak-e-*	*nai*
Passive	*		*	*rareru*
Causative	*	*	*	*sas(er)u*
Formal nonpast				*masu*
Past/TE				*ta/te*
Nonpast affirmative				*ru*
Provisional				*reba*
Potential	*		*	*rareru*
Imperative			*	*ro*
-ō form			*	*yō*

* Indicates that the form is not used.

2.2   Vt (transitive verbs) and Vi (intransitive verbs)

Transitive verbs take a direct object word followed by the object particle *o*, and sometimes also an indirect object word followed by the particle *ni*.

*Tarō wa doa **o** aketa.*	Taro opened the door.
*Tarō wa Hanako **ni** hon **o** ageta.*	Taro gave Hanako a book.

Most Vt-Vi pairs take slightly different forms: *ageru* "to raise" and *agaru* "to rise," *akeru*(Vt) and *aku*(Vi) for "to open."

For a partial list of Vt and Vi pairs, see Appendix § 4.1.

Note that Japanese tends to use Vi in a situation where English would be more likely to use Vt.

Kabin ga kowarete(Vi)-iru. *	Someone broke(Vt) the vase! The vase is broken!

> * Vi-*te-iru* denotes a state, while Vt-*te-iru* indicates an on-going action. See below, § 2.5.1 for details.

One reason why Vi is preferred in this kind of situation may be that Japanese tends to avoid mentioning the performer of actions, especially when there might be a chance of offending someone. Japanese in general prefers to avoid confrontation and leave things vague and indirect wherever possible—a consequence of the premium placed on harmonious human relations.

2.3 Passive and Spontaneous Forms

2.3.1 Passive Voice

The function of the Japanese passive is considerably different from that of the passive voice in Western languages. It is used primarily to describe events that cause conditions of **adversity**.

Kodomo ga sarawareta(Vt).	The child was kidnapped.
*Kodomo ga jitensha **ni*** **butsukerareta**(Vt).*	The child was hit by a bicycle.

> * The agent which caused the action is marked by *ni*.

The "adversative" passive can be made with Vi as well, which is not possible in Western languages where the direct object of Vt becomes the subject of the passive voice.

Kare wa sansai no toki ni haha ni shinareta(Vi).	He was affected by his mother's dying when he was three.
Tenisu o shitakatta noni ame ni furareta(Vi).	Although I wanted to play tennis I couldn't because of the rain.

Benkyō shite-iru toki ni tomodachi ni korareta(Vi).	I was disturbed by my friend's coming (to my house) when I was studying.
Kodomo ni nakareta(Vi).	I was troubled by the child's crying.

These examples show that the adversative passive cannot simply be translated by the ordinary English passive, as in: "I was cried by the child." Japanese use of the kind of passive found in Western languages is relatively recent, becoming more frequent in the Meiji Period when Western literature was translated into Japanese.

Kore wa Mōtsuaruto ni yotte sakkyoku-sareta.	*This was composed by Mozart.*

Such usage of passive in a non-adversative situation occurs mainly in written language — in newspaper articles as well as in some academic writing.

Hatsuka kara kokkai ga saikai sareta.	The national diet was resumed from the twentieth.

Note that the passive form can be used as a kind of honorific form (more frequently used in male speech).

Dochira e ikaremasu ka (as the equivalent of *Dochira e irasshaimasu ka*).	Where are you going (honorific)?

2.3.2 Spontaneous Form

The spontaneous form is the same as the passive form (*-areru* for CVs and *-rareru* for VVs). It is limited to verbs whose meaning has to do with the speaker's perception of or feelings toward something, such as *kangae-ru* "to think," *omo-u* "to think," *kanji-ru* "to feel, to sense," *mi-ru* "to see, to recognize," or *mitome-ru* "to recognize, to consider."* The spontaneous voice is neither "active" or "passive" but is something like the "middle voice" of the verb in ancient Greek, whose meaning lies somewhere between the two.

* Some other verbs that can take the spontaneous form: *kik-u* "to hear," *omoidas-u* "to recall," *shinob-u* "to recollect," *wasure-ru* "to forget," *odorok-*

u "to be surprised," *shinpai suru* "to worry," *anji-ru/anzuru* "to be anxious, to worry," *kui-ru* "to repent," *ajiwa-u* "to taste," *sōzō suru* "to imagine," *mats-u* "to wait for."

While the passive voice is used when there is a definite agent who performs the action (even when it is not mentioned explicitly), the spontaneous voice does not require any specific agent. The meaning of the spontaneous form is something like "It is naturally possible to feel, think, worry . . ." or "it feels somewhat like . . . , it seems that . . ."

The sense is that a feeling arises as if the result of some external power, regardless of the speakers intention—a manifestation of the Japanese fondness for indirectness (see ch. 3, § 9.2). The spontaneous form was used extensively in classical Japanese, a language particularly given to the poetic expression of emotions and to references to a realm beyond visible reality.

Arishi hi no koto shinobaruru.	Things of days gone by are (somehow) recollected in memory.
Mono omohoyu.	I somehow think about things (without my trying).

Some modern Japanese retains this kind of poetic quality. The following are examples from *Yama no oto* by Kawabata Yasunari.

Kaze no oto ka, miminari ka to Shingo wa reisei ni kangaeta tsumori datta ga, sonna oto nado shinakatta no de wa naika to omowareta.	Shingo thought he had calmly considered whether it could have been the sound of the wind or a rushing in his ears, and yet it felt as if he didn't hear any such sound at all.
Tsuki no yo ga fukai yō ni omowareru.	There is a sense of depth to the moonlit night.
Fukasa ga yokomuke ni tōku e kanjirareru no da.	It feels as if its (= the night's) depth stretches horizontally into the far distance.

In formal writing the use of the spontaneous form suggests a speculative statement and is a device through which the writer avoids taking credit for the statement—often an expression of humility on the part of the author.

| Nihon-rettō wa Asia tairiku to rikutsuzuki deatta to kangaerareru. | It seems that the Japanese archipelago was connected to the Asian Continent. |

When we need to express the same statement in the passive form *V-teiru* is used: . . . *to kangaerarete-iru* "it is considered that . . . , it has been thought that . . ."

It is interesting to note that *miru* (Vt) "to see, look" and *kiku* "to listen, hear" have Vi forms which have a kind of potential meaning: *mieru* "can be seen, appear" and *kikoeru* "can be heard" (without the speaker's effort of trying to do so). In this sense they function somewhat like the spontaneous forms for *miru* and *kiku: mi-rareru* and *kik-areru*. The meanings of the two forms overlap to some extent.

The spontaneous forms of those Vt's given in this section seem to function somehow as intransitive versions of those verbs. Even though the person feels or thinks (Vt) about something, the subject (the thinker) is withdrawn grammatically, suggesting that the person is somehow made to think or feel in a certain way, and the object of thinking or feeling itself becomes "subjective" as if the matter referred to is itself doing the thinking or feeling.

In fact there are some intransitive Vs of this type, which are also called spontaneous verbs: *ure-ru* "(things) sell" (as in "This car sells well"), *nake-ru* "(spontaneously) cry," *sazukar-u* "be granted," *osowar-u* "to learn, be taught."

| Kono hanashi wa chotto kiita dake de mo nakete-kuru. | As for this story, one comes to feel like crying just by hearing a little of it. |
| Ojiisan to obaasan ni wa chiisana otoko no ko ga sazukatta. | To the old man and woman a small baby boy was granted. |

2.4 The Nature of Tense and Verb Types

2.4.1 Tense

Japanese tenses work quite differently from those of English. What matters is whether the action has been completed or not.

The past tense in Japanese does not actually mean that something happened in the past but it indicates that an action was completed sometime in the past or has been completed now. The focus is on completion, which is why the terms "perfect" and "nonperfect" are often used. The time covered by past tense is from the infinite past right up to the present.

The nonpast tense indicates that an action is not completed but is going to take place between now and sometime in the future. It covers the present and future tenses of English.

Consider the following examples:

Shigoto o shimasu ka.	Are you going to work?

This question actually refers to a future possibility. If you want to say "Do you work?" or "Do you have a job?" you say:

Shigoto o shite-imasu ka.	Are you working?

using the progressive form, or:

Shigoto ga arimasu ka.	Is there a job? (meaning "Do you have a job?")

The nonpast can also be used to refer to a habitual act, as in:

Ano hito wa gorufu o suru.	He plays golf.
Kare wa yoku nihon e iku.	He often goes to Japan.
Mainichi ha o migaku.	(I) brush my teeth everyday.

↳ Note that there is no tense agreement in Japanese.

*[Nihon e **iku**] toki papaiya o **katta**.*

In this sentence even though the tense of the main verb (the predicate of the sentence) is past, iku is nonpast and indicates that the action of going has not been completed but is going to take place. So, the meaning of this sentence is: "When I went to Japan (before I left) I bought papayas."

Compare this with the next sentence:

*[Nihon e **itta**] toki papaiya o **katta**.*

The tense of this sentence is past, too. However, itta *indicates that the action of* going was completed; in other words, the person was in Japan. So the meaning is: "When I went to Japan I bought papayas (there)."

> [Nihon e **itta**] toki papaiya o **kau**.

The tense of this sentence is non-past, which means that the buying will take place between now and the future. However, **itta** indicates that the action of going is completed and therefore the person is in Japan. Thus it means: "When I go to Japan (= when I get there), I will buy papayas."

The above examples show that the tense of a verb in a subordinate clause is not affected by the tense of the final predicate.* The *V-ta* form concerns whether the action is completed or not. In this sense Japanese verbs do not have tense but are rather marked by aspect.

* Except in the case of V-*te*, which assumes the tense of the final verb.

Ha o migaite neta.	I brush**ed** my teeth and **went** to bed.

Note the special uses of *V-ta*:

Chotto **matta**!	Wait a minute! *or*: Stop! (URGENT REQUEST)
Miitingu wa tashika niji kara **datta**.	The meeting **will be** from two o'clock. (CONFIRMATION)*

*The idea is: "It **was** decided that it will be at two."

Doko ni aru ka na. A, koko ni **atta**.	Where is it? Oh, here it is!*

*It **was** here all along.

2.4.2 Verb Types

A. Durative Verbs

Durative verbs are also called continuative verbs and signify activities that take place over a period of time such as eating, drinking, reading, writing, seeing, walking, and waiting. Action verbs belong to this type. Most durative verbs are Vt, though some are Vi, such as *hataraku* "to work," *tsutomeru* "to work at, hold a post," *naku* "to cry," and *suberu* "to slide."

B. Momentary verbs

Momentary or punctual verbs are such verbs as going, coming, leaving, arriving, dying, and falling that signify a change in state, a momentary transition from one state to another. They do not refer to actions that take place over a period of time, and the majority are Vi.

For a partial list of momentary verbs, see Appendix § 4.3.

C. Stative Verbs

Stative verbs are such verbs as *aru* "(inanimate) exist," *iru* "need," *dekiru* "be able to," *mieru* "be visible," *kikoeru* "be audible," and *-sugiru* "be excessive" — as in *muzukashi-sugiru* "too difficult." These verbs do not need to take *-te iru* (see § 2.5) to indicate a state.

2.5 *-te* Forms

-te forms, sometimes called Gerund Forms, are *V-te* for verbs, *ADJ-kute* for adjectives, and *AN de and N-de* for adjectival nouns and nouns.

Verb-*te* forms are made in the same way as the past tense form, except that the final vowel is changed to *-e* instead of *-a*. They are used to form various grammatical structures with auxiliaries.

See § 7.4 for *V-te ageru/yaru/kureru*; and § 13 for *V-temo* and *V-te wa*.

2.5.1 *V-te-iru*

A. On-going action (= action in progress) ". . . is doing . . . now"

i. The majority are durative Vt:

| *Jon wa ima sono hon o kaite(Vt)-iru.* | John is writing the book now. |

ii. Other than durative Vt:

    a. Durative Vi:

| *Kodomo wa ima naite(Vi)-iru.* | The child is crying now. |

    b. Momentary Verb (and therefore Vi):

| *Ima ame ga futte-iru.** | It's raining now. |

* *Furu* is a momentary happening and yet it takes a certain amount of time before the raindrops actually touch the ground. In this sense it is a combination of durative and momentary. *Koboreru* "spills," and *chiru* "(flower petals) fall" are other examples. The *V-te-iru* form of these verbs can also indicate a state.

B. State: something happened and the effect or the experience of it remains.

i. Momentary V (and therefore Vi):

Mado ga shimatte-iru.	The window is closed.
Ame ga futte-iru.	It has rained (and the result—for example: wet ground—remains).
Jon wa yōroppa e itte-iru.	John has gone to Europe and the resulting state remains (= he is still there).*
Sono hikōki wa Tōkyō ni tsuite-iru.	The plane has arrived in Tokyo (= it is there now).

* This could also mean: "John has been to Europe (= his experience of going there remains)."

In English both writing (durative verb) and arriving (momentary verb) refer to an action that is taking place at the moment, while in Japanese *tsuite-iru* means a state after the action of arriving has been completed: "someone is in the state of being here or there as a result of arriving."

"He is dying" in English means that the person is still alive but about to die. The equivalent of this in Japanese is not *shinde-iru*—which means that the person has already died and is in the state of death—but something like *shini-sō da* "looks as if he is dying" or *shini-tsutsu aru*, literally "is in the process of dying."

ii. Occasionally a durative Vt can be used to indicate a state:

John wa sono toshi sono hon o kaite-iru.	John wrote the book that year (and the result remains—the written book or his experience of writing it).

C. Habitual action

i. Durative action verbs:

Tenusu o shite-iru.	I play tennis.
Mainichi hashitte-iru.	I run everyday.

ii. Momentary motion verbs that signify motion from point A to B, such as *iku* "to go," *kuru* "to come," *kaeru* "to return," and *modoru* "to return, to back up."

Daigaku ni itte-iru.[*]	I go to college. *or:* I am a college student.

  [*] This could also refer to a state, in which case it means: "(Someone) has gone to the university (and so is there now)."

2.5.2 *V-te aru*

A. Most of the verbs used in this construction are durative Vt.

This construction is used to indicate that someone has performed an action and the state resulting from it persists. It is usually best translated as "Something has been done." The speaker is aware that there is an agent involved, though it is not explicitly mentioned since the object has become the subject of the sentence.

To ga* akete(Vt)-aru.	The door has been opened (by someone, and it is still open).

  [*] The original direct object particle *o* has been changed to the subject particle *ga*.

Compare this with:

To ga aite(Vi)-iru.	The door is open.

The agent of the action of opening is not the speaker's concern: it does not matter whether the opening of the door was caused by a person, an animal, or a natural force such as wind.

B. With durative Vi (except for verbs of natural phenomena)

This construction appears to be a *V-te-aru* construction on the surface, but it can be considered as an extension of *V-te oku* ("to put aside") "do something in advance or for future use" to form *V-te (oite)-aru* (see § 2.5.5). The *oite*, "put aside," does not appear, but the idea is at the back of the speaker's mind.

Yoku nete(Vi)-aru.	Sleeping has been done (for future use).[1]
Nihon ni itte(Vi)-aru.	Going to Japan has been done (I went to Japan).[2]

[1] This could mean: "I have slept, so I am rested and am thus ready now to do something else.

[2] This could mean: "I have the experience of having gone to Japan (so I know about the place and am now ready to do something with this experience.)"

In this last example, the speaker is not in Japan right now, but what persists here and now is the experience "available for future use," as it were.

Compare this with the state expressed by *Nihon ni itte-iru*. "(He) has gone to Japan (and is now there)." In order to express "He has been to Japan" neutrally and without any concern for future purpose, *V-ta koto ga aru* is used:

Nihon e itta koto ga aru.	I have been to Japan.

Exception: verbs associated with natural phenomena, such as the falling of rain or snow, **cannot** be used in the *-te aru* construction.

↪ Vt can also be used with respect to future use. In such cases the direct object particle *o* after the original direct object is **not** changed to the subject particle *ga*:

*To **o** ake**te-aru**.*	Opening the door has been done (so that people can come in later).
*Gohan **o** takusan tabe**te-aru**.*	Eating a lot (of rice) has been done (so I am now ready to engage in some other activity).

Compare this with:

*Gohan **ga** takusan tabe**te-aru**.*	Much rice has been eaten (and little is left).

2.5.3 *V-te iku/kuru*

A. Since *iku* means "to go," *V-te iku* has the meaning of a motion taking place away from "here" (where the speaker is), or of performing an action and going away from the speaker, or of a motion or action taking place continuously or gradually into the future.

Watakushi wa aruite-iku.	I will go on foot. (I will walk.) AWAY FROM THE SPEAKER
Watakushi wa tabete (kara) iku.	I will eat and then go. ACTION + GOING AWAY
Kore kara zutto Nihongo o benkyōshite-iku.	I will continue to study Japanese from now on. CONTINUOUS ACTION INTO THE FUTURE
Kore kara atatakaku natte-iku.	It will get warmer gradually from now on. GRADUAL OCCURRENCE

B. Since *kuru* means "to come," *V-te kuru* has the meaning of a motion toward "here" (where the speaker is), or of performing an action and coming toward the speaker, or of a motion or action taking place continuously toward the present, or — in the case of momentary verbs — of a motion's beginning.

Watakushi wa hashitte-kita.	I came running. COMING TOWARD WHERE THE SPEAKER IS
Watakushi wa tabete-kita.	I ate and came.[1] ACTION + COMING HERE
Mainichi piano o renshū shite-kita.	I have been practising (continuously) every day. CONTINUOUS ACTION UP TO NOW
Byōnin wa jojo ni kaifuku shite-kita.	The patient is gradually recovering. GRADUAL OCCURRENCE
Ame ga futte[2] kita.	It began to rain. BEGINNING OF A MOTION

[1] This is the literal translation but the actual meaning is more like "I went out to eat (and came back)."

[2] *Furu* is a momentary verb.

Note the following "psychological" use of *V-te kuru*: If the speaker/writer is personally involved with the issue, *V-te kuru* can be used for a future occurring instead of *V-te iku*. For example:

*Sekai no jinkō wa masumasu fuete-**kuru** darō.*	The world population will continue to increase.

The use of *-te-kuru* here indicates that the speaker/writer is a concerned member of the world population who feels that the increase is going to affect us (= is coming toward us).

2.5.4 *V-te shimau*

"do something completely" (often accompanied by some emotion – normally regret or sadness, occasionally joy):

Ano hito wa itte-shimatta.	Unfortunately that person has gone.

This expresses COMPLETION + sadness, while *Ano hito wa itta* "That person went" simply states what happened.

Sono hon o zenbu yonde-shimatta.	I have read the entire book. COMPLETION
Mata machigaete-shimatta.	(I'm afraid) I have made a mistake again. REGRET
Hyakuten o totte-shimatta!	I scored a hundred! JOY

2.5.5 *V-te oku**

This construction means "do something in advance" (leaving the result for the time being, so that it can be used in the future):

* *Oku* means "to put, place"

Tesuto no benkyō o shite oku.	I will study for the test.
Yasai o aratte oku.	I wash the vegetables in advance.

2.5.6 *V-te miru*

V-te miru means "try doing something, do something and see":

Unagi o tabete-mita.	I tried eating eel.
Sono otera made itte-miyō.	I will go as far as the temple and see (what it is like).

For a list of idiomatic phrases and grammatical constructions using *V-te*, see Appendix § 2.

2 6 V-stem

The stem of the verb is the form of the I-row in the case of Consonant Verbs (*kaki*, *yomi*, etc.) and the form to which suffixes are attached in the case of Vowel Verbs (*tabe*, *shirabe*, etc.). It is the form that results from dropping the -*masu* suffix from the formal form. Verb stems are used in various constructions and compounds, some of the most important of which involve auxiliaries that are "bound forms" (forms that do not appear by themselves but are always attached to other words, as with -*masu*, the formal present ending of a verb, in *kaki-masu*).

1. V-stem + *tai**: "Want to do"

> * -*tai* is ADJ, and with a V-stem it forms Vi and takes the subject particle *ga*. However, the direct object particle *o* is widely accepted nowadays.

*Shi **ga**/o kaki-tai.*	I want to write poems.

"Want N" is expressed also by an adjective (. . . *ga hoshii*) instead of a verb. Again the object particle *o* may be used in place of *ga*.

-*tai* can take a further bound form -*garu* when the speaker/writer expresses an observation about a third person's feeling or desire. See § 2.7.

2. V-stem   *nagara* "while doing something" SIMULTANEOUS ACTION or "while/although . . ."

Hanako wa warai-nagara sō itta.	Hanako said so while smiling.
Hanako no hō ga Jon yori keiken ga ari-nagara misu ga ōkatta.	Although Hanako is more experienced than John is, she made more errors.

Karera wa chōjō chikaku made iki-nagara mo akutenkō no tame hikikaesanakereba naranakatta.	Even though they climbed almost to the summit, they had to turn back owing to bad weather.
Hanako wa Jon ga Amerika e kaeru koto o shitte-i-nagara shiranai furi o shita.	Although Hanako knew about John's going back to America, she pretended that she didn't.

V-te oki nagara (mo) "While having done . . ." or "even though one has done . . .":

Jon wa kuru to itte-oki-nagara konakatta.	John didn't come, even though he said he would.

⇨ N/AN and ADJ-stem can be used with *nagara (mo)*. See Appendix § 1.

3. V-stem + *tsutsu* "while doing something" (SIMULTANEOUS ACTION), "be in the process of doing something" followed by *aru*.

kōgi o kiki-tsutsu nōto o toru	take notes while listening to a lecture
Jon wa ima shōsetsu o kaki-tsutsu aru.	John is in the process of writing a novel right now.
Ie ga ima deki-tsutsu aru.	The house is nearing completion.

V-stem + *tsutsu (mo)* means "notwithstanding, even though, in spite of."

Warui to shiri-tsutsu (mo) damatte motte-kite-shimatta.	Although I knew it was wrong, I took it without telling anyone.

4. V1-stem + *tari* V2-stem *tari suru*: "do things such as V1 and V2":

Jisho o mi-tari sankōsho o shirabe-tari suru.	I do things such as looking in the dictionary and checking in the reference book.

See § 4.1.2 for V/ADJ-stem or AN followed by *sō/ge*. For a list of Verb Compounds, many of which involve V-stems, see Appendix § 3.

2.7 Verbalizers

Certain suffixes are attached to words to make them into verbs. The following usages are limited to certain verbs:

N + *bamu*	a state becomes visible
ase-bamu	start perspiring
ki-bamu	grow yellowish

N + *baru**	assume the air of . . .
yoku-baru	be greedy
kenshiki-baru	assume an air of importance

* *Baru* comes from the verb *haru* "to stretch, slap":

mie o haru	show off
ki o haru	be tense

↪ Note that *ganbaru* "to hold out, do one's best," which consists of the kanji *gan* meaning "stubborn, greedy" and *baru*, is now one word.

N + *biru*	start looking like . . .
otona-biru	start looking like an adult

N + *buru*	act as if . . . , pretend that . . .
otona-buru	act like an adult
shinsetsu-buru	pretend that one is kind

ADJ-stem* + *garu*, "feel strongly, be anxious to do something," is used when the speaker/writer guesses a third person's feeling or desire. It can be attached to *V-tai*(ADJ) and *N ga hoshii*(ADJ) as well as to other adjectives: *samu-garu* "feel terribly cold"

Kodomo wa okashi o kai-ta-gatta.	The child really wanted to buy the candy.

Kodomo wa okashi o hoshi-gatta.	The child wanted the candy very much.
Kodomo wa obake o kowa-gatta.	The child was very scared of the ghost.

Some ADJs or Ns followed by *gari*, the stem of *garu*, make a N meaning someone who has a low tolerance of certain state: *atsu-gari* "a person who cannot tolerate heat," *kowa-gari* "a person who is easily scared," *yoku-bari* "a miser."

N + datsu (= tatsu)	erect
awa-datsu	to bubble up
hara-datsu	to get angry

N + doru	take
kata-doru	model after
tema-doru or: *hima-doru*	take time, be detained

Related N forms: *kaki-tori* "dictation" (from *kaki-toru* "write down")

N + gomoru	be confined*
kuchi-gomoru	mumble
mi-gomoru	become pregnant

* This usage is rather limited.

N + jimiru	penetrate
shotai-jimiru	become domesticated
inaka-jimiru	be rusticated

N + meku	become like . . .
haru-meku	become more like spring
toki-meku	be influential/prosperous
zawa-meku	become noisy

N + *tsukeru*	attach
chikara-zukeru	encourage
iro-zukeru	color

Related N forms: *aji-tsuke*, "seasoning"

N (or Manner Word) + *tsuku/zuku*	be attached-Vi
ki-zuku	come back to consciousness
kizu-tsuku	be hurt, get injured
ne-zuku	take root
fura-tsuku	feel dizzy, stagger, wander about
gata-tsuku	to be shaky
*guzu-tsuku**	remain unsettled

* As in the expression *Tenki ga guzu-tsuku.*

N + *yagu*	become
hana-yagu	become gay/florid/flowery
waka-yagu	be rejuvenated, grow younger

3. Nouns

This section deals with common nouns, **futsū-meishi**, such as *hon* "a book," *shinri* "truth."

3.1 Derivation of Nouns

A. Abstract Ns may be derived from ADJs by replacing the final *i* with *-sa*: *fuka-sa* "depth," *ama-sa* "(degree of) sweetness," *omoshiro-sa* "joy, fun"

Some ADJs also take *-mi** to derive Ns that are less abstract: *fuka-mi* "deep place, depth," while *fuka-sa* means how deep something is; *ama-mi* "sweetness, sweet taste," while *ama-sa* means the degree of sweetness; *omoshiro-mi* "interest, (degree of) interestingness" while *omoshiro-sa* means "joy."

> * *-mu*(Vi)/*-meru*(Vt) can be attached to some ADJs to derive Vi and Vt respectively, but it is not consistent: *ita-mu* (Vi) "something aches," *ita-meru* (Vt) "to harm, to injure," from *itai* (ADJ); *shira-mu* (Vi) "becomes white (=light)," but not *shira-meru* (Vt), from *shiroi* (ADJ); and from *hiroi* (ADJ) *hiro-maru* instead of *hiro-mu* (Vi) and *hiro-meru* (Vt) "spread, preach."

To say that one measures the depth of a pond one would say: *Ike no fuka-sa o hakaru*, and not *Ike no fuka-mi o hakaru*. The latter would mean that one measures the deep place of the pond. Insofar as the *-mi* suffix is used to make nouns that are more concrete, such nouns are often used in metaphorical senses:

Kare no geijutsu ni fuka-mi ga dete-kita.	His art has gradually gained in profundity.

One wouldn't say . . . *fuka-sa ga dete-kita*, since that would mean that his art had become literally deeper. Similarly, one does not use the abstract *-sa* suffix in a case such as the following:

| *Geijutsu no taka-mi ni noboru.* | One climbs to the heights of art. |

"Measures how high the tree is" would be *Ki no taka-sa o hakaru*, and not *taka-mi o hakaru*.

B. Most ANs take *-sa*: *shizuka-sa** "quietness," *aware-sa* "pitifulness," *oroka-sa* "stupidity," *yutaka-sa* "richness"

> * *Shizukesa* means "silence, stillness, tranquility, calmness," whereas *shizukasa* refers to a degree of quietness.

C. Some V-stems can be nouns: *oyogi* "swimming," *asobi* "playing," *hanashi* "story," *tatakai* "battle."

3.2 Verbal Nouns

Verbal nouns are nouns used with the following verb *suru* "to do." They can also be used with the direct object particle *o*: *benkyō suru* "to study" or *benkyō o suru* "engage in the study of . . ."

Examine the following:

| *Nihongo no benkyō **o** suru.* | I engage in the study of Japanese. |
| *Nihongo **o** benkyō* suru.* | I study Japanese. |

> * *Benkyō* cannot be followed by *o* here because *o* is used only once within a sentence.

The majority of verbal nouns are Chinese compounds (used with *suru*) such as *kaimono* "shopping," *shigoto* "job," or *kantoku* "supervision."

There are a few native verbal nouns: *dakko suru* "to embrace," *onbu suru* "to carry on one's back," *namida suru* "to weep," *tomadoi suru* "to get lost, be puzzled" (also used as one verb *tomadou*).

Words from Western languages are also used as verbal nouns, such as: *chekku suru* "to check," *esukareeto suru* "to escalate," *purinto suru* "to print out," *sutoraiki suru* "to go on strike."

Some foreign words are "Japanized" as verbal nouns: *gōruin* ("goal-in") *suru* "to reach the goal in a race; finally get married," *kurankuin* ("crank-in") *suru* "to begin filming," and so on.

Some foreign words can be made into real verbs by adding a *-ru* ending such as *dabu-ru* "to overlap," and *sabo-ru* "to goof off" (from the French *sabotage*). These verbs follow the Consonant Verb conjugation.

⮑ There are quite a few verbs consisting of a single Chinese character and *suru**
but *they cannot take the direct object particle before suru*: *ka* 課 *-suru* "to assess" but not *ka o suru*. As for their negative forms, they take either *-sanai*
(Vowel Verb conjugation) or *-shinai* (Irregular Verb *suru* conjugation) depending on the degree of assimilation: *kasuru/kasu* "to assess" takes *kas-anai* but
ze 絶 *ssuru* "to exhaust, to surpass" (as in *gengo ni zessuru* "be beyond words")
takes *ze-sshinai*.

> * Many of them also take *su* as well as *suru*, such as: *teki* 適 *-suru/su* "to
> fit/suit," *yoku* 浴 *-suru/su* "to receive one's favor," *geki* 激 *-suru/su* "to get
> excited," *gū* 遇 *-suru/su* "to treat," *haku* 博 *-suru/su* "to win (applause),"
> *soku* 即 *-suru/su* "to conform." When the head nouns end with a nasal
> sound, they take *zuru/jiru* — as in *zon* 存 *-zuru* "to know" — and follow the
> Vowel Verb conjugation (see § 2.1.2).

3.3 Time Words

Basically time words are Ns, though some are ADVs. Time words that are Ns
take *ni*.

NOUNS:

n-*ji*, n-*fun* "(n o'clock, n minutes,)" D-*yōbi* "(day of the week)," n-*nichi* "(day
of the month)," M-*gatsu* "(name of the month)," nn-*nen* "year." All of these
are followed by the time particle *ni*. *Ni* can be omitted in *(kotoshi no) haru
(ni)* "in the spring (of this year)," *mikka mae (ni)* "three days ago."

ADVERBS:

ima "now," *kyō* "today," *(ashita no) asa* "(tomorrow) morning," *konshū* "this
week," *kongetsu* "this month," *kotoshi* "this year."

See ch. 1, § 3.1.1A for various time related adverbial phrases.

3.4 Nouns used as Adverbs of Quantity

Sukoshi/takusan *no okane* "a little/a lot of money," **ōzei** *no hito* "a lot of people," **zenbu** *no kuruma* "all the cars."

COUNTERS:

> *Rōjin ga* **hitori** *iru.* "There is one old man."
> *hon o* **sansatsu** *kau* "buy three books"

While counters are normally used as adverbs, as in the above examples, they
can also be used in a noun form: **hitori** *no rōjin* "one old man"; **sansatsu** *no hon*
"three books."

3.5 Loan Words

Japanese has numerous loan words which reflect the history of Japan's contact with foreign countries (and which are written in *katakana*). Some examples:

from Portuguese: *pan* "bread," *birōdo* "velvet"

from Dutch: *garasu* "glass" (as material), *kokku* "a cook," *chokki* "a vest"

from German: *karute* "a patient's (medical) card," *arerugii* "allergy"

from French: *butikku* "boutique," *gurume* "gourmet", *baree* "ballet," *dessan* "sketch," *ankeeto* "a questionnaire," *toire* "toilet"

from English: *hoteru* "hotel," *dezain* "design," *terebi* "TV," *hurūtsu* "fruit," *konpyūtā* "computer," *tomato* "tomato (from British English)"

Some are used somewhat differently from the original word: *manshion* "a condominium" from the English "mansion"; *arubaito* "a part time job" from the German *Arbeit* ("work"); **ga**rasu "glass" (in general, as material) from the Dutch (**gu**rasu "a cocktail glass" comes from the English "glass"); *koppu* "a tall drinking glass" from the English "cup"; etc.

Some loan words are a combination of two words shortened: *masukomi* "mass media" from "mass communication," *wāpuro* "a word processor," *maruchoi* "multiple choice test" from "multiple choice."

↪ Some of these may be used as verbs with *suru* (see § 3.2 above).

3.6 Pronouns

3.6.1 Personal

Personal pronouns are derived from location words: as *kare* "over there" (third person singular), *kochi* "this side" (first person singular), and so on. Some of their meanings have changed over the course of time. *Kisama* "honorable you" used by *bushi* (samurai warriors) is now used as male "you" (vulgar). The third person singulars *kare* ("he") and *kanojo* ("she") began to be used only in the Meiji Period when Western literature was introduced and translated. The following are considered personal pronouns:

watakushi "I"

anata "you" (equal or lower/younger; normally used among women), or "darling" (used by women to refer to a husband or lover) *kare* "he," *kanojo* "she" (these are also used to mean "a boyfriend/girlfriend")

dare "who"

In the informal male speech style, *boku* is used for "I" and *kimi* for "you."

Plurality, though not normally indicated, can be expressed by attaching a suffix: either *-tachi* or *-ra*. "Who-(plural)" is *dare-tachi* but not *dare-ra*. *"We" is watakushi-tachi*, or *wareware* (literary, or in speech), or *watakushi-domo* (humble and exclusively referring only to in-group members); "you" (pl.) is *anata-tachi/ra*; "they" is *kare-tachi/ra* (male or female) or *kanojo-tachi/ra* (female).

> ⇨ Since Japanese topics and subjects are often omitted, *watakushi* is rarely used in either speech or writing. In formal or academic writing *hissha/chosha* "author" or *wareware* "we" is used.
>
> *Anata* "you," which is derived from the classical *anata* which meant "far distance" or "you (higher/older)," is also rarely used in conversation, except in informal female speech. If used at all in the formal speech style, it refers only to an equal or to someone of lower status.
>
> In conversation, surnames are normally used instead of the 2nd and 3rd person pronouns: *Tanaka-san* "you, he/she or Mr./Mrs./Mr.& Mrs./Ms. Tanaka, or *Tanaka-san tachi* "Mr. Tanaka and others." A person is frequently referred to by his or her title, rank, position, or occupation—often with the suffix *-san* or *-sama* (even more polite): *buchō(-san)* "department head," *sensei* "teacher" (for professors, doctors, teachers, or specialists in any field), *okyakusama* "clients or passengers," *otōsan* "dad," *oneesan* "older sister," *ojisan/obasan* "uncle/aunt" (to address adult male/female), *denkiya-san* "appliance shop owner or repairman," and so on.

3.6.2 K-S-A-D Series

Ko-:

Spatial/visible: an item closest to the speaker.
Temporal: what is happening at the moment. In writing it refers to what was just mentioned or what is just about to be mentioned.

So-:

Spatial/visible: an item close to the speaker.
Temporal: what has happened in the past, "aforementioned" in writing.

A. *Sengetsu chichi ga nyūin shimashita.*	My father got hospitalized last month.
B: **Sore** *wa taihen deshita ne.*	That was too bad.

A-:

Spatial/visible: an item farther from both the speaker and the listener.
Temporal/spatial: an item both the speaker and the listener know about.

↳ The distinction between *sore* and *are* for visible things is relative: depending
on the context, either can be used.

Do-:

Interrogative

kore	sore	are	dore	this/that/that/which?
kono[1]	sono	ano	dono	this (+ N) PreN
koko	soko	asoko	doko	here
kochira[2]	sochira	achira	dochira	this side/direction
kocchi[3]	socchi	acchi	docchi	this side
koitsu	soitsu	aitsu	doitsu	this item/person (vulgar)

[1] While English pronouns have the same forms when they are **used before Ns**, their Japanese counterparts not only take different forms but also
are classified separately. They are **Prenouns** and are bound forms that can
occur only with a following noun. The pronominal *no* "one" cannot be attached to these prenouns: *kono no* cannot be made to mean "this one": instead, one simply uses *kore* "this."

[2] *-chira* is also used to refer to an item/person politely. *Kochira* "this
item" (polite), "this person" (polite), or "I" (humble); *dochira* "which item"
(polite) or "who" (polite). The suffix *-sama* can be attached in order to refer
to persons even more politely as *dochirasama* "who" (often used in phone
conversations).

[3] *-cchi* is the colloquial equivalent of *-chira*.

While the following are not pronouns, they conform to the K-S-A-D pattern:

kō[1]	sō	ā	dō	this/that/which way
kōshita[2]	sōshita	āshita	dōshita	this kind of
kōshite[2]	sōshite	shite	dōshite	in this way
konna[3]	sonna	anna	donna	this kind of (+ N)
konna ni[3]	sonna ni	anna ni	donna ni	like this, this much

[1] *kō, sō, ā, dō* are ADVs and do not take a following particle.

[2] *-shita* is used as an adjective, while *-shite* is used adverbially. They should not be confused with the predicate of a clause or a component of a multiple predicate respectively.

[3] *-nna* is AN and is used adverbially with *ni*.

4. Adjectival nouns

ADJECTIVAL NOUNS (ANs) are like ADJs insofar as they describe the characteristics of something, yet grammatically they are Ns. (See Appendix § 4.4 for a list of the more common ANs.)

ANs take *na* before N, while Ns take *no*:

| *kirei na e* | a beautiful picture |
| *byōki no hito* | a sick person |

The *na* and *no* are derived from the copula *da/dearu* as the predicate of an original modifier clause:

| *[. . . kirei da/dearu] e* | a picture that is beautiful |
| *[. . . byōki da/dearu] hito** | a person who is sick |

> * The original copula *dearu* is occasionally retained in the literary style, as in: *byōki dearu hito.*

Kirei (AN) *na* means "clean; beautiful, pretty" whereas *utsukushii* (ADJ) means "beautiful" but not "clean."

AN with particle *ni* makes an ADV: *kirei ni* "beautiful"; *shizuka ni* "quietly." *Ōkii/ōkina* "big," *chiisai/chiisana* "small," and *okashii/okashina* "funny, strange" are ADJs even though they sometimes take *na* before Ns. Their negative forms are not *dewa nai* but *kunai*, the ADJ negative form.

4.1 Special ANs: *-yō*, *-sō*, and *-ge*

These special ANs are bound forms which cannot stand by themselves but always appear with another word. Since they take *na* before N they are considered as ANs in this book.

4.1.1 *-yō da/na/ni* "appearance, state, shape, way"

PreN, *N no/dearu, AN na/dearu,* V/ADJ-plain + *yō da/na/ni*

sono (PreN) **yō na** *hanashi*	a story that is something like that
yume (N) no **yō na** *hanashi*	a dream-like story
*Kyō wa suzushii (*ADJ*)* **yō da***.	It seems to be cool today.
*[Bureeki no guai ga hen (*AN*) na] yō da.*	It seems that the condition of the brakes is not good.
[Taifū ga kuru (V)] **yō da***.	It seems that a typhoon is coming.
kodomo no **yō ni** *furumau*	act like a child

4.1.2 *-sō da* and *-ge da*

A. AN or ADJ/V-stem + *sō da/na/ni*: "it looks as if, it seems"

*Kono mondai wa muzukashi(*ADJ*)-* **sō da***.	This problem looks as if it is hard.
Muzukashi- **sō na** *mondai*	a problem that looks hard
*kantan(*AN*)-* **sō na** *mondai*	a problem that looks simple
Ame ga furi(V)- **sō da***.	It looks as if it's going to rain
[ame ga furi- **sō na***] hi*	a day when it looks as if it's going to rain
[muzukashi- **sō ni** *mieru] mondai*	a problem that appears to be difficult

⤳ Note: This *sō* is different from the *sō* of hearsay, which requires a plain form instead of a stem. Compare the following.

*[Ame ga **furu**] sō desu.*	I **hear that** it is going to rain.

Idiomatic phrase:

. . . *-sō ni nai/-sō ni mo nai/-sō mo nai* "not look as if there's a chance of something's happening"

Ame ga yami sō ni nai.	It doesn't look as if it's going to stop raining.

B. ADJ-stem + *ge*: "looks as if"

This construction is used when the speaker guesses another's state or desire. It cannot be attached to all ADJs.

*kurushi-**ge na** yōsu*	a pained expression
*ureshi-**ge na** kao*	happy face

but **not**:

utsukushi-ge na keshiki	view that looks beautiful
tsumeta-ge na nomimono	a drink that looks as if it's cold

Instead one says:

utsukushii keshiki	a beautiful view
tsumeta-sō na nomimono	a drink that looks as if it's cold

This *-ge* construction is generally used only in connection with animate beings:

*Kodomo wa motto okashi ga hoshi-**ge na** kao o shite-iru.*	The child appears to be wanting more candies.
Kodomo wa hahaoya to issho ni iki-ta-**ge na** yōsu datta.*	The child looked as if he wanted to go with his mother.

* *-ta* is the stem of the ADJ *-tai* "want to."

⮑ *-ge* is used with V-stem only idiomatically:

imi-ari-ge na kao	an expression that looks as if it means something

5. The uses of *wa*, *ga*, and *mo*

Japanese particles are post-positional; that is, the particle **follows** the noun to relate the word to other elements of the sentence, and particularly to the predicate. Theoretically speaking, since *ga* is a case particle (like *o*) it is in a different category from *wa* and *mo*, which have the function of highlighting an element in a sentence. However, this section begins with a discussion of *wa* and *ga* together, since the differences between them are a constant source of confusion for students, whereas the functions of *mo* are relatively straightforward.

5.1 *WA*

5.1.1 Topic *wa*

The main way in which *wa* highlights the element it is attached to is by indicating the topic or theme of the sentence. The topic of a sentence is normally placed at the beginning.

*Kore **wa** bara da.*	This is a rose.

The particle *wa* indicates that the PRECEDING NOUN is the topic of the sentence. The exact meaning of this sentence is more like "As for this thing, it is a rose," or "Speaking of this item, it is a rose."

It helps to distinguish two different kinds of predication:

DESCRIPTIVE:

Hana ga kirei da.	Flowers are beautiful.
Jon ga aruite-kuru.	(Look!) John is walking toward me/us.

The speaker simply describes a scene or an event as a whole and as he sees it, without undertaking preparations for stating something about a certain component of the scene. The speaker presents the person and the action — or the item and its state — together as a unit.

DECLARATIVE:

Hana wa kirei da.	The flowers (or: Flowers in general) are beautiful.
Jon wa aruite-kuru.	As for John, he is coming on foot.

In these cases, the speaker takes up a particular item as a theme, separating it from any scene or situation, and makes a statement about it. The item or person is not presented "in a package" with its action or state.

In Japanese declarative sentences the TOPIC or the theme is presented by *N* (or noun-phrase) + *wa*. Descriptive sentences present the SUBJECT by *N* (or noun-phrase) + *ga*. The topic word governs the entire sentence, while the subject word governs "locally" (governs clauses, which are sentences within a sentence), unless the main predicate requires a subject rather than a topic.

Another way to explain the differing functions of *wa* and *ga*, though it does not fully explain them, is by using the analogy of the English indefinite article "a" and the definite article "the." Consider the following passage from the folk tale *Momotaro*, "The Peach Boy."

*Mukashi mukashi, ojiisan to obsan **ga** imashita.*	Once upon a time, there was **an** old man and **an** old woman.
*Ojiisan **wa** yama e shibakari ni ikimashita.*	**The** old man went to the mountain to gather firewood.
*Obsan **wa** kawa e sentaku ni ikimashita.*	**The** old woman went to the river to wash clothes.

While the subject particle *ga* is used to introduce something or someone for the first time in a discourse, the topic particle *wa* is used to refer to the same thing from the second time on. *Ga* is used to introduce **new information** (as is the English indefinite article "a") while *wa* is used to refer to **old information** (as is the English definite article "the").

In general the distance between the topic and its predicate is greater than that between a subject and its predicate. Normally the closest predicate to the right of a subject is its predicate. In the case of clauses, the closest subjects and predicates are grouped together. On the other hand, the end of the sentence is where the the main predicate for the topic is located, except in the case of *toiu* clauses and quotation clauses in which TOPIC + *wa* can appear (see ch. 1, § § 3.1.1B and 3.1.2A).

⇨ There is normally only one topic for the main predicate. However, there are cases where there is more than one topic:

Kyō wa Jon wa atama ga itai.	Today John has a headache. (As for today, speaking of John, his head aches.)

5.1.2 Contrast *wa*

The particle *wa* may also be used to show contrast, regardless of whether the contrasted element is actually mentioned or not.

A.

Densha wa anzen da keredo, hikōki wa abunai.	Trains are safe but airplanes are dangerous.

Trains and airplanes are here contrasted with respect to safeness.

B.

Kōhii o nomimasu ka.	Do you drink coffee?
Iie. Nihoncha wa nomimasu ga, . . .	No. I drink Japanese tea but (not . . .)

Japanese tea is contrasted here with other drinks that are not mentioned. The original particle *o*, the direct object particle, has been replaced by the contrast *wa*. **Thus, the original relational signification (between object and verb) in the above sentence is concealed by the contrast *wa*.**

The contrast *wa* may also replace the subject particle *ga*:

Senshū ame ga futta ga yuki wa furanakatta.	It rained last week but it didn't snow.

The first *ga* is a regular subject particle, while the second is a conjunction. The *wa* has replaced an original *ga* marking *yuki* as the subject of the second part of the sentence.

*Niku **wa*** tabenai ga yasai **wa*** taberu.*	I eat vegetables but I don't eat meat.

* Here the contrast *wa* has replaced the particle *o*.

*Furansugo wa yasashii. Nihongo **wa*** muzukashii.*	French is easy. Japanese (by contrast) is hard.

* The contrast *wa* has replaced an original topic *wa*.

The contrast *wa* tends to be used more often in negative sentences, though not invariably. In this context the contrast implied has the effect of softening the negative statement, and is thus an instance of the euphemism of which Japanese discourse is so fond.

Pen ga irimasu ka.	Do you need a pen?
*Iie, pen **wa** irimasen ga . . .*	[I'm sorry] I don't need a pen [in spite of your kind offer], but . . . [actually I need something else]

C. *Wa* can be attached to other particles to show contrast:

*Tōkyō e iku ga, Ōsaka **e wa** ikanai.*	I am going to Tokyo, but not to Osaka.
*Koko de tabako o sū ga, ofisu **de wa** suwanai.*	I smoke here, but not in my office.
*Ichiji kara kōgi ga atte, niji **kara wa** tōgi ga okonawareru.*	There will be a lecture at one o'clock, and from two there will be discussion.

*X **made wa***	until or as far as X
*X **de wa***	at X *or:* with X
*X **ni wa***	in X

D. The contrast particle *wa* can be inserted even when there was originally no particle:

1. After an ADV.

*Kyō **wa** koraremasu ka.*	Can you come today (as compared with other days)?

2. Within a V: V-stem + *wa* + *suru*

*Inu wa kuruma ni butsukerareta keredo, shini(V-stem) **wa** shinakatta.*	Although the dog was hit by a car, it did not die.

The contrast implied is, perhaps, that the dog was badly injured.

*Sono tegami o ake **wa** shita.*	I did open the letter (but, for example, did not read it).

The contrast implied is perhaps that I didn't read it.

3. Within ADJ: ADJ-*ku* + *wa* + *aru*

*Omoshiroku **wa** nai ga, . . .*	It is not amusing (but is, for example, challenging).

4. Within N/AN *dearu:* AN de + *wa* + *aru*

Byōki de wa aru ga . . .	I am sick (but at least I can work at home).

Wa can appear at the end of a sentence, but it functions there quite differently from the *wa* which comes after N to show the topic or contrast.

In female speech the sentence final particle *wa* can be attached to the end of a statement for slight emphasis.

Polite Formal Style:

*Watakushi ga itashimasu **wa**.*	I (female) will do (humble) it.

Informal Style:

*Mada tegami wa konai **wa** ne.*	I suppose the letter hasn't come yet.

5.2 *GA*

*A, asoko ni **akai bara** ga saite-iru.*	Look! A red rose is blooming over there.
Kore wa bara da.	This is a rose.

"A red rose" in the first sentence and "this" in the second sentence are both the subjects of their respective sentences in English. However, only words followed by *ga* are subjects in Japanese. Therefore, "a red rose" in the first sentence is the subject.

The particle *ga* indicates the subject of a "descriptive" sentence, but it tends to be omitted when understood. It is important for reading comprehension to be constantly aware of the possibility of omitted subjects.

5.2.1 Immediate Description of a Scene or Event

Ame ga hutte-kita.	(Oh) it has started raining.
Aa, atama ga itai.	Oh, my head hurts!
Hora, koko ni kirei na hana ga saite-iru!	Look, a pretty flower is blooming here!

The subject particle *ga* appears in sentences in which a speaker describes the current state of something, or what is happening right at the moment in front of her eyes, or else at some definite point in the past — as in story telling.

Suruto totsuzen ōotoko ga arawareta.	And then, suddenly a giant appeared.

5.2.2 Subject Emphasis

Ano hito wa Tanaka-san da.	That person is Mr.Tanaka.
*Ano hito **ga** hannin da.*	**That person** is the culprit. *or:* It is **that person** who is the culprit.

In the first example *wa* indicates that *ano hito* "that person" is the topic of the sentence, while in the second the *ga* indicates that *ano hito* is the **subject** in focus. In a question—***Dare*** *ga hannin desu ka.* "**Who** is the culprit?"—***dare*** is the focused element and is therefore followed by the subject emphasis *ga.*

⮡ In cases where other elements are focused on, the particles remain the same.

*Ano hito wa **nani o** nomu ka.*	What is he going to drink?
*Ano hito wa **doko e** iku ka.*	Where is he going?

5.2.3 Subject in a Location Sentence with *aru/iru*

*Koko ni denwa **ga** aru.*	Here is a telephone.
*Ōsaka ni oji **ga** iru.*	I have an uncle in Osaka. or: My uncle is in Osaka.

In the location pattern the subject particle *ga* is used to describe the location of something with *aru* "there is/exists (an inanimate object)" or with *iru* "there is/exists (an animate being)." These sentences are all descriptive.

LOCATION *ni* N* ***ga*** *aru/iru.*

> * This subject word can be topicalized by replacing the subject particle *ga* with the topic particle *wa* (and usually also placing it at the beginning of the sentence).

Compare the following.

*Asoko ni **haha ga** iru.*	There is my mother over there.
***Haha wa** asoko ni iru.*	As for my mother, she is over there.

A sentence such as *Watakushi wa oji ga iru* can be considered to have come from a location sentence:

Watakushi ni wa oji ga iru.	At me an uncle exists (= I have an uncle).

Possession is normally expressed by a location pattern in which the location particle *ni* is often omitted:

Jon (ni) wa kuruma ga aru.	John has/owns a car.

5.2.4 Other Cases requiring Subject *ga*

A. AN requiring *ga* for the direct object in English:

*Suteeki **ga suki** da.*	(I) like steak [= steak is likable].
*Gakusei wa shiken **ga kirai** da.*	As for students, they dislike exams.

B. ADJ requiring *ga* for the direct object in English:

*Supōtsukā **ga**/o* **hoshii**.*	I **want** a sports car [= a sports car is desirable].
*Yasai **ga**/o* tabe-**tai**.*	I **want to** eat vegetables.

    * By analogy with English, *o* is used widely nowadays.

Others:

*Obake **ga kowai** desu.*	I **am scared** of ghosts [= ghosts are scary].
*Me **ga kayui**.*	My eyes are itchy.
*Ha **ga itai**.*	I have a toothache.

C. Intransitive Vs: All Vi's take a subject rather than a topic, though the *ga* may be replaced by the topic or contrast *wa*.

*Mizu **ga koboreru**.*	Water spills.
*Byōki **ga naotta**.*	The illness was cured.
*To **ga aita**.*	The door opened.

D. Intransitive Vs whose English equivalents are transitive:

*Hanako-san wa chūgokugo **ga wakaru**.*	Hanako **understands** Chinese [= Chinese is understood by Hanako].
*Kongetsu wa mō sukoshi okane **ga iru**.*	As for this month, (I) **need** a little more money [=money is needed].

*Yama **ga mieru**.*	Mountains can be seen.
*Tonari no heya kara ongaku **ga kikoeru**.*	Music can be heard from the next room.

E. Potential Vs:

*Hanako wa tenisu **ga dekiru**.*	Hanako can play tennis.
*Nanshii wa nihongo **ga hanaseru**.*	Nancy can speak Japanese.

F. Passive form:

*Kuruma **ga nusumareta**.*	A car was stolen.

G. Spontaneous form:

*Fuan **ga kanjirareru**.*	I somehow feel anxiety.

H. In subordinate clauses (when the subject of a clause is different from that of the main sentence):

Noun Modifier Clause:

*[Watakushi **ga**/no katta] hon wa kore da.*	The book I bought is this one.

Adverbial Clause:

*[Ame **ga** futtara], watakushi wa ikanai.*	If it rains, I won't go.

↪ Note that *no* cannot be used in place of the subject *ga* in adverbial clauses.

5.3 *MO*

5.3.1 "Also," "both . . . and," "neither . . . nor"

The particle *mo* means "also" — or, when repeated — "both . . . and." When used with negative verbs it means "not . . . either . . . or," or "neither . . . nor." It can replace the particles *ga*, *o*, or *wa*.

| Nihongo ga suki da. Chūgokugo **mo*** suki da. | I like Japanese (language). I **also** like Chinese. |

* *ga* has been replaced by *mo*.

| Nihongo **mo** chūgokugo **mo***benkyō shita. | I studied **both** Japanese and Chinese. |

* *o* has been replaced by *mo*.

| Hanako wa nihonjin da. Tarō **mo***nihonjin da. | Hanako is Japanese. Taro is **also** Japanese. |

* The topic *wa* has been replaced by *mo*.

Other particles are retained when used with *mo*.

Nihon e itta. Chūgoku **e mo** itta.	I went to Japan. I went to China too.
Nihon de benkyō shita. Chūgoku **de mo** benkyō shita.	I studied in Japan. I studied in China too.
Nihon **de mo** chūgoku **de mo** benkyō shita.	I studied both in Japan and in China.
Pen de kaku. Enpitsu **de mo** kaku.	I write with a pen. I also write with a pencil.
Nihon **ni mo** chūgoku **ni mo** kojinshugi wa nai.	Individualism does not exist in either Japan or China.

5.3.2 Emphasis *mo*

A. Quantity ADV + *mo*

emphasizing largeness:

| Tōkyō made ichijikan **mo** kakarau. | It takes **as long as** one hour to Tokyo. |

emphasizing smallness:

| Tōkyō made ichijikan **mo** kakaranai. | It doesn't take **even** an hour to Tokyo. |

| *Sukoshi/chitto* **mo** *omoshiroku nai.* | It's not at all interesting. |
| *Kyōshitsu ni wa gakusei ga hitori* **mo** *inakatta.* | There wasn't even one student in the classroom. |

B. Interrogative Word + *mo* + Negative

Jon wa nani **mo** *tabenai.*	John doesn't eat anything.
Heya ni dare **mo** *inai.*	There is no one in the room.
Dare ni **mo** *sono koto o hanasanakatta.*	I didn't tell anyone about it.
Ojiisan wa doko ni **mo** *inakatta.*	The old man was nowhere.
Nan no kōka **mo** *nakatta.*	There was no effect whatsover.
Gan wa kare no i zentai ni hirogatte-ite dō suru koto **mo** *dekinakatta.*	The cancer had spread all over the stomach, so they were unable to do anything.
Jon wa itsu **mo** *uchi ni inai.*	John is never home.
Jon wa itsumo * *uchi ni iru.*	John is always home.

* *Itsumo* is ADV meaning "always."

C. Interrogative + *demo* + Affirmative

Dare **demo** *kono tsuā ni sanka dekiru.*	Anyone can join this tour.
Kare wa nan **demo** *shitte-iru*	Whatever it is, he knows it.
Karinui wa itsu **demo** *ii.*	Any time is fine for fitting.
Yatou no wa nanijin **demo** *ii.*	Any nationality is fine for hiring.

D. Quantity Interrogative

Quantity interrogative + *mo* + Affirmative, "ever so much"
+ Negative, "ever so little"

| *Jon wa nansatsu* **mo** *hon o yonda.* | John read ever so many books. |

*Jon wa nansatsu **mo** hon o yomanakatta.*	John read very few books.
*Tōkyō made nanjikan **mo** kakaru.*	It takes ever so many hours to Tokyo.
*Tōkyō made nanjikan **mo** kakaranai.*	It takes only a few hours to Tokyo.
*Okane wa ikura **mo** nai.*	I have ever so little money.

The following examples with *demo* + AFFIRMATIVE are slightly different from the above examples. *N + demo* means "even if it is N":

*Jon wa nansatsu **demo** hon o yonda.*	John read any number of books.
*Jon wa nanjikan **demo** benkyō shita.*	John studied for whatever amount of time (=John studied hour after hour).
*Nedan wa ikura **demo** ii kara kono e ga/o kaitai.*	No matter how high the price may be, I want to buy this painting.

See ch. 1, § 3.2.1 for *ikura/donnani* + *V-temo*: "no matter how much one may do."

E. Emphasis: "even, indeed"

*Jon **mo** kore de yatto hitoridachi dekiru.*	John can finally become independent from now on.
*Kare **mo** nakanaka yaru ne.*	He does indeed do it well.
*Kore dewa kujō ga deru no **mo** tōzen da.*	It is indeed understandable that (people) complain if this is the situation.
*Sonna koto wa mezurashiku **mo** (nan to mo) nai.*	That kind of thing is not at all unusual.
*Sono gakusei wa hon o yomi **mo** shinai de wakaranai to iu.*	That student doesn't even read the book—and then says he doesn't understand.

F. Emphatic Adverbial

ADJ-ku mo:

hayaku mo	as early as this, already	from *hayaku* (ADV)	early, fast
imijiku mo	aptly	from classical *imiji* (ADJ)	extreme, extraordinary
iyashiku mo	[if you do it] at least . . .	*iyashii* (ADJ)	lowly, humble, base
karaku mo	barely	from classical *karashi* (ADJ)	(spicy) hot, cruel, painful
osore ōku mo	graciously	from *osore* (N)	fear, awe, and *ōi* (ADJ), many

AN + ni mo:

kōun/saiwai ni mo	quite fortunately
fuun/fukō ni mo	quite unfortunately
gūzen ni mo	quite coincidentally

For idiomatic expressions using *mo*, see Appendix § 1.

6. The uses of no

6.1 *N no N:*

no in between nouns connects them in different ways.

6.1.1 "of (genitive)," or simply connecting two nouns:

*Nihongo **no** hon*	a book of Japanese, a Japanese book
*rekishi **no** kurasu*	a class in history, a history class
*Nihon **no** yama*	a mountain in Japan, a Japanese mountain
*futari **no** musuko*	two sons (quantity)
*ōzei **no** hito*	many people (quantity)
*chūgurai **no** ōkisa*	medium size
*ishi **no** ie*	a stone house (quality)

6.1.2 Possessive

*Hanako **no** hon*	Hanako's book

The second N may be omitted, in which case the meaning is simply "Hanako's":

*Kore wa Hanako **no** da.*	This is Hanako's.

6.1.3 The COPULA *da* is changed to *no/dearu* after N at the end of a modifier clause:

This is the same kind of operation as with V/ADJ/AN:

Hanako wa Tōkyō e iku.	Hanako is going to Tokyo.
[Tōkyō e iku] Hanako	Hanako who is going to Tokyo
Hanako wa utsukushii.	Hanako is beautiful.
[utsukushii] Hanako	Hanako who is beautiful *or:* beautiful Hanako
Hanako wa kirei da.	Hanako is pretty.
[kirei na/dearu] Hanako	Hanako who is pretty *or:* pretty Hanako
Hanako wa byōki da.	Hanako is sick.
*[byōki **no**/dearu] Hanako*	Hanako who is sick *or:* sick Hanako

A. Apposition:

Tarō wa musuko da.	Taro is my son.
*[musuko **no**/dearu]* **Tarō**	Taro (who is) my son *or:* my son Taro

Ambiguous case:

*isha **no** musume*	POSSESSIVE: a doctor's daughter
*[isha **no**/dearu]* **musume*****	APPOSITION: (my) daughter who is a doctor.

    * The sense of this *musume* is particular, referring to "my daughter" rather than "daughters (in general)" as in: [*isha **no**/dearu*] *Tanaka-san* "Mr. Tanaka who is a doctor" or: "Mr. Tanaka, a doctor."

B. Others (any predicate, depending on the context):

*[eigo **no**] Yamada-san*	Mr. Yamada who teaches / studies / speaks / likes English

Any predication concerning the N is possible depending on the context; in other words, any predicate can be contracted to *no*:

[Tōkyō made **no***] kippu*	a ticket to Tokyo

The *no* here represents the predicate *ikeru*, "with which one can go."

6.2 Subject in a Modifier Clause as the Equivalent of *ga*

*[watakushi ga/***no*** katta] hon*	the book that I bought
*[ame ga/***no*** furu] hi*	the day it rains

6.3 Sentence-Final Particle in Informal Speech Style

A. QUESTION with rising intonation:

Doko e iku **no**.	Where are you going?

B. SOFTENING of the meaning with falling intonation (more commonly used by women and children):

Kaimono ni iku **no**.	I am going shopping . . .

⮑ Note that *no* can be attached to the end of a sentence in the formal feminine speech style as well.

6.4 Emphasis or Softener in a Predicate: *V/ADJ* + *no da*, *N/AN* + *na no da*

No in a predicate (*N/AN na* or Verbal plain + *no/n˙* + *da*) carries a special meaning. Depending on the context it either intensifies the meaning of the sentence (EMPHASIS) or else softens it (SOFTENER). The latter sense is common in speech, since it conveys a sense of the speaker's being humble or indirect or accommodating. The softener *no* thus has an important euphemistic function.

* In conversation, *no* is frequently contracted to just *n* to form *n da/ desu*: *Byōki datta n' desu.* "I was ill, you know . . . "

In the plain style (or informal speech style) *da/dearu* is omitted when followed by the question *ka*, as in:

Nihonjin wa doko kara kita **no** *ka.*	Where did the Japanese come from?
Mita **no** *ka.*	You mean you saw it? *or:* Is it that you saw it?

Consider the following dialogue:

A: *Naze nanben mo denwa o shita* **no** *desu ka.*	Why did you call so many times?

EMPHASIS: if A is truly surprised by the fact that B did call so many times.
SOFTENER: if A doesn't want to appear too inquisitive.

B: *Fuan datta* **no** *desu.*	It was that I felt anxious.

EMPHASIS: if B was truly very anxious
SOFTENER: if B is reluctant to give the reason, or B feels apologetic about disturbing A with this information.

Ii-nikui **n** *(EMPH) desu ga, Tanaka-san wa ochita* **no** *(SOFT) desu.*	It's really hard for me to say this, but Mr. Tanaka has failed.
Kare no seiseki wa maamaa datta **no** *desu ga . . .* SOFT	His grades were so-so, but . . .
Ittai nani ga shōnen hanzai no gen'in na **no** *ka.* EMPH	What in the world is the cause of juvenile delinquency?
Jūnengo tsuini kare wa seikō shita **no** *dearu.* EMPH	Finally he did succeed after ten years.
Oyatachi no mukanshin ga* *gen'in na* **no** *da.* EMPH	The indifference of the parents is indeed the cause.

* The emphasis *no* often occurs in the same sentence with the **subject emphasis** particle *ga*, as in this case.

6.5 Pronominal: "one (person, thing, place, etc.)"

The pronominal *no* replaces a noun and is usually followed by a particle (*wa, ga, o, e, kara,* etc.) or by the copula *da.*

Kurasu o yasunda no wa Jon da.	The one (= person) who missed the class is John.
Watakushi ga katta no wa Amerika no conpyūtā da.	The one (= computer) that I bought is an American computer.
Nihon ni hajimete kanji ga tsutawatta no wa yonseiki goro da to iwarete-iru.	It has been said that the time when Chinese characters were first transmitted to Japan was around the 4th century.
Orinpikku ni sanka shinakatta no wa Soren da.	The one (= country) that did not participate in the Olympics was the U. S. S. R.
Jon ga tsukatta pen wa sono atarashii no da.	The pen which John used is that new one.

6.6 Nominalizer: Plain V (nonpast) + *no*

The nominalizer changes a V into a N to mean "to (do) V" or "V-ing."

Tegami o kaku no wa mendō da.	Writing letters is troublesome.
Oyogu no wa karada ni ii.	Swimming is good for one's health.
[Kare ga naku]* no o mita.	I saw him crying.

  * This is basically a noun modifier construction; see ch. 1, § 3.1.1A.

↪ The *no* of *V-ta no* is sometimes regarded as a nominalizer. In this book, however, this *no* is treated as a pronominal, on the grounds that the nominalizer *no* is only attached to the nonpast tense of V. For example:

Kare ga soko e itta (V-past) no* wa yokunakatta.	It was not good that he went there.

  * This *no* is the pronominal *no* replacing *koto* "the fact," and *toiu* has been omitted after the *toiu* clause: [*Kare ga soko e itta*] *(toiu) koto wa yokunakatta.*

7. The particle ni

7.1 Time

For time Ns that take *ni* and those that do not, see above § 3.3.

7.2 Location + *aru/iru*:

Aru/iru: location

*Kōkyo wa Tōkyō **ni** aru.*	The imperial palace is in Tokyo.
*Jon wa uchi **ni** iru.*	John is at home.

Vt-te-aru / Vi-te-iru: location where something is done or has been done

*Kuruma ga uchi no mae **ni** tomatte-iru.*	The car is parked in front of the house.
*Kuruma ga uchi no mae **ni** tomete-aru.*	The car has been parked in front of the house.
*Oka no ue **ni** ki ga haete-iru.*	A tree is growing on the hill.
*Kokuban **ni** nanika ga kaite-aru.*	Something has been written on the blackboard.

↪ Note that:

A. In the case of an on-going action *de* is used:

*Soto **de** kodomo ga naite-iru.*	A child is crying outside.

B. The location of an event is expressed by *de*:

| *Koko **de** kaigi ga atta.* | The conference was held here. |

C. The verb *umareru* normally takes place + *de* to indicate a place:

| *Nihon **de** umareta.* | I was born in Japan. |

However, it can also take location + *ni* to indicate a situation or fate one is born into:

| *Kanemochi no uchi **ni** umareta.* | I was born into a wealthy family. |

See above § 5.2.3 for possession expressed by a location pattern.

7.3 Location + Other Verbs:

*teeburu no ue **ni** hana o oku*	place flowers on the table
*Ōsaka **ni** sumu*	live in Osaka
*mizuumi no soba **ni** uchi o tateru*	build a house beside a lake
*mizu **ni** moguru*	dive into the water
*isu **ni** suwaru/kakeru*	sit on a chair
*kyanbasu **ni** e o kaku*	paint a picture on a canvas
*hangā **ni** fuku o kakeru*	put clothes on hangers
*niwa **ni** hana o ueru*	plant flowers in a garden
*yama **ni**/o noboru*	climb a mountain

⤳ Places one moves **through** are marked by *o*:

michi o aruku/tōru	walk/go along the street
hashi o wataru	cross the bridge
marason kōsu o hashiru	run along the marathon course

7.4 Direction or Goal

A. With MOTION VERBS:

*Amerika **ni** iku/kuru/kaeru/modoru/hikikaesu*	go/come/return/return/turn back to America
*Haneda **ni** tsuku**	arrive at Haneda
*Kariforunia **ni** itaru*	reach California
*Orinpikku **ni** deru*	participate in the Olympics
*uchi **ni** hairu*	enter the house

* But note the following:

*Haneda **o** deru*	leave Haneda
*uchi **o** deru*	leave the house

B. Verbs of GIVING and RECEIVING:

*A wa B **ni** X o ageru/yaru/ kureru.**	A gives X to B.
*B wa A **ni**/kara X o morau.*	B receives X from A.
*A wa B **ni** . . . V-te ageru/ yaru/kureru.*	A performs an action for B *or:* A does something for B.
*B wa A **ni** . . . V-te morau.*	A has B do something = A receives [the effect or benefit of] B's doing something

* *-yaru* is used when the recipient is younger or of lower status, an animal, or an inanimate object; *-kureru* is used when something is given to the speaker, whether by an outsider or an in-group member, or else by an outsider to an in-group member—typically one's family, or member(s) of a group one belongs to, such as a section of a company, a firm where one works, a club, church, or a school.

*Haha **ni** hana o katte-ageta.*	I bought some flowers for my mother.
*Inu **ni**/to asonde-yatta.*	I played with the dog [for him].

| Sakaya **ni** sake o todokete-moratta. | I had the liquor shop deliver sake. |

⇨ Note that this is a grammatical device peculiar to Japanese — perhaps a product of a society concerned with such ideas as *giri*, "an obligation," and *on*, "a debt of gratitude." People's actions tend to be perceived as the objects of giving or receiving.

C. With PASSIVE, CAUSATIVE, and CAUSATIVE-PASSIVE:

*Tarō wa Hanako **ni** hikareru.*	Taro is attracted to (by) Hanako.
*Kodomo **ni** piano o narawaseru.*	(I) have the child take piano lessons.
*Kodomo wa oya **ni** piano o narawaserareta.*	The child was made to take piano lessons.

D. Change of State:

*X (N/AN) **ni** naru*	become X (but *ADJ-ku naru*)
*Hawai wa gojūbanme no shū **ni**/to natta.*	Hawaii became the fiftieth state.
*Heya wa kirei **ni** natta.*	The room became clean.
*X **ni** kawaru/kaeru*	change into X
*X **ni** ketteisuru/suru*	decide on X
*X **ni** kimaru*	be decided on X
*X **ni** suru*	make, set (decide on) X
*Kaigi no jikan wa ichiji **ni** shita.*	They made the conference time one o'clock.

*Y o X **ni** suru*	change/make Y into X *or:* punish someone by X
*Kare wa musuko o isha **ni** shita.*	He made his son a doctor.
*Ō wa otoko o shikei **ni** suru yō meijita.*	The king ordered the man to be put to death.

7.5 Purpose

A. V-stem *ni* + Motion Verb: "go/come/return/leave (in order) to do . . . "

*Honya e hon o kai **ni** iku.*	I'm going to the bookstore to buy a book.

☞ Often *(shite)* + *mo*[EMPHASIS] follows *ni* when the circumstance is one of impossibility, as in:

Denwa o kakeru ni (shite) mo kozeni ga nai (kara kakerarenai).	Even though I just want to make a phone call, I don't have any change (so I can't do so).

B. "for the purpose of, in order to . . . "
V-ru (no) ni:

*Sore o kau no **ni** okane ga iru.*	(I) need money to buy it.
*Muzukashii kanji wa oboeru no **ni** jikan ga kakaru.*	Difficult kanji take a long time to memorize.
*Kono gakko wa kayou no **ni** benri da.*	This school is convenient to commute to.

N *ni*:

*kenkyū (no tame) **ni** kikin o morau*	receive funds for research
*Undō wa kenkō (no tame) **ni** ii.*	Exercise is good for one's health.

N *no tame ni* is an idiomatic phrase which means "for the purpose/sake of N." It can also means "due to" or "owing to":

*Byōki **no tame ni** kurasu o yasunda.*	I missed the class due to illness.

C. "as/for . . . "

*rei **ni** X o ageru*	raise X as an example

*orei **ni** X o okuru*	send X as an appreciation
*nagusami **ni** gitā o hiku*	play the guitar for amusement

7.6 Manner ADV: *X + ni*

A. *AN + **ni***

kanzen ni "perfectly" (See also § 4.4.1.)

B. Others:

> *ichiretsu ni (narabu)* "(line up) in a row," *gen ni* "actually," *jissai (ni)* "actually," *jojo ni* "slowly, gradually," *koto ni* "especially," *sara ni* "furthermore," *shidai ni* "gradually," *tagai ni* "mutually," *tsune ni* "always, constantly," *sengiri ni suru* "slice something thin."

In the following examples the *ni* is optional:

dandan (ni/to*)	gradually
sugu (ni)	immediately
tachimachi (ni)	suddenly

* See ch. 4, § 8.2 for the omission of *to*.

7.7 Subject for *dekiru* and *wakaru*

These verbs are Vi in Japanese and their meanings are literally "can be done" and "can be understood." Their English equivalents are Vt and therefore when they are translated they take the direct object.

*X **ni** (wa) Y ga dekiru.*	Y is possible for X (= X can do Y).
*X **ni** (wa) Y ga wakaru.*	Y is understandable for X (= X can understand Y).

7.8 Addition

*San **ni** go o tasu to hachi ni naru.*	If you add 5 to 3, you get 8.
*jagaimo **ni*** ninjin*	potatoes and (moreover) carrots

* The *ni* in this context emphasizes the idea of adding an item or items to the thing first mentioned. If one is simply listing out, then *to* is used: *A to B* "A and B"

Presenting things in contrast as a pair:

*take **ni** tora*	bamboo and tiger
*azuma-otoko **ni** kyō-onna*	a man from Eastern Japan and a woman from Kyoto*

* The idea is that masculine qualities are best found in a man from Edo and feminine beauty in a woman from Kyoto.

7.9 Sentence-Ending for Wish, Prayer, etc.

*Dōzo, Jon ga kachimasu yō **ni**.*	Please let John win.

7.10 "per [number]"

*jyūnin **ni** hitori*	one person out of every ten people
*ichinichi **ni** sando*	three times a day

7.11 Honorific: *o*-V-stem *ni naru*:

o-kaki ni naru	to write

The humble form is made with *suru*:

o-kaki suru	(I) humbly write for you

↪ Not every verb can take this polite form because of the meaning of "humbly do something for the hearer" in case of the humble form. For example, one doesn't say: *Uchi e okaeri suru.* "I humbly go home for . . ." The action of going home cannot be done for a hearer who isn't a member of one's in-group.

7.12 Partial list of other verbs that take *ni*

X ni ataru	hit X
nagaredama ni ataru	be hit by a stray bullet

X ni ataru	correspond to, be poisoned by, take charge of X
Kyō wa jiko no hi kara chōdo ichinenme ni ataru.	Today falls exactly on the first anniversary of the accident.
oji ni ataru hito	a person related to me as my uncle
sakana ni ataru	be poisoned by fish
shinnyūshain no shidō ni ataru	take charge of guiding newly entered employees

Y ga X ni au	Y suits/matches X
Shiroi kutsu ga shiroi doresu ni au.	White shoes match the white dress.

X ni butsukaru/butsukeru	hit/strike X or collide with X
denshinbashira ni butsukaru	hit a utility pole

X ni chakushu suru	take up
X ni chikau	swear by X
kami ni chikau	swear by God

X ni denwa (o) kakeru/suru	call (= phone) a person
X ni deru	to take part in X
X ni hairu	to enter (into) X
X ni iu/hanasu/miseru/okuru	say/speak/show/send to X
Contrast: *X to hanasu*	talk with X

X ni kabureru	have a rash due to
urushi ni kabureru	be poisoned by lacquer
kyōsanshugi ni kabureru	be infected with communism

X ni kakeru	lack X
Kare wa shinsetsushin ni kakeru.	He is lacking in kindness.

X ni kakeru	bet on X
X ni/kara kariru	borrow from X
X ni kasu	lend to X
X ni megumareru	be blessed with X
X ni mieru	be seen as X
Ano kumo ga ryū ni mieru.	That cloud looks like a dragon.

X ni/kara motomeru	request/seek from X
X ni wabi o motomeru	seek an apology from X
X ni motozuku	be based on X
X ni motozuite	based on X ∽
X ni mukau	to face/head toward X
X ga Y ni niau	X looks good on Y
X ni/to niru	resemble X
X ni nureru	get wetted by X
X ni odoroku	be surprised at X
X ni oshieru	teach something to X
X ni osowaru/narau	learn from X
X ni sanka suru	to participate in X
X ni sōdan suru	consult with X
Contrast: *X **to** sōdan suru*	confer with X

X ni sōtō suru (=ataru)	correspond to X
X ni taeru	endure X
X ni tanomu	request/order from X
bōi ni kōhii o tanomu	order coffee from a waiter

X ni tayoru	rely on X
X ni tazusawaru	be engaged in X
X ni tomu	be rich in X
X ni (tori)kakaru	take up X
X ni zokusuru	belong to X

Proverbs:

manaita ni koi	be doomed
buta ni shinju or: *neko("cat") ni koban("gold")*	throw pearls before swine
tasuke ni fune	the right help in time of need
watari ni fune	a timely offer

8. The particle *to*

8.1 Quotation Particle

A.

Kodomo wa sono otoko o papa **to** *yonda.*	The child called the man papa.
Kodomo o Hanako **to** *nazuketa.*	(We) named the child Hanako.
Kono hito wa Nanshii **to** *iu.*	This person is called Nancy.
Tōkyō wa edo **to** *yobareta.*	Tokyo was called Edo.

B. *X toiu N   "N called X":*

Takada **toiu** *hito / machi*	a person / town called Takada
X **to***(ka*[*]*)***iu** *yō na N* or: *X* **to***(ka)***itta** *N*	N such as X or something like that

* The additional *ka* conveys a stronger sense of indefiniteness.

8.2 Manner: . . . + *to*

A. Sound imitation (=*giseigo*) or description of state/action (=*gitaigo*):

Where English often uses verbs to talk about things making sounds, Japanese uses *giseigo* followed by *to*:

Doa ga **gii tto** *iu.*	The door squeaks.

Where English uses ADJ or ADV to describe a state or the manner of an action, Japanese uses *gitaigo* + *to*:

*Te ga **betobeto to** suru.*	(My) hands are sticky.

In general voiceless consonants represent lighter and more pleasant sounds or feelings, while voiced consonants represent heavier, stronger, and less pleasant ones.

After manner words consisting of reduplication of sounds the particle *to* may be omitted, but after other manner words it is obligatory.

1. Sound:

***ton** to kata o tataku*	pat someone's shoulder
*Taihō no oto ga **don** to narihibiita.*	The sound of a cannon resounded.
*to o **tonton** (to) tataku*	knock on the door
*to o **dondon** (to) tataku*	bang the door

2. State or action:

   a. One syllable: followed by *tto*.

***ji**tto shite-iru*	stay still
***ji**tto mitsumeru*	stare at
***ha**tto odoroku*	be astonished
***ho**tto anshinsuru*	be relieved

   b. Two syllables and *-ri*. These are followed by *to*, but when the final *-ri* is dropped they are followed by *tto* instead:

bikuri **to** suru* or: *biku **tto** suru*	be startled at

   * There is a verb *bikkuri suru* from *bikuri*.

An alternative form can be made by repeating the entire two syllables, which are followed by an optional *to*: *bikubiku (to)*.

Daiyamondo no yubiwa ga **kira** *tto kagayaku.*	A diamond ring sparkles.
Hoshi ga **kirakira** *(to) kagayaku.*	Stars twinkle.
Kaijū no me ga **giragira** *(to) hikatte-iru.*	The monsters eyes are glaring.
furafura *(to) suru*	feel dizzy
Kyū ni tatta node **fura** *tto shita.*	I felt dizzy because I stood up suddenly.
burabura *(to) suru*	browse
noronoro *to aruku*	walk slowly
sura *tto shite-iru hito*	a person with a slender figure
surasura *to yomu*	read fluently

c. Chinese Compounds:

danko *to shite*	absolutely
azen *to suru*	be totally astonished
kakuko *to shita (ishi)*	firm/solid (will)
totsujo *to shite*	suddenly
yūzen *to shite-iru*	be composed
bōzen *to suru or* **bō** *tto suru*	feel blank

B. Words such as the following can be adverbs by themselves, and the following *to* is optional:

yukkuri *(to) aruku*	walk slowly
yanwari *(to) iu*	speak softly/indirectly
atafuta *(to) hashiri-mawaru*	run around in a hurry

C. Set phrases:

QUANTITY *to* + Negative "not even . . .":

*Hanako no joggingu wa mikka **to** tsuzukanakatta.*	Hanako's jogging didn't even last three days.

INTERROGATIVE counter* + *to naku* "ever so many . . .":

*Haha wa ko ni sono hanashi o ikudo **to** naku shite-yatta.*	The mother told the child the story ever so many times.

     * See also Quantity Interrogative + *mo*, § 5.3.2D above.

8.3 Other Functions of *to*

A. "and":

A to B to C (to) * . . .	A and B and C . . .

     * The final *to* is normally omitted.

*Kamera **to** nōto (to) o motte-iku.*	I will take a camera and a notebook (with me).

This *to* can connect only nouns and noun phrases, but not sentences.

*Tsukue no ue **to** sofā no waki (to) ni sutando ga oite-aru.*	Lamps have been placed on the desk and beside the couch.

But

Jon ga kite, kore o oite-itta. or: *Jon ga kita. Soshite kore o oite-itta.*	John came and he left this.

For less exhaustive listings *ya* or *toka* is used:

A ya B or *A toka B (toka)*	A, B, and so forth

B. "with"

X to (issho ni)	(together) with X
tomodachi to asobu	play with friends
X to hanasu/sōdan suru	talk/confer with
X to kenka/giron suru	quarrel/argue with
X to shōtotsu suru	collide with
X to kekkon/rikon suru	get married to/divorced from
X to mazeru	mix with X
X to wakareru	be separated from

↪ In *X to no hanashi*, "a talk with X," there is a *no* after *X to* because X and *to* form a noun phrase to constitute *N(=X to) no N*.

Similar examples are:

haha e no tegami	a letter to my mother
Tōkyō kara no hikōki	a plane from Tokyo,

C. "the same as" or "different from"

A wa B to/ni hitoshii or: . . . *onaji da*	A is the same as B
A wa B to X o hitoshiku suru	A is equal to B with regard to X
A wa B to chigau	A is different from X
A wa B to/ni nite-iru	A resembles X

D. *A wa B to/ni naru*, "A becomes B"

E. *A o B to suru* "make A into B," "suppose that A is B"

Tennō wa Yoritomo o shōgun to shita.	The emperor made Yoritomo (the) Shogun.

| *Kono bōru o chikyū **to** suru.* | Suppose that this ball is the earth. |

⇨ *to* is used when the resulting state is temporary or is a role or position or rank; while in a similar expression, *A o B ni suru* "make A into B," A is changed or transformed into B, and *ni* indicates the direction or end-point of the change of state. (See above, § 7.4D.)

X toshite "as X"

| *Shizen o shi **toshite** mananda.* | I learned from nature as a master. |

F. A *o* B *to (tori)kaeru,* "exchange A for B"

Compare:

| *A o B ni kaeru* | change/transform A into B |

G. Idiomatic constructions using *V-ō* (volitional form) + *to*:

1. *V-ō **to** omou* "think one **will** do . . ."

| *Nihon e rainen iku **to** omou.* | I think I'll be going to Japan next year (if the company sends me; if I save enough money, or whatever). |
| *Nihon e rainen ikō **to** omou.* | I think I really will go to Japan next year (regardless of what else happens). |

2. *V-ō **to** suru* "try (hard) to do . . ."

*Jon wa kanji o masutā shiyō **to** shite-iru.*	John is trying hard to master kanji.
*Mainichi hashirō **to** suru ga nakanaka dekinai.*	I try hard to run every day.
*Kanji o hayaku masutā shiyō **to** suru nara kono hon o tsukattara ii.*	If you are going to try to master kanji quickly, you should use this book.

3. *V-ō* **to** *shite-iru (tokoro da)* "be about to do . . ."
   V-ō **to** *shita toki (ni)* "about to do . . . when "

Ima dekakeyō **to** *shite-iru (tokoro da).*	I am just about to leave.
Doa o akeyō **to** *shita toki naka kara aita.*	I was about to open the door when it opened from inside.

An idiomatic construction with a similar meaning is *V-(r)u* (nonpast*) *tokoro da*:

Denwa o kakeru tokoro da.	I am about to make a phone call.

> * *V-ta* (past) *tokoro da*: "to have just finished doing . . ." (See below, § 10.2.)

4. *V-ō* **to** *shita hazumi/totan ni* "at the moment of trying to . . ."

Hako o mochiage-yō **to** *shita hazumi ni koshi o itameta.*	Just as I tried to lift the box I injured my back.

5. *V-ō* **to**/ga *V-mai* **to**/ga *(kamawanai)* "(no matter) whether one does . . . or not"

Ame ga furō **to** *furu-mai* **to** *kasa o motte-iku.*	Whether it will rain or not, I will take an umbrella.

6. *ikani/ikura/donnani V-ō* **to**/ni *(mo)* "no matter how much . . . may do . . ."
   ikani/ikura/donnani V-ō **to** *shite mo* "no matter how much . . . may try to do . . ."

Ika ni neyō **to** *shite mo (= sure domo) nerarenai.*	No matter how much I may try, I can't sleep.
Gaikokugo wa ikura benkyō shiyō **to** *(mo) kesshite bokokugo no yō ni wa naranai.*	No matter how much one may study a foreign language, it never becomes as familiar as one's mother tongue.
Donnani tanomō **to** *(mo) (= tanonde mo) tetsudatte-yaranai.*	I will not help you no matter how much you may ask.

See Appendix § 1 for *tomo*.

9. The use of *mono*

Mono is a N meaning "a thing, matter," and also "a person"—usually in a general or a humble sense:

Chikagoro no wakai mono wa . . .	Young people nowadays . . .
Watakushi wa Yoshida toiu mono desu.	I am (a person) called Yoshida.

However, *mono* is also used in various grammatical constructions where it does not function as a common noun signifying a thing or a person. (This kind of noun is sometimes called *keishiki meishi* or "pseudo-noun." Other such nouns are: *koto, tokoro, wake,* and so on.)

9.1 (. . . *toiu mono/no*) *wa . . . mono da*: general expectation or understanding:

Gakusei toiu mono/no wa yoku benkyō suru mono da.	Students are supposed to study hard.
Yakusoku (toiu mono/no) wa mamoru mono da.	It is a matter of course that one keep a promise.
Josei no hō ga [*] *dansei yori nagaiki suru mono da.*	Women generally live longer than men.

* This *ga* is a subject emphasis particle.

Tabako nado toiu mono wa suu mono dewa nai.	You shouldn't do such a thing as smoking.

9.2 Past Tense + *mono da*: past habit

*Mukashi wa kono kawa ni mo sake ga nobotte-**kita mono da**.*	Salmon used to come up to this stream.
*Geta nado **yasukatta mono da**.*	Such things as clogs used to be inexpensive.

9.3 *mono de/dakara* or *da mono:* indicates REASON*

* More common in spoken than in written Japanese.

*Soko ni inakatta **mono de** kuwashii koto wa wakaranai.*	Because I wasn't there, I don't know the details.
*Tarō wa mada kodomo **da mono** wakaru hazu ga nai.*	Since Taro is still a child, there is no reason to expect him to understand.
A: *Naze sore o yomanai no.*	Why don't you read it?
B: *Datte tsumaranai n **da mono**.*	Because it's boring.

9.4 . . . *mono da/ka/o*: expresses emotional involvement

*Jinsei to (iu mono/no) wa muzukashii **mono da**.*	Life is hard indeed.
*Gakushi o eru tame ni shinbun haitatsu o suru to wa kanshin na **mono**/koto da.*	It is admirable to deliver newspapers in order to earn money to go to school.
*Sono karee wa karakute taberareta **mono** de wa nai.*	That curry is so hot that there is no way that we can eat it.
*Sonna hazu ga aru **mono ka**.*	It cannot be so.
*Sō to wakatte-itara tasukerareta **mono o**.**	If only I had known it, I could have helped.

* This *o* is a special exclamatory use of *o*. *Mono o* can be replaced by *noni*.

Obake nante (= nado toiu mono wa) kowai **mono ka**.	How can something like ghosts be scary?
Kore kara motto ōku no hito ni kankyō mondai o kangaete-morai-tai **mono da**.	We certainly want more people to think about the issue of ecology.

9.5 *V-ō mono nara*: emphatic provision

Kaisha de sonna koto o shiyō **mono nara** *sugu yamesaserareru darō*.	If (you) should ever do such a thing in your office, you would immediately be fired.
Sonnani hakkiri mono o iō **mono nara** *nihon shakai de wa ukeirerarenai*.	If one were ever to speak so outspokenly, one would not be accepted in Japanese society.

9.6 . . . *mono no* or *to wa ie* "even though"

Itsuka tomodachi no uchi o tazuneyō to omotte-iru **mono no** *nakanaka ikenai*.	Even though I intend to visit my friend one of these days, I am never able to go.
Kodomo wa soko made hitori de iku ni wa itta **mono no** *kaerenaku natte-shimatta*.	Although the child went up there all by herself, she ended up not being able to make it back.

9.7 . . . *mono to V*:

Mono can be inserted between a clause and the quotation particle without really adding any substantial meaning but giving a feeling of "officialness" or "weight." Some of the verbs used with *to* this way are: *suru, minasu, mitomeru, omou,* and *kangaeru.*

[Todokede nashi ni sando ijō yasunda baai, sono mono ga kono kurabu o yameta] **mono to** *minasu/minasareru.*	If anyone misses more than three meetings without informing us, the person will be considered to have withdrawn from the club.

See also the example using the potential form of *omowareru* in § 14.1, below.

10. The use of *tokoro*

10.1 *tokoro* (N) "a place, point (spatial or 'feature'), residence"

*Soko no **tokoro** o hidari ni magatte-kudasai.*	Please turn to the left **there.**
*Daigaku kara (aruite) gofun no **tokoro** ni apāto o karita.*	I rented an apartment (in a **place**) five minutes (on foot) from the university.
Koko ni o **tokoro** to o*namae o kaite kudasai.*	Please write in here your **address** and name.

* *O* is the honorific prefix for Ns.

*Machigatte-iru **tokoro** o naoshinasai.*	Please correct the **part** that is wrong.
*Narubeku hito no ii **tokoro** o mite-yaru to yoi.*	It is good to try to see a person's strong **points** as much as possible.
*Shoshinsha dattara sukoa wa konna **tokoro**/mono darō.*	If one is a beginner, the score will probably be just about **this.**

10.2 *V + tokoro* "at the point where . . ."

A. *V-ru + tokoro* (an action about to take place):

*Ima taberu **tokoro** da.*	I am about to eat.

B. *V-te-iru tokoro* (in the middle of an action):

*Ima tabete-iru **tokoro** da.*	I am in the midst of eating.
*Tabeyō to shite-iru **tokoro** da.*	I am just getting ready to eat.
*Hanako ga odotte-iru **tokoro o** video ni totta.*	I took a video of Hanako while she was dancing.
*Dekakeyō to omotte-iru **tokoro** e/**ni** ame ga furi-dashita.*	Just as I was thinking about going out it began to rain.
*Watakushi ga Hanako ni denwa o kakeyō to shite-iru **tokoro** e/**ni** denwa ga atta.*	Just as I was going to call Hanako, there was a phone call from her.

C. *V-ta tokoro da* (an action has just taken place):

*Jon wa tabeta **tokoro**/bakari* da.*	John has just eaten.

> * *Bakari* "merely, only" can also be used in this context, though not in others where *tokoro* is appropriate (see § 12.1D below).

*Senshu ga zen'in nyūjō shita **tokoro de** kokka seishō ga atta.*	At the point where all the athletes had entered (the arena) the national anthem was sung.

D. *V-ru tokoro datta* (something almost happened)

*Mō sukoshi de mae no kuruma ni butsukaru **tokoro** datta.*	I almost hit the car just in front.

10.3 Other Uses of *tokoro*

A. *V-ta tokoro (ga)* or *V-tara* "when . . . , it turned out that . . .*":

* usually something unexpected

*Mazusō na tabemono datta ga tabete-mita **tokoro** (ga) totemo oishikatta.*	The food didn't look good, but when I tried it, it turned out to be delicious.
*Jon no uchi o tazuneta **tokoro** (ga) kare wa rusu datta.*	When I visited John's house, he wasn't home.
*Sono hon o kai ni itta **tokoro** (ga) urikire de nakatta.*	When I went to buy the book, it was sold out and there weren't any.

⮑ *Tokoroga* at the beginning of a sentence is used as a conjunction meaning "however."

B. *V-ta tokoro de, V-te mita tokoro de,* or *V-ta to shite mo* + Negative "even if one does something (the result will be negative)":

*Imasara monku o itta **tokoro** de dō ni mo naranai.*	Even though (you) complain now, nothing can be done.
*Kodomo no kenka ni oya ga dete-itta **tokoro** de dō ni mo naranai.*	Even if the parents show up when children are fighting, it's of no use.

⮑ *Tokorode* at the beginning of a sentence is used as a conjunction meaning "by the way."

C. *V-ru/ta tokoro/kagiri de wa* or *V-ru/ta tokoro ni yoruto/yoreba* "according to . . .":

*watakushi ga shirabeta **tokoro** de wa . . .*	according to my checking . . .
*Jon ga iu **tokoro** ni yoruto ichidoru wa sonouchi hyakuen gurai ni naru sō da.*	According to what John says, the dollar will eventually become about one hundred yen.

| *Watakushi no shitte-iru* **tokoro**/*kagiri dewa Hanako wa mada nihon e kaette-inai.* | As far as I know, Hanako hasn't come back to Japan yet. |

D. N Modifier clause + *tokoro no N* "N which . . .":

The *tokoro* in this construction functions somewhat like the English relative pronoun "which," although this usage is not very common. (See also ch. 3, Example 1.)

| *[Saikaku ga arawashita]* **tokoro** *no sekai* | the world that Saikaku depicted |

F. *tokoro* "in spite of a certain condition":

| *(O)isogashii* **tokoro** *irashatte-kudasatte arigatō gozaimashita.* | Thank you for coming, in spite of your being so busy. |
| *Oyasumi-chū no* **tokoro** *o (ojama shite) shitsurei shimashita.* | I am sorry to have disturbed you while you were resting. |

G. *kono tokoro** "recently, these days"

> * Not "this place" which would be *koko*.

| **Kono tokoro** *warui kaze ga hayatte-iru.* | A bad cold has been going around lately. |

11. The use of *wake*

11.1 "reason" (= *riyū*):

Atsumari ni shusseki dekinai **wake** *o setsumei shita.*	I explained (the reason) why I can't attend the gathering.

11.2 . . . *(toiu)* wake da*, "that is why, no wonder, that means . . ."

* *toiu* often precedes *wake*.

Jon wa jūnen mo nihon ni sunde-ita kara nihongo ga umai **wake** *da.*	Because John lived in Japan for as long as ten years, (that is why) his Japanese is good.
A: *Tetsuya de shigoto o shita n(o) desu yo.* B: *Dōri de nemu-sō na* **wake** *desu ne.*	I worked throughout the night. No wonder you look sleepy.
Nihon no en ga agareba nihon-seihin no nedan mo agaru **wake** *da.*	If the Japanese yen goes up, that means that the cost of Japanese goods will go up too.
A: *Kekkonshiki wa Hawai de agemashita.* B: *Sore de, hirōen wa Nihon de nasatta* to iu* **wake** *desu ne.* A: *Hai, sonna* **wake** *desu.*	We had the wedding ceremony in Hawaii. I assume, then, that you had the reception in Japan. Yes, that's how it was.

* *Nasaru* is the honorific form of the verb *suru*, "to do."

Nagai aida kurō shita kai ga atte, kare mo tsuini shachō toiu **wake** *da.*	His long hard work paid off, with the result that he has finally made it as the president (of a company).

11.3 . . .* *(kanarazushimo)* . . . *(toiu)* **wake** *dewa nai* (or: *to wa kagiranai*) "it doesn't necessarily mean that . . ."

* Often preceded by an "although . . ." or "even though . . ." clause.

Nihon no sarariiman wa taisha-jikan ni natte mo sugu uchi e kaeru **wake** *de wa nai.*	It doesn't necessarily mean that Japanese company employees go home immediately, even when the time comes to leave.
Mukō no iu koto ni sansei shinai **wake** *de wa nai.*	(It) doesn't necessarily mean that I don't agree with what the other party says (= I do agree but . . .)

11.4 . . . *wake/hazu wa/ga nai* "it cannot be (there is no reason to expect) that . . ."

Hanako wa byōki da kara ikeru **wake**/*hazu ga nai.*	Since Hanako is ill, there is no reason to expect that she can go.

↳ this should not be confused with the idiom *wake wa/ga nai* "easy, nothing special":

Kaji nado **wake** *(wa) nai.*	Things like domestic chores are easy (= nothing to it).
wake *no nai koto*	a simple/easy matter

11.5 Emphasis

This is an equivalent (informal speech) of the emphasis *no*, and is often not translated:

A: Ikanai **wake**? B: Un, sō iu **wake**.	"You mean you aren't going?" "Yeah, that's right.
Ano otoko ga hannin datta toiu **wake** desu.	That man **was** the culprit (after all).

11.6 ... *wake ni wa ikanai* "can't very well ..."

Shiranai hito ni okane o kasu **wake** ni wa ikanai.	I can't very well loan money to someone I don't know.

Negative + *wake ni wa ikanai* "must ... " (synonymous with: *V-zaru o enai*)

A o maneitara B mo manekanai **wake** ni wa ikanai.	If we've invited A, we must invite B as well (= we can't very well not invite B).

12. Emphatic particles

The emphatic particles treated in this section include: *Dake, nomi, kiri, bakari, shika, koso, sae, sura, made, mo,* and *demo* (= *datte*). These are special particles which emphasize or focus attention on the preceding word. They can replace *wa, ga,* and *o*.

12.1 Restrictives: "only"

A. *DAKE* "only"

*Hanako **dake** (ga) sore ga yometa.*	Only Hanako could read it.
*Hanako wa yasai **dake** (o) tabeta.*	Hanako ate only vegetables.

V-(r)eba, V-stem *dake/hodo* . . . "the more . . . , the more . . ."

*yomeba yomu **dake**/hodo wakaranaku naru*	The more I read, the more I get confused.

(sasuga ni) . . . *dake atte/ni* "indeed"

*Sasuga ni meishō no chi (to iwareru) **dake** atte fuyu nanoni kankōkyaku mo ōi.*	As one would expect with a place famous for its beautiful scenery, there are many tourists even in winter.

B. *NOMI* "only" (slightly more literary than *dake*)

*Shiken no koto **nomi** (ga) ki ni naru.*	Only the matter of the exam bothers me (= I can't help thinking about it).
*Kare wa chichi no kataki o toru koto **nomi** (o) kangaeta.*	He thought about nothing but taking revenge on his father.
*Kōnattara hara o kiru (V-ru) **nomi** da (= shika nai).*	Since the situation has come to this, the only thing left [for us to do] is to commit harakiri.

Idiomatic phrase:

*ki**nomi** kino mama*	with nothing but the clothes on one's back.

C. *KIRI* + Negative "only this much, that's it" (replaces *wa*, *ga*, and *o*)

*Yasai (k)**kiri*** tabenai.*	I eat only vegetables.
*Okane wa kore (k)**kiri** (shika) nai.*	As for the money, that's all we have.

* *kkiri* with an extra *k* is the spoken form.

*Sore (k)**kiri** (de*) tsuru wa kaette-konakatta.*	Since then, the stork has not returned (and that's it).
*Kare wa arigatō to hitokoto itta **kiri** nani mo iwanakatta.*	He said just one word, "thank you," — and nothing more.

* This *de* is the instrumental meaning "with."

D. *BAKARI* "only, nothing but"

*Sono kodomo wa okashi **bakari** (o) tabete-iru.*	The child is eating nothing but sweets.

V-ru bakari da or: *V-te bakari iru* "do nothing but . . ."

*Kodomo wa naku **bakari** da.* or: *Kodomo wa naite **bakari** iru.*	The child does nothing but cry.

V-ru *bakari ni natte-iru* "be just about ready to do something"

*Karera wa mō taberu **bakari** ni natte-iru.*	They are just about ready to eat.

V-ru *bakari no tokoro e* "when just about to . . ."

*Taberu **bakari** no tokoro e kyaku ga kita.*	A visitor showed up when we were just about to eat.

V-n* *bakari da* "be on the verge of . . ."

*Jon wa (ima ni mo) naki-dasan **bakari** da.*	John is on the verge of crying.

  * -*mu* is the classical auxiliary for the volitional. It is now pronounced and written as -*n*: *utawamu* as *utawan*, "will sing."

V-ta *bakari da*, have just finished doing . . .

*Ima tabeta **bakari** da.*	I have just finished eating.
*Jon wa nihon e kita **bakari** da ga kanari yoku nihongo ga hanaseru.*	John came to Japan only recently, but he can speak Japanese fairly well.

In this kind of example *tokoro* cannot be used. *Tokoro* refers more to the immediate occurrence of an action, while *bakari* emphasizes the limitedness of the action or experience.

*Kare wa sansai ni natta **bakari** de piano ga totemo yoku hiketa.*	He was able to play the piano so well even though he just turned three.

See above, § 10.2C, for a similar construction: *V-ta tokoro da.*

E. *SHIKA* + Negative "only + affirmative" (replaces *wa*, *ga*, and *o*)

*Jon **shika** soko ni inakatta.*	Only John was there.
*Hanako wa yasai **shika** tabenai.*	Hanako eats only vegetables.
Kō nattara jibun de itte-miru ***shika** nai.*	Now that the situation has come to this, the only thing left is to try going myself.

12.2 Non-restrictives

A. *KOSO* (focus on one item out of many)

A: Sore wa sumimasendeshita. *B: Iie, kochira **koso***	I am sorry about that. Oh no, it's I who has to apologize.
*Jon **koso** (wa) masani kantoku ga sagashite-ita haiyū da.*	John is just the actor the director has been looking for.
*Bungaku **koso** (wa) watakushi ga isshō benkyō shitai mono da.*	Literature is the very thing I want to study throughout my life.
*Kyōto e **koso** iku beki da.*	You should go to Kyoto (of all places).

-te koso "only if": *V-te koso,* ADJ-*kute koso,* N/AN *de koso*

Kimono wa (gara ga) jimi (AN) ***de koso** nagaku kirareru.*	One can wear a kimono for many years only if the pattern is quiet.

See also Appendix § 2.2 for *V-te koso.*

V-stem *koso sure* "even if one does . . . "

Kodomo wa naki(V stem) **koso sure** *kesshite sore o koi wa shinakatta.*	Even though the child cried, she didn't ever beg for it.

B. *SAE* "even" (replaces *ga, o,* and *wa*)

Kare no sōshiki ni wa jitsu no kodomo **sae** *konakatta.*	Not even his own children came to his funeral.
Onna wa namida **sae** *ukabete rei o itta.*	The woman expressed gratitude even with tears in her eyes.

V-stem *sae sureba* "only if one does . . ."

Kodomo wa naki **sae sureba** *omoi dōri ni naru to omotte-iru.*	The child thinks that only if he cries can he get what he wants.
Koko made ki **sae sureba** *mō daijōbu da.*	Since we have come this far, we are already safe.

N or *V-te* + *sae areba* "if only, only if, now that . . . "

Kuruma **sae** *areba kayou no ga motto raku na no ni.*	If only I had a car, commuting would be much easier.
*Yoku junbi shite-***sae** *areba shiken wa daijōbu da.*	Only if one is well prepared will one do all right in the exam.
Kono chizu **sae** *te ni haireba takara wa kochira no mono da.*	Now that we have the map, the treasure will be ours.*

> * Compare the similar use of the subjunctive mentioned earlier in ch. 1,
> § 3.2.1.

C. *SURA* "even" (more or less equivalent to *sae,* but not used after V-stem)

Jon wa Hiragana **sura** *kakenai.*	John can't even write Hiragana.

D. *MADE* "even"

*Sono kekkon wa oya **made** (ga) hantai shita.*	Even the parents opposed that marriage.
*Kodomo no nyūgakushiken ni oya **made** (wa/ga) tsuite-ikanai mono da.*	Parents don't usually (go so far as to) accompany their children for their entrance examinations.
*Hanako wa otōto no bun **made** (o) tabete-shimatta.*	Hanako ate up even her brother's portion.
*Sō **made** shinakutemo ii no ni.*	You don't need to go that far (= do that much).
*Kare wa naki (V-stem) **made** shite sore o tanonda.*	He begged for it, even to the point of crying.

See also Appendix § 1 for *made **ni**.*

E. *DEMO (= de sae mo)* "even"

*Sore wa kodomo **demo** dekiru.*	Even a child can do it.

13. -te mo and -te wa

A. *V-te, ADJ-kute, N/AN de + mo ii/kamawanai* "It is all right (even) if . . . "

Jon ga kite mo ii.	It is all right if John comes. or: John may come. PERMISSION
Kusuri ga nigakute mo kamawanai.	It is all right (even) if the medicine is bitter.
Ie ga apāto de mo kamawanai.	It is all right even if (my) home is an apartment.
Tenki ga hen de mo ii.	It is all right even if the weather is bad.

B. *V-nakute, ADJ-nakute, N/AN de mo + ii/kamawanai* "It is all right (even) if . . . not . . . "

Jon ga konakute mo ii.	It is all right even if John doesn't come. *or:* John doesn't have to come.
Nedan ga yasukunakute mo ii.	Even if the price is not cheap, it is all right.
Basho ga benri de nakute mo kamawanai.	It is all right even if the location is not convenient.

C. *V-te wa, ADJ-kute wa, N/AN de wa + ikenai/komaru/dame da* "It is not all right if . . . "

Kodomo ga haitte wa ikenai.	It is not all right if children come in. or: Children may not come in. PROHIBITION

*Machigai ga ō**kute wa** dame da.*	There shouldn't be many mistakes.
*Iro ga chairo **de wa** ikenai.*	The color shouldn't be brown.
*Katachi ga hen **de wa** ikenai.*	It is not good if the shape is strange.

D. *V-nakute wa, ADJ-kunakute wa, N/AN de nakute wa + ikenai/komaru/ dame da* "It is not all right if . . . not . . ."

*Ryōshin ga shusseki shi**nakute wa** ikenai.*	It is not all right if both parents do not attend. or: Both parents must attend. OBLIGATION
*Mi ga aka**kunakute wa** dame da.*	The fruit should be red.
*Iro ga chairo **de nakute wa** komaru.*	The color has to be brown.
*Setsumei ga kantan **de nakute wa** ikenai.*	The explanation has to be simple.

14. Sentence-ending expressions

Japanese has a variety of sentence ending expressions that express subtle nuances of the degree of the writer's commitment or certainty regarding her assertions. Just as expressions such as "It is said/thought that" or ". . . is considered to be . . ." are used to qualify assertions in Western academic writing, the passive voice is used in Japanese too.

However, Japanese employs in addition a wide range of other auxiliaries and constructions to express humility and soften assertiveness, many of which (such as the spontaneous form discussed earlier) reflect conditons in which the subject does not experience itself as clearly separated from the objective world.

The need to give an impression of humility extends even into the most scientific and "objective" writing, where readers in the West would think it unnecessary and out of place. Because of the structural emphasis on the end of the sentence in Japanese, the combination of passive forms, spontaneous forms, euphemisms and other rhetorical devices makes for a rich—and often bewildering—variety of sentence-ending expressions (see the examples in ch. 3, § 9.2.). These expressions may also appear at the end of certain subordinate clauses.

14.1 Basic

A. NOUNS, ADJECTIVAL NOUNS, and ADJECTIVES

N/AN:

*1. Uso **dearu**/da.*	It is a lie.
*1n. Uso **dewa nai**.*	It is not a lie.
*1e. Uso **na no dearu**.*	It is surely a lie.

n = NEGATIVE   e = EMPHASIS

2. *Uso **dearō**.*	It may be a lie. (The writer thinks it *is* a lie.)
*2n. Uso **dewa naidearō/ nakarō/arumai**.*	It may not be a lie. (The writer thinks it is not a lie.)
*2e. Uso **na no dearō**.*	It might be a lie.

In this last example the emphasis *no* actually serves to increase the uncertainty.

3. *Uso **dearō ka**.*	Is it perhaps a lie? (The writer thinks it probably isn't a lie.)
*3n. Uso **dewa nai dearō/ nakarō ka**.* or: *Uso dewa arumai ka.*	Is it not perhaps a lie? (The writer thinks it probably is a lie.)
*3e. Uso **na no dearō ka**.*	Could it really be a lie? (The writer thinks it is probably not a lie.)

4. *Uso **dewa nai ka**.*	Isn't it perhaps a lie? (The writer thinks it is a lie.)
*4n. Uso **dewa nai dewa nai ka**.*	It is indeed not a lie.
*4e. Uso **dewa nai no dewa nai ka**.*	Could it really be a lie? (The writer thinks it probably isn't.)

This last example is actually "softer" than 4n, for the same reason as with 2e.

5. Uso ***deatta/datta** + **rō*** is considered to be the equivalent of *uso **deatta/ datta** + **dearō***, "I suppose that . . . (past)." It is called the "presumptive" or "probable past" and is becoming obsolescent. *-rō* can be attached to *ADJ-katta* and *V-ta* as well.

migoto deatta/datta-rō	I suppose . . . was magnificent
omoshirokatta-rō	I suppose . . . was interesting
kangaeta-rō	I suppose one thought . . .

ADJ

1. Yoi (= ii).	It is good.
1n. Yoku nai.	It is not good.
1e. Yoi no dearu.	It is surely good.

2. Yoi dearō. or: *yokarō.*	It may be good. (The writer thinks it is good.)
2n. Yoku naidearō/nakarō/ arumai.	It may not be good.
2e. Yoi no de arō.	It might be good.

3. Yoi dearō ka.	Is it perhaps good? (The writer thinks it is not good.)
3n. Yoku nai dearō ka, nakarō ka. or: *Yoku arumai ka.*	Is it not perhaps good? (The writer thinks it is good.)
3e. Yoi no dearō ka.	Might it be good? (The writer thinks it is probably not good.)

4. Yoi dewa nai ka.	Isn't it perhaps good? (The writer thinks it is good.)
Yoku nai ka.	Is it not good?
4n. Yoku nai dewa nai ka.	It is indeed not good
4e. Yoku nai no dewa nai ka	Could it really be good? (The writer thinks that it is probably not good.)

5. Yokatta rō/dearō.	I suppose it was good.
5n. Yokunakatta rō/dearō.	I suppose it was not good.

B. VERB

1. . . . to kangaeru	I think that . . .
1n. . . . to (wa) kangaenai*	I don't think that . . .

* Contrast *wa* may be inserted.

2. . . . to kangae**rareru** (POTENTIAL)	One can think that . . .
2n. . . . to (wa) kangae**rarenai**	One cannot think that . . .

3. . . . to kangae**ru koto ga dekiru**	One can think that . . .
3n. . . . to (wa) kangae**ru koto ga dekinai**	One cannot think that . . .

4. . . . to kangae-**uru**	It is possible to think that . . .
4n. . . . to (wa) kangae-**enai**	It is not possible to think that . . .

5. . . . to kangae**rarete-iru** (PASSIVE/STATE)	It has been thought that . . . or: It is thought that . . .
5n. . . . to (wa) kangae-**rarete-inai**	It has not been thought that . . .

6. . . . to kangae**rareru** (SPONT)	(somehow it seems) one can think that . . .
6n. . . . to (wa)kangae**rarenai**	(somehow it doesn't seem) one can think that . . .

7. . . . to kangae**ta-rō**	I suppose one thought that . . .
7n. . . . to kangae**nakatta-rō**	I suppose one didn't think that . . .

The above endings (except for no. 7) can further take: . . . **dearō** or Stem + (y)ō "probably"

. . . **dearō ka**	probably not
. . . **no dewa nai ka**	probably (softer than the first one)
. . . **no dewa nai dearō ka**	might be (softer than the above)
. . . **no dewa nakarō ka**	(same as the above)

EXAMPLES:

. . . to kangaeru dearō	One may think that . . .
. . . to kangae-yō	One may think that . . .
. . . to kangaerareru (POTENTIAL) *dearō*	Perhaps one can think that . . .
. . . to kangaeru koto ga dekiru dearō ka	Is it really possible to think that . . . ? (The writer thinks that one cannot think that . . .)
. . . to kangae-uru no dewa nai ka	Isn't it perhaps possible to think that . . . ? (The writer thinks it is possible to think that . . .)
. . . to kangaerareru (POTENTIAL*) no dewa nai dearō ka* or: *. . . to kangaeru koto ga dekiru no dewa nakarō ka*	Wouldn't it be possible that one could think that . . . ? (The writer thinks that one can think that . . .)

These expressions can be further qualified by *to omou*, "to think that . . . " *to omowareru* (SPONT) "Somehow it feels as if one can think that . . . " and by other idiomatic expressions given in the next section.

. . . to kangaeru koto ga dekiru no dewa nakarō ka to omowareru.	Somehow it feels as if it may be that it is possible to think that . . .

⇨ Note that in actual practice, most of these expressions are translated relatively simply, by means of "perhaps" or "one might think that . . . " or else omitted completely. The important thing is to be clear about—and the context helps here—is whether the force of the expression is affirmative or negative.

14.2 Other Endings that can be attached to the Predicate

The following auxiliaries express a simpler indirectness or sense of uncertainty:

. . . kamoshirenai "perhaps/maybe . . ."

Sensō ga okoru kamoshirenai.	There may be a war.

... *yō da* (colloquial equivalent: *mitai da*) "it seems that ..."

Chūkintō no jōsei ga kinpaku shite-kita. Sensō ga okoru yō da.	The situation in the Middle East has intensified. It seems that a war may break out.

... *sō da*, I hear that ... ,, I understand that ...

Nyūsu ni yoruto sensō ga okoru sō da.	According to the news (I understand/hear that) a war is going to break out.

V-stem + *sō da* "it looks as if ..." (through direct observation):

Jōkyō ga akkashite-kita. Ima ni mo sensō ga okori-sō da.	The situation has worsened. It looks as if a war is going to break out at any moment.

(through indirect information or judgment:) ... *rashii* "it seems that ..."

Nyūsu ni yoruto sensō ga okoru rashii.	According to the news it seems that a war is going to break out.

The following expressions are used rhetorically as "assertion softeners":

Negative + *koto wa nai* "it is not that ... not (= it is possible that ...)"

Kakusensō ga okoranai koto wa nai.	It is not that a nuclear war is not going to take place.

Negative + *demo nai* "it may after all be possible to ... (if one tries)"

Umaku yotei o tatereba Nyūyōku made ikenai demo nai.	It may after all be possible for me to go as far as New York if I plan well.

. . . to (ieba)* ienai koto wa/mo nai "it may be possible after all to say (if I may say so) . . . "

> * The *-ba* form is often omitted in this construction.

Amerika to kurabeta toki Nihon de wa jinshu sabetsu ga hotondo nai to ieba ienai koto mo nai.	It may be possible after all to say (if I may say so) that there is hardly any racial problem in Japan by comparison with the U. S.

. . . to itte mo sashitsukaenai dearō or: *. . . to itte mo yoi dearō* "it may be all right to say that . . . "

Sekai keizai no jidai dearu imaya kakusensō wa mohaya okori-enai to itte mo sahitsukaenai dearō.	Now that we are in the era of a global economy, it may be all right to say that nuclear war is no longer possible.
Josei no chingin no mondai o hajime (toshite) Nihon no josei kaihō no michi wa mada mada tōi to itte mo sahitsukaenai dearō.	Quite apart from the issue of (lower) wages for women, it may be all right to say that women's liberation in Japan still has a long way to go.

Note that even emphatic expressions can take the above endings to soften the statement:

N + ni hokanaranai ("it is precisely") *(mono) to ieyō* "It may be possible to say that . . . is precisely . . . "

Nihon ga busshitsushugi no heigai ni kurushimi-hajimeta no wa Nihon no dentō-teki na kachi no keishō ga sengo umaku okonawarenakatta kara ni hokanaranai to ieyō.	It may be possible to say that the reason why Japan began to suffer from the ills of materialism was precisely that traditional Japanese values were not properly transmitted after the war.

. . . ni chigainai ("it is certain that") *(mono) to itte mo sashitsukaenai dearō* or: *. . . ni chigainai (mono) to omowareru* (= spontaneous form) "It may be all right to say that it is certain that . . . " (See the example above.)

| *... ni chigainai to itte mo sashitsukaenai dearō to omowareru.* | Somehow it seems that we can think that it is all right to say that it is certain that ... |

Here are some more expressions showing different degrees of the writer's commitment to the certainty of the assertion:

... to ii-uru	one can say that ..., it is possible to say that ...
... to ieru	one can say that ...
... to ieba ieru	(if one tries) one may be able to say that ...
... to ieba ienai koto wa/mo nai	(if one tries) it's not impossible to say that ...
... to iu koto ga dekiru	one can say that ...
... to iwarete-iru	it has been said that ..., it is said that ...
... to mieru	it appears that ...
... to omowareru/kangaerareru	somehow (it seems that) one can think that ...
... to omowarete-iru	it is / has been thought that ...
... to sarete-iru	it is / has been considered as ...
... to mirarete-iru	it is / has been seen/considered as ...
... to minasarete-iru	it is / has been regarded as ...
... to mitomerate-iru	it is / has been seen/recognized as ...

The following four expressions can be added to any of the above. For example: *... to ieru*

| + *dearō ka* | I wonder whether one can say that ... |

+ *no dewa nai dearō/ darō ka* or: *no de wa nakarō ka*	I think one can say that . . .
+ *yō da/rashii*	It seems that one can say that . . .
+ *kamoshirenai*	Perhaps one can say that . . .

. . . *to ieyō*	one may be able to say that . . .
. . . *to iu ki ga suru*	I have a feeling that . . . , it seems to be that . . .
. . . *to ka kiita*	I have heard that . . . (or something to that effect)

Appendix

1. IDIOMATIC EXPRESSIONS 307

2. IDIOMS USING *-TE* FORMS

    2.1 Idiomatic Phrases 337

    2.1 Idiomatic Constructions 342

3. COMPOUNDS USING V-STEM

    3.1 V-stem + V 345

    3.2 Other V-stem Compounds and Phrases 359

4. GRAMMAR LISTS

    4.1 Transitive/Instransitive Verb-Pairs 362

    4.2 *-i* (Vowel) Verbs 365

    4.3 Momentary Verbs 369

    4.4 Adjectival Nouns 371

    4.5 Conjunctions 377

5. OLD KANA 379

1. Idiomatic expressions

The lists that follow are by no means exhaustive. I have simply tried to include the more common idiomatic expressions that tend to obstruct reading comprehension when they are not known.

The following signs are used in entries under idiomatic expressions:

[ ] Clause

[-ka] Interrogative Clause

( ) Items enclosed in parentheses are optional elements.

Most of the constructions involving such particles as *ni* or *to* are listed under the respective particles rather than under other elements in the expression.
 For constructions involving-*V-te* forms, see § 2.

A

[ ] **aida** and [ ] **aida ni**. See ch. 1, § 3.1.1A.

X mo **arō ni** "of all X, (the worst) . . ."

Basho mo arō ni hannin wa jitaku de taiho sareta.	The culprit was arrested at—of all places—his own home.
Hito mo arō ni sabotta kurasu no kyōshi ni dekuwashita.	I ran into—of all people—the teacher of the class I skipped.

aru + *N* "a certain N" (not to be confused with the plain form as a predicate) — as in, *aru toki, aru tokoro ni* "at a certain time, in a certain place"

aruiwa (ADV) "perhaps, possibly"

A **aruiwa** *B* "A or B"

X ni **atai** *suru* "deserve X"

Kare no kono bunya e no kōken wa shōsan ni ataisuru.	His contribution to this field well deserves praise.

atakamo . . . *(ka no) gotoku* "as if . . ."

(*V-ta*) **ato de**. See ch. 1, § 3.1.1A.

B

-ba. See ch. 1, § 3.2.1.

[ ] **baai** (ni) "in the case of . . ." See ch. 1, § 3.1.1A.

baai ni yotte	according to the circumstances

A **bakari ka** *B mo*, *A* **bakari de naku** *B mo*, or *A* **nominarazu** *B mo* "not only A but also B"

For **bakari**, see ch. 4, § 12.1D.

V-ru **beki** *da* "one should do . . ."

V-ru **beku** "in order to do . . ."

C

. . . **chigainai**. See *ni chigainai*.

X o **chūshin** *to suru* "to take X as the center"

Kono mondai o chūshin toshite giron o susumeyō.	Let us proceed with our discussion, making this the central issue.

D

dake and **dake ni**. See ch. 4, § 12.1A.

N/AN/V-plain no + **de mo** *nan de mo nai* "it's just nothing, not even . . ."

Nyūin to itte mo shujutsu o suru no de mo nan de mo nai. Kensa dake da.	Even though it's hospitalization, it's not even for an operation. It's just for a test.

For ADJs: *ADJ-ku mo nan to mo nai* "not in the least . . ."

Chūsha wa itaku mo nan to mo nai.	The injection isn't painful in the least.

X **de wa/mo** *arumai shi* "because one can hardly be X"

Kodomo de mo arumai shi sonna ni itsumade mo nakanaide.	Don't keep crying like that since you're hardly a child.

Negative **de mo nai**. See ch. 4, § 14.2.

N/AN or V/ADJ-plain-no **de wa naku(te)** "it is not (that) . . . and/but . . ."

Sango wa kōbutsu de wa nakute seibutsu da.	Coral isn't a mineral but rather something living.

N/AN (na) or V/ADJ-plain + **dokoro** *de wa nai* "too . . . to (do) . . ."

Isogashikute shokuji/taberu dokoro de wa nai.	I am too busy to eat.

N/AN (na)/V-plain + **dokoro** *ka* "not only . . . but moreover"

Isogashikute shokuji/taberu dokoro ka neru hima sae nai.	I am so busy that I not only have no time to eat but moreover no time to sleep.

V-e **do mo** *V-e* **do mo** = *V-te mo V-te mo*. See ch. 4, § 13.

[*-ka* **dō** *ka*]. See [**-ka** *dō ka*], below.

E

V-(a)zaru o **enai** See **zaru** *o enai*.

*V-stem-***eru/uru**. See below, § 3.1C.

F

[   ] **furi** *o suru* "pretend . . ."

G

*ADJ-***garu**. See ch. 4, § § 2.6 and 2.7.

V-stem **gatai** "hard/difficult to do . . ." See below, § 3.2.

*ADJ-***ge** *da* "look as if . . ." See ch. 4, § 4.1.2.

N(TIME) or *V-ru* **goto** *ni* "every time/whenever . . ."

nichiyō goto ni	every Sunday
Kodomo wa au goto ni ōkiku natte-iru.	Every time I see the child he is bigger.
Kashita okane o kaesu yō ni kare ni au goto ni saisoku suru.	I urge him to pay back the money I loaned him every time I see him.

V-ru (ga) **gotoki** + *N* "such a *N* as to . . . "

Shūwai o ukeru ga gotoki seiji ka wa kibishiku basserareru beki dearu.	Politicians who take bribes should be severely punished.

N no or *V-ru (ga)* **gotoku** "like/as . . ."

ijō/ika no gotoku	as above / as follows

gyaku *ni (iu to)* "conversely, (speaking) from another point of view"

(*X no*) **gyaku** *ni* "in contrast to X, opposite X"

H

X (o) **hajime** *(toshite)* "not to speak of X, including X, from X on"

Jon no uchi de wa chichioya o hajime zen'in ga dai no shinnichi ka da.	In John's family the whole family, including his father, are enthusiastically pro-Japanese.

[ ] **hanmen** *(de)* "on the one hand . . . , on the other hand"

Bunmei ga shinpo suru hanmen ningen no kokoro no mondai wa izen toshite kaiketsu sare nai mama ni nokotte-iru.	On the one hand civilization advances, and yet the issue of the human soul remains unresolved.

V-ru ga **hayai** *ka* "as soon as . . ." (Syn. *V-ru ya inaya)*

[ ] **hazu** *da* "is supposed to . . ."

[ ] **hazu**/*wake ga nai* "it cannot be that . . . , there is no way that . . ."

V-ō to shita **hazumi** *ni* "just as one did . . ." See ch. 4, § 8.3G.

dō shita **hazumi** *ka* "by some chance"

rei o **hiku** *(ageru)* "give an example"

X ni/to **hitoshii** "is equal to X" (but *to onaji* "the same as"; *to chigau* "different from") (See also ch. 4, § 8.3C.)

hitotsu *ni wa* "for one thing"

[ ] **hodo/kurai** "so . . . that . . . , to the extent that . . ." See ch. 1, § 3.1.1A.

[ ] **hodo** *no koto wa nai* "it is not such (=so serious) that one needs to . . ."

Kono kurai no kega nara byōin e iku hodo no koto wa nai.	With this kind of injury it isn't necessary to go into hospital.

N/AN deareba or *V/ADJ-ba* + same word repeated in plain form + **hodo** "the more . . . the more . . ."

Muzukashikereba muzukashii hodo yari-gai ga aru.	The harder it is, the more worthwhile it is to do it.

V-ru (yori) **hoka** *nai.* See below, **igai** *(ni) nai.*

X ni **hokanaranai** "is precisely X, must be X"

V-ta* **hō** *ga ii* "you'd better do . . ."

Kaze o hiite-iru nara suibun o ōku totta-hō ga ii.	You'd better take lots of liquids if you have a cold.

* For a negative suggestion or advice *V-nai* is used.

Byōki ga mada naotte-inai kara dekakenai hō ga ii.	You'd better not go out since you aren't well yet.

V₁-ru **hō** *ga V₂-ru(or V₁-nai) yori (ii)* "(is better) to do V₁ than V₂ (or not do V₁)"

Gaikokugo wa kaku yori hanasu hō ga yasashii.	It's easier to speak foreign languages than to write them.

I

igai *ni* "unexpectedly"

X **igai** "other than X"

N or *V-ru/nai* + **igai** *(ni) nai* or *(yori)hoka nai* "have no choice but to . . ."

Kō nattara honnin ni chokusetsu kiku igai ni nai (or . . . kiku yori hoka nai).	Since the situation has become this serious, the only thing left is to ask the person directly.

N or *V-te* + **igo** "after, since . . ."

N **ijō** "more than . . ."

sore ijō	more than that
futsuka ijō	two days or more

Cf. *Ijō . . .* "as stated above"; *Ijō da* "That's all."

[   ] **ijō** "since, now that . . ."

Nihon no rieki ni kakawaru ijō Nihon wa kono koto ni kainyū sezaru o enai.	Since it has to do with Japanese interests, Japan cannot help intervening in this matter.
Kono himitsu o shitta ijō ikashite wa okenai.	Now that you know this secret (we) cannot let you live.

N **ika** "below . . ." " . . . and less"

V-te wa **ikenai.** See ch. 4, § 13C.

[ka] **inaka** "**whether or not . . .**"

X **inai** "within X"

([ ]) **imaya** "now, now that"

V-ru ya **inaya.** See *V-ru ga* **hayai** *ka.*

([ ]) **ippō** *(de wa)* "while on the one hand . . ." or "at the same time . . ." (*Tahō (de wa)* . . . "On the other hand . . .")
　　See ch. 3, § 8.2.

N or *V-te* **irai** "since (doing) . . ." See also below § 2.2.

to **iwan** *bakari ni.* See below, **to** *iwan bakari ni.*

([ ]) **izen** *(ni)* "before . . ."

izureniseyo or **izurenishiro**, "in any case, in either case" (*izure* "which, which of the two; one of these days")

J

X **jō** = *X no ue de* "in X, from the viewpoint of X, in terms of X": *rekishi jō* "in history"

K

[**ka dō ka**] "whether or not . . ."

[**ka**] **no yō na/ni** "(almost) as if . . ."

Hajimete mita yuki wa utsukushiku, marude otogi no kuni ni kita ka no yō ni kanjirareta.	The first time I saw snow it was so beautiful that it felt as if I were in a fairyland.

[**ka] to omou to** "just as one thinks (that something happens), then . . ."

Kaminari ga natta ka to omou to ame ga furidashita.	Just as I thought I heard thunder it began to rain.

N$_1$/AN$_1$/ADJ$_1$/V$_1$-plain **ka to omou to** (or **omoeba**) + N$_2$/AN$_2$ *dattari suru*, ADJ$_2$-*kattari (mo) suru* or V$_2$-*tari (mo) suru* "sometimes things are one way (or one does one thing) and other times they are a different way (or one does something else)"

Sensei wa Nihonjin ka to omou to Amerikajin dattari suru.	The teachers may be Japanese or Americans.
Kare wa ocha o tanoshimu ka to omoeba futtobōru mo shi-tari suru.	While he enjoys tea ceremony, he also does things like playing football.
Hon o yonde-iru hito ga iru ka to omou to hanashite-iru hito mo iru.	There are some people who are reading books while there are others who are talking.
Kare wa kurasu e kuru ka to omou to konakattari suru.	Sometimes he comes to class, and sometimes he doesn't.

[   ] *to wa* **kagiranai.** See below, **to wa** *kagiranai.*

X **kagiri** "only (for), from, as of"

kondo kagiri	(for) this time only
tōka kagiri de yameru	to resign as of the tenth (of the month)
ichinichi kagiri no seeru	one-day sale
Sono hi kagiri de oni wa sugata o keshita	From that day on, the ogre has not been seen.

[   ] **kagiri** "as long as . . ." See ch. 1, § 3.1.1A.

N no **kagiri** *de wa*   "as long as . . ." or "as far as . . . is concerned, according to"

Kesa no happyō no kagiri de wa sore wa hakkiri shite-inai.	As far as this morning's announcement is concerned, it is not clear.

N or *V-ru/nai (no)* + **ni kagiru**   "be the best thing (to do)" See also ch. 4, § 8.10.

Samui toki wa sake o nomu ni kagiru.	When the weather is cold, the best thing is to drink sake.

. . . **ni mo kakawarazu**   *See* **ni** *mo kakawarazu.*

kamoshirenai. See ch. 4, § 14.2.

kanarazushimo + Negative   "not always, not necessarily" See also ch. 4, § 11.3.

X to **kankei** *ga aru*   "be related to X, be connected to X"

[   ] **kankei** *ni tatsu*   "be related insofar as . . ."

[   ] **kankei** *jō/de*   "in connection with, because of, due to . . ."

X ni **kanshin** *o motsu*   "be interested in X"

X ni **kansuru** *N*   "N regarding X"

sekai heiwa ni kansuru kaigi	a conference on world peace

X **kara**   "from, since"

X **kara shite**   See below, § 2.1.

V-te **kara**   "since, after doing . . ." (Be careful to distinguish this from *V-ta kara:* REASON.) See also ch. 1, § 3.2.2.

[   ] **kara**   "because . . ."

[   ] **kara** *koso*   "precisely because"

[   ] **kara** *ni wa*   "now that . . . , since/once . . ." or "precisely because . . ."

| *Yakusoku suru kara ni wa (= kagiri) mamoru.* | As long as I make a promise, I will keep it. |

[ ] **kara** *to itte*   See below, § 2.1.

. . . *ni* **karande**   "in connection with . . ."

kari *ni . . . toshite*   "supposing that . . ."

[ ] **kashira**.   "I wonder if . . ."   (female speech style)

[ ] **kawari** *ni*   "instead of doing . . ."

X no **kawari** *ni*   or: *X ni* **kawatte**   "in place of X"

N no or *V-ta* + **kekka**   "as a result of . . ."

V-ru **ki** *ga aru*   "have the intention of doing . . ."

N ni **ki** *ga aru*   "be interested in something, take a fancy to (a person)"

[ ] **kirai** *ga aru*   "tend to do . . ."

koso   See ch. 4, § 12.2A.

V-reba **koso**   "all the more because . . ."

V-te **koso**   See below, § 2.2.

X no **koto**   "a matter of/about X, things about X"

X to Y *o* **koto** *ni suru*   "differ from X with respect to Y"

[A] (*toiu*) **koto** *wa* [B] (*toiu*) **koto** *dearu*.   "(The fact) that A means that B."

[ ] **koto** *ga aru*   "there are times when . . ." "sometimes . . ."

V-ta **koto** *ga aru*   "have the experience of having done . . ."

V-ru **koto** *ga dekiru*   "can do, be able to do"

V-ru **koto** *(mo) naku*   "without doing . . ."

ADJ, AN na, V-ta + **koto** *ni (wa)*   [EMPHASIS: contrary to what one would expect]

omoshiroi koto ni wa	interestingly
fushigi na koto ni	strangely
odoroita koto ni	to [my] surprise

[   ] *(toiu)* **koto** *ni naru*   "it is decided that . . ."

Kyōshitsu de wa tabako o sutte wa ikenai (toiu) koto ni natte-iru.	It has been decided that there will be no smoking in the classroom.

V-ru/nai **koto** *ni shite-iru*   "to have made it a practice to / not to . . ."

Maiasa taisō o suru koto ni shite-iru.	I have made it a rule to do exercise every morning.

V-ru/nai **koto** *ni suru*   "decide to / not to . . ."

Kotoshi wa Nihon e ikanai koto ni shita.	I decided not to go to Japan this year.

V-ta **koto** *ni suru*   "pretend that (one did . . .)"

Kono koto wa nakatta koto ni shiyō.	Let us pretend that this didn't happen.
Ryokō shita koto ni shite sono okane o chokin shita.	I simply pretended that I went traveling and so saved the money.

(nanimo/betsu ni) V-ru (hodo no) **koto** *wa nai*   "it isn't necessary to do . . . , one shouldn't do . . ."   See above [   ] *hodo no koto wa nai* and [   ] *kara to itte* in § 2.1 below.

. . . *-ba* . . . *nai* **koto** *wa nai.* See ch. 4, § 14.2.

X ni kuraberu to   "as compared with X"

[   ] **kurai** See [   ] **hodo**.

. . . **kuse** *ni*   "in spite of doing . . ."

Kare wa yakusoku shita kuse ni konakatta.	In spite of having promised (to come) he didn't come.

X wa Y ni **kyōtsū suru**   "X is common to Y"

Gaikokugo ni yowai toiu no wa Nihonjin ni kyōtsū suru koto da.	Being weak in foreign languages is something common to Japanese people.

M

N no or *V-ru* + **ma** *mo naku* "having no time to do, without doing . . ."

Kare wa aisatsu suru ma mo naku dekaketa.	He left without having time to greet us.

TIME N or [   ] **made ni** "by such-and such a time, by the time . . ."

Niji made ni uchi e kaeru.	I will go home by two o'clock.
Fuyu ga kuru made ni kono seetaa o amiageyō.	I will finish knitting this sweater by the time winter comes.

[   ] **made ni** "to the point where . . ."

Kodomo wa hitori de yomeru made ni jōtatsu shita.	The child progressed to the point where she could read by herself.

V-ru-**mai** (1) negative volitional: *Taberu-mai.* "I will not eat it."; (2) negative tentative: *Kare wa taberu-mai.* " He probably won't eat it." (See also ch. 3, Example 53.)

*N demo/dewa aru***mai** *shi/ni* "because one is hardly . . ."

Eiga haiyū demo arumai shi sonna sangurasu nado kakenakute mo ii noni.	You're hardly a movie star, so you shouldn't wear those dark glasses.

N no, V-ru + **mama ni** "as is, as . . ."

shizen no mama ni shite-oku	leave things as natural as they are
ki ga muku mama ni	as one pleases
toki ga/no nagareru mama ni	as time passes

| *Naku mama ni saseta.* | I left him/her weeping. |

(*moshi*) **mangaichi** + hypothetical. See ch. 1, § 3.2.1.

A **mata wa** *B* "A or B" (Syn. *aruiwa*)

. . . *mo* **mata** "also"

| *Kore mo mata machigai da.* | This, too, is an error. |

N no/AN na, ADJ or [ ] *toiu* + **me** *ni au* "come across a circumstance such that"

| *Densha ga konde-ite hidoi me ni atta.* | I had a terrible time because the train was so crowded. |
| *Enjin no koshō de kinai de nijikan mo matasareru toiu me ni atta.* | It so happened that I had to wait inside the plane for as long as two hours due to engine trouble. |

X o **megutte** "concerning X"

. . . *to* **mieru** "it seems, apparently"

| *Jon wa gakkō e ikanakatta to mieru.* | Apparently John didn't go to school. |

Compare with:

| *Jon wa Nihonjin* **no yō ni mieru**. | John looks like a Japanese. |
| *Jon wa Nihonjin* **ni mieru**. | John looks (as if he really is) Japanese. |

A o B to **minasu** or [ ] *(mono) to* **minasu** "regard/consider A as B"

| *Kono kotae o seikai to minasu.* | I will consider this answer correct. |
| *Kijitsu made ni henji ga nai baai wa kore ni sanka shinai (mono) to minasu.* | In case there is no reply by the due date we will take it that (the person) is not going to participate. |

. . . **mitai** *da* = *yō da* "seems, looks as if . . . , as/like . . ."

[   ] **mitōshi** *da* "the prospect is that . . ."

Idioms with **mo** (see also ch. 4, § 5.3.2):

Ichi mo ni mo naku hikiuketa.	I undertook it without a moment's hesitation.
Mukashi mo ima mo hito no kokoro wa kawaranai.	Past or present, human feelings never change.
Jon wa nihongo mo benkyō sureba chūgokugo mo benkyō suru.	(It is impressive that) John studies not only Japanese but also Chinese.
ne mo ha mo nai uwasa	groundless rumor
mie mo gaibun mo nai	have no pretentions whatsoever
Sonna koto wa itaku mo kayuku mo nai.	That kind of thing doesn't bother me a bit.

Interrogative + **mo** repeated: "every, any . . ."

Sono koto wa dare mo kare mo (ga) shitte-iru.	Anybody knows about it.
Doko mo kashiko mo gomi darake da.	There is rubbish everywhere.
Nani mo ka mo ushinatta.	He lost everything.

V-te **mo**, *V-nakute* **mo** or *V-naku to* **mo**. See ch. 4, § 13 and below § 2.2.

ADJ-ku **mo**, and *ADV/AN* + *ni* **mo:** see ch. 4, § 5.3.2F.

mono See ch. 4, § 9.

[   ]**mono no** See ch. 4, § 9.6.

A **moshiku** *wa B* "A or B"

N no **moto** *de/ni* "under the guidance of N"

Yamada sensei no shidō no moto de/ni kenkyū o tsuzuketa.	I continued my research under the guidance of Professor Yamada.

Asuka bunka wa bukkyō no eikyō no moto ni hanahiraita.	Asuka culture flourished under the influence of Buddhism.

(*aruiwa*) **mushiro** "or rather"

A ya B ya C **nado** "A, B, C, and so on"

[ ] **nado** *to wa (yume ni mo) omowanai* "not even dream of doing . . ."

Kare ga hannin da nado to wa yume ni mo omowanakatta.	I didn't even dream of his being the culprit.
Ichinichi de sonna ni takusan no kanji o oboeyō nado to wa omowanai.	I wouldn't dream of trying to memorize that many kanji in a day.

X **nado** (derogatory) "such a thing as X"

Omocha no kuruma nado hoshikunai.	I don't want such a thing as a toy car.

N or *V/ADJ-plain* + **nado/nante** *V-ru mono ka* "would ever do such a thing as . . . ?"

Teki no enjo o nado (dare ga) ukeru mono ka.	Who would do such a thing as accept help from one's enemy?
Kare ga tadashii nado to dare ga omou mono ka.	Who could ever think that he is right?

V-stem + **nagara**. See ch. 4, § 2.6.

N/AN, ADJ/V-stem **nagara mo** "even though"

Kare wa kodomo nagara mo marason o kansō shita.	Even though he is a child he finished the marathon.

See ch. 4, § 2.6 for examples with V-stem.

*V-***naide** "without doing something" (See ch. 1, § 3.2.2) (Syn. *V-zu ni*)

A **naishi** *B* "A or B"

X no **naka** *de wa* "among X"

nan *to itte mo* "after all"

nani wa tomokaku/*tom(o)are*/*sateoki* "anyhow, in any case, nevertheless"

Nani wa tomoare kanpai!	Anyhow, cheers!

[ ] **nara** See ch. 1, § 3.1.3.

N_1/AN_1 or V_1/*ADJ-plain* + **nara** N_1/AN_1 or V_1-plain + *de* "if one does / it is . . . at all"

Iya nara iya de hajime kara sō ieba yokatta.	If you don't like it at all, you should have said so from the beginning.
Ayamaru nara ayamaru de hayaku shita hō ga ii.	If you are to apologize at all, you should do so soon.

A **narabi ni** *B* "A and B"

. . . *to* **narabi**/*heikō shite* "as well as, in parallel with"

N/*AN* **nari** : classical equivalent of the copula *da*/*dearu*.

V-ru/*ta* **nari** "as soon as . . ."

Kare wa koko e tsuku nari denwa o kake-hajimeta.	As soon as he got here he began calling (people).

iu/*iwareru*/*meirei-sareru* **nari** *ni naru* "do as (one is) told/ordered to"

V_1-*ru* **nari** V_2-*ru* **nari** "(do something) such as V_1 or V_2"

Wakaranakereba jibun de shiraberu nari sensei ni kiku nari shitara ii.	If you don't understand you should do things like looking it up on your own or asking the teacher.

N/*AN ni* **naru** or *ADJ-ku* **naru**. See ch. 4, § 7.4D.

ni and *X* **ni** *V*. See ch. 4, § 7.

V-stem **ni** V(the same V repeated)-*ru* "do something excessively"

make ni makeru	be totally defeated

V-ru (no) **ni** "in order to do . . ." See ch. 4, § 7.5B.

V-ru **ni** V-negative-potential "be unable to do something (due to the circumstances)"

| *hiku ni hikenai* | cannot withdraw (due to the circumstances) |
| *iu ni iwarenu** | indescribable |

> * *-nu* = *-nai*; see ch. 4, § 2.1.

[　] ni chigainai "it is certain that . . . , it must be that . . ."

| *Kare wa hontō no koto o itta ni chigainai.* | It is certain that he told the truth. |

X **ni itaru** "reach X" See ch. 4, § 7.4A.

V-ru **ni itaru** "reach the point where, end up doing . . ."

| *Nihon wa chūgoku-tairiku o shinryaku suru ni itatta.* | Japan ended up invading the Chinese continent. |

N or *V-stem* **ni kakaru** or **torikakaru** "take up, begin" See ch. 4, § 7.12.

[　] **ni koshita** *koto wa nai* "it would be best if . . ."

V-ō **ni mo** + V-negative potential "be unable to do something no matter how much one may try"

| *Yoyaku ga ippai de, kippu o torō ni mo torenai.* | It is all booked, so no matter how much I try I can't get a ticket. |

[　*] **nimokakawarazu** "nevertheless, in spite of . . ." See ch. 1, § 3.1.3.

> * The *dearu* can be omitted from *N/AN dearu*.

[　] **ni** (**mo**) *seyo* "even if"

o-V-stem **ni naru** : honorific form of the verb; see ch. 4, § 7.11.
　　Humble form is *o-V-stem suru*.

X **ni okeru** + *N* "N at/in X"

V-ru **ni oyobi**. See *oyobi*.

A **ni seyo/shiro** *B* **ni seyo/shiro** "regardless of A or B"

[ ] **ni seyo** [ ]* **ni seyo** "regardless of whether one does something or not"

Iku ni seyo ikanai ni seyo hayaku shiraseta hō ga ii.	Regardless of whether you go or not, you'd better let (them) know.

* The second clause is often negative.

X **ni seyo/shiro/shitemo** or *X* **ni shita tokoro de** : expresses the moderate degree or quality of X, contrary to expectation:

(Nihon o yoku shitte-iru to iwareru) Jon ni shita tokoro de ichinen Nihon ni sunda ni suginai.	Even John (who is said to know Japan very well) has only lived in Japan for a year.

N or *V/ADJ-plain* **ni shita tokoro de** or *V-ta/V-te mita tokoro de* + Negative "even though it is or one does . . ."

Iinchō ni shita tokoro de ii an o motte-iru wake de wa nai.	Even the chairman doesn't have a good plan.
Shiken no mae no ban ni awatete benkyō shita tokoro de dō ni mo naranai.	Even if one studies the night before the exam, nothing can be done (= no good result is expected).

X **ni shite** See below, § 2.1.

[ ] **ni suginai** "merely . . ."

ni suru. See ch. 4, § 7.4D.

X **ni te o yaku** "be troubled about X"

Shi wa hikōshōnen no taisaku ni te o yaite-iru.	The city is troubled about what to do with juvenile delinquents.

ni umareru. See ch. 4, § 7.2C.

V-ru **ni wa** *V (the same verb)-(r)u/ta* **ga** "one does something anyway, but . . ."

Sono hito ni au ni wa au ga yatou to wa kagiranai.	I will see the person anyway, but it doesn't mean that I'll hire him.

V-ru **ni wa** *oyobanai* "not be necessary to do . . ."

Sonna koto wa ayamaru ni wa oyobanai.	You don't have to apologize for such a thing.

V-ru **ni wa** *shinobinai* "not have the heart to do . . ."

Teki no mono to wa ie sonna chiisana kodomo wa korosu ni wa shinobinai.	Even though he belongs to our enemy, it would be unthinkable to kill such a small child.

X **ni yoru to** "according to"

X **ni yotte** *naritatsu* "consist of X"

V-stem **nikui** "hard/difficult to do . . ." See below, § 3.2.

node. See ch. 1, § 3.1.3.

no de wa *naku(te)*. See **de wa** *naku(te)*

nomi. See ch. 4, § 12.1B

A **nominarazu** *B mo* "not only A but also B" (Syn. *A bakari ka B mo*).

noni. See ch. 1, § 3.2.2.

O

PHRASES USING *V-ō*

V-ō. "will do . . ." or "probably" See ch. 4, § § 8.3G and 14.

V-ō **ga nai** "there is no way of doing . . ."

V-ō **mono nara** See ch. 4, § 9.5.

V-ō **ni/to mo** + Negative. See above, *V-ō* **ni mo** and ch. 4, § 8.3G.

[*-ka*] *to* **omou** *to*. See [   ]-**ka** *to omou to*

[   ] *to* **omowareru** "it seems that, somehow it makes me feel that." See also ch. 4, § 2.3.2 for the spontaneous form of verbs.

[   ] **osore** *ga aru* "there is a possibility that (something negative happens)"

V-ru **ni** *(wa/mo)* **oyobanai** "not be necessary to . . ."

A **oyobi** B "A and B"

N or *V-ru* **ni oyobi**/*oyonde* "when it comes to the point of . . ."

tabidatsu ni oyobi	upon leaving for a trip

R

TIME **+ rai** "since . . ." or "for these . . ."

sakunen-rai	since last year
koko jūnenrai	for these ten years

N/AN or *V-plain* **+ rashii** "it seems to be (that) . . ."; see also ch. 4, § 14.

Y o X no **rei ni** *ageru* "give Y as an example of X"

[X] *toiu no wa* [Y] *toiu* **riyū** *kara dearu* "The reason for X is that Y"

S

. . . **sae** (*V-ba* . . .) See ch. 4, § 12.2.

V-te-iru **saichū** *ni* "in the midst of doing . . ."

V-ta ga **saigo** "once one does something (that's the end of it)"

Jigoku wa ochita ga saigo kaerenai.	As for hell, once you fall in it's impossible to come back.

N or *V-ta no* **+ o saigo ni** "after . . . ," "since . . ."

Kashu wa sono risaitaru o saigo ni intai shita.	The singer retired after that recital.

. . . *to* **sareru** "it is considered/assumed that . . ." (passive of . . . *to suru* "consider/suppose that . . .")

Henji o shinakereba kyanseru shita mono to sareru.	It will be assumed that you have cancelled unless you reply.

N no or [ ] **sei** *da* "due/owing to, because of"

Taifū no sei de densha ga okureta.	Owing to the typhoon, trains were delayed.

[ ] **sei** *ka* "perhaps due to . . ."

Kibishiku shikatta sei ka kodomo wa totemo otonashikatta.	Perhaps due to my severe scolding the child was very quiet.

V_1-*ru* **shi** V_2-stem *mo suru* "not only do . . . but also do . . ."

(Negative: V_1-*nai* **shi** V_2-stem *mo shinai*)

. . . **shika.** See ch. 4, § 12.1E.

ADJ-kute or *V-takute* **shikata ga nai/tamaranai/yarikirenai** "be unbearable, unable to stand (owing to a condition or desire)"

Nemukute tamaranai.	I'm unbearably sleepy.
Kuruma ga hoshikute/kaitakute tamaranai.	I am dying to get a car.

V-**shimeru** (= -*(s)aseru*). See ch. 3, § 1.1.4, Example 8, note 4.

X ni **shiro/seyo/shitemo.** See above, *X* **ni seyo.**

to **shitara** See ch. 1, § 3.2.1.

. . . **shite** See below, § 2.1.

N mo **sokosoko** *ni* "hurriedly, hardly having time for N"

Kare wa aisatsu mo sokosoko ni shuppatsu shita.	He left in such a hurry that he hardly had time to greet them.

AN or *V/ADJ-stem* **sō da.** See ch. 4, § 4.1.2.

[ ] **sō** *da* "I hear that . . . , they say that . . ." See ch. 4, § 14.2.

... *ni* **sotte**   See ... *ni* **sokushite** in § 2.1 below.

N or *V-ru ni* **suginai**   "merely/simply, no more than"

AN or *V/ADJ-stem* **sugiru**   "too much, excessively"   See ch. 4, § 2.4.2C, and below, § 3.1C.

sukoshi *mo* + negative   "not ... at all"

X ga **sukunaku nai**   "there are many X's"

X **sura**   See ch. 4, § 12.2.

to **sureba**   See ch. 1, § 3.1.3, *to* **suru to**.

ni **suru**   See ch. 4, § 7.4D.

to **suru**   See ch. 4, § 8.3E.

to **suru to**   See ch. 1, § 3.1.3.

T

N no or [   ] **tabi** *ni*   "every time that ..." (Syn. *goto ni*)

X no **tagui** *(no mono)*   "(a thing) of X kind/sort"

Anna tagui no ningen to wa tsukiai-takunai.	I don't want to associate with that sort of person.

X to **taihi** *suru*   "to contrast/compare with X" (*X to no* **taihi** "a contrast with X")

X ni **taisuru**   "to oppose X" or "regarding X"

[   ] **tame** *ni*   "for the purpose of, in order to, for the sake of" and "because of, due to the fact that"

[X] *toiu no/koto wa* [Y] ***tame*** *dearu*.   "It is due to Y that X." or "X is for the purpose of Y."

tamaranai.   See **shikata** *ga nai*.

-**tara.**   See ch. 1, § 3.2.1.

N **tarashimeru**   "cause someone/something to be ..." (literary)

V_1-**tari** V_2-**tari**   "do things such as V_1 and V_2"   See ch. 1, § 3.2.2 and ch. 4, § 2.6.

(ikani/ikura/donna ni/nando) + *V-***te mo**. See ch. 1, § 3.2.1.

*V-***te mo** *V-***te mo**. See ch. 4, § 13.

*V-***te** For more expressions with *V-te*, see ch. 4, § 2.5 and below § 2.

X o **tegakari** *ni (shite)* "with X as a clue (to go on)"

. . . **teido**/*gurai da* (derogative) "be limited to . . ."

Kare no yamanobori no keiken to itte mo daigaku jidai ni Nihon Arupusu o nobotta teido da.	His mountaineering experience is limited to his having climbed in the Japan Alps when he was a college student.

*X-***teki** *ni wa* "from the perspective of X"

seijiteki ni wa	politically (speaking)

(kono) **ten** *de* "in (this) respect"

CONSTRUCTIONS WITH *TO*   See ch. 1, § § 3.1.2A and 3.1.3, and ch. 4, § 8.

tō *no N* "said N, the very N" (*tō-nin* "the very person, in person")

*CONSTRUCTIONS WITH **TOIU***

[   ] **toiu** *hanashi/koto da* (or [   ] *to no koto da)* "I understand/hear that . . . ."

[Jon wa shiken ni ukatta] **toiu hanashi*** *da* **toiu koto*** *da* **to no koto** *da*	I hear/understand that John passed the exam.

> * *Hanashi da* and *koto da* may be omitted, in which case the content of the clause is followed simply by *toiu*.

A **toiu ka** *B* "A or B"

. . . **toiu** *ki ga suru* "I have a feeling that . . . ."

. . . **toiu** *koto dake de wa* "just by the fact that . . . ."

Kijitsu made ni henji o shinai toiu dake de wa kyanseru shita koto ni naranai.	It doesn't necessarily mean that you cancelled it if you simply didn't reply by the due date.

. . . **toiu** *wake*. See ch. 4, § 11.

. . . **toiu** *yō ni* "in such a manner that . . ."

Kotoba ga wakaranakattara jibun de jisho de shiraberu toiu yō ni susunde benkyō su(ru) beki da.	One should study on one's own initiative, in such a way that one immediately consults a dictionary if there are any words one doesn't understand.

. . . **to iwan** *bakari ni* "as if to say . . ."

Onna wa mō hanasu koto nado nai to iwan bakari ni doa o batan to shimete dete-itta.	The woman slammed the door and left as if to say that there's nothing more to talk about.

. . . **to ka** See ch. 1, § 3.1.2A.

A **toka** *B* "A, B, and so on"

tokoro. See ch. 4, § 10.

. . . **to mieru** See . . . *to* **mieru**.

X **tomo** EMPHASIS:

Sannin tomo konakatta.	All three of them failed to show up.
Bengoshi tomo arō hito ga taiho sareta to wa . . .	(It is indeed a surprise that) a person who is actually a lawyer was arrested!
Yakusoku suru tomo.	(Of course) I do promise! (STRONG ASSERTION)
Tashika ni watakushi ga yarimashita tomo.	Certainly I did it!

ADJ-ku **tomo**/*(te mo)* "even if . . ." See ch. 1, § 3.2.1.

V-ru **tomo**/*towa nashi ni* "without intending to . . ."

Kiku tomo/towa nashi ni kiite-shimatta.	I happened to hear it without meaning to.

N or *V-ru to* **tomo ni** "together with, at the same time as"

tomodachi to tomo ni	with friends
Soto de katsuyaku suru to tomo ni katei de mo yoki chichioya da.	He is very active outside and at the same time is also a good father at home.
toki ga tatsu to tomo ni	as time goes on

(*nani wa*) **tomoare** or *tomare* "anyhow."

tomokaku = tonikaku "at any rate, anyway"

. . . *wa tomokaku (toshite).* See below, § 2.1, *betsu toshite.*

N or *V-plain no* + *wa* **tomokaku** *(toshite)* "leaving aside . . ."

Shiki no naiyō wa tomokaku (toshite) mazu hinichi to basho o kimeyō.	Leaving aside the content of the ceremony, let's decide on a date and place first.

N *no* or V-plain affirmative **tōri** *ni (suru)* "(do) just as . . ."

Setsumeisho no tōri ni tento o kumitateta.	I put up the tent just as the instructions say.
Kodomo wa oya no iu tōri ni shita.	The child did exactly as the parents told him.
Hokkaidō wa gaidobukku ni kaite-aru tōri ni subarashikatta.	Hokkaido was as wonderful as the guidebooks say.

X ni torikakaru. See **ni kakaru.**

. . . *(mono)* **toshite**:

a. "granted that . . ." (The speaker is doubtful, but willing to concede that the assertion might be true.)

Kakusensō ga nakunaru toiu kangae ga tadashii toshite, de wa kakuosen no mondai ni tsuite wa dō taisho shite-ittara yoi ka.	Granted that the idea that there will be no more nuclear war is valid, then how shall we deal with the problem of nuclear pollution?

b. "supposing, on the assumption that . . ."

Sobieto ga sanka shinai (mono) toshite keikaku o tateta.	We made our plans on the assumption that Russia will not participate.
[Moshi kari ni] kare ga mada ikite-iru (mono) toshite hanashi o susumeyō.	Let us proceed with our talks on the assumption that he is still alive.

N **toshite** "as N"; see also ch. 4, § 8.3E.

. . . **to shitara**/*sureba* "supposing that" or "if . . . should happen"

Kono mama chikyū ga atatakaku nari-tsuzukeru to shitara hyakunengo kaimen wa yaku nisenchi agaru darō.	If the earth continues to get warmer at this rate, sea level will have risen about two centimeters a hundred years from now.

. . . **to shite mo** "even if"

Kare ga kuru toshite mo kuji sugi ni naru darō.	Even if he comes, it will be after nine o'clock.
Kakusensō ga nakunaru toshite mo kaku osen no mondai wa nokorō (= nokoru darō).	Even if there is no more nuclear war, the problem of nuclear pollution will probably remain.

V-ta **totan** *ni* "at the moment something happened" (Syn. *V-ru to totan ni*)

V-ru to **totan**/*totsuzen ni* See ch. 1, § 3.1.3.

tōtei + negative "hardly, by no means"

   TO WA

. . . **to wa** *ie* "even though . . ."

Haru to wa ie kyō wa zuibun atatakai hi da.	Even though it is spring, it is still a warm day today.

. . . **to wa** *iu/omou mono no* "even though (one may say/think) . . ."

Haru to wa iu mono no mada zuibun samui.	Even though it is spring, it is still very cold.

. . . **to wa** *kagiranai* "it does not necessarily mean that . . ."

Kare ga un to itte mo sō suru to wa kagiranai.	Even though he says Yes, it doesn't necessarily mean that he will do it.

V-*ru* **to wa** *nashi ni* See V-*ru* **tomo**.

V-*plain* **tsuide** *ni* "taking the opportunity to . . ."

Kaimono ni itta tsuide ni tomodachi no uchi e yotta.	I stopped by at my friend's house and took the opportunity to (go on to) do some shopping.

V-*ru* **tsumori** *da* "intend to (do) . . ."

V-*ta* **tsumori** *da* or *ni naru* "pretend that (one did) . . ."

V-*ta* **tsumori** *de* + Negative "have thought that one has done . . . (but didn't)"

Doa no kagi o kaketa tsumori de, jitsu wa kakete-nakatta.	I thought I'd locked the door but in fact I hadn't.

V-stem + **tsutsu** See ch. 4, § 2.6.

U

[ ] **uchi** *ni* "while . . ." See ch. 1, § 3.1.1A.

X *no* **uchi** "in/among X"

X *no* **ue** *de* or X *jō* "in (the perspective of) X" (Syn. . . . *ni oite*)

V-*ru* **ue** *de/ni* "in/on/for doing . . ."

Amae no gainen wa nihon bunka o rikai suru ue de daiji da.	The concept of *amae* is important for understanding Japanese culture.

V-*plain* **ue** *ni* "on top of doing . . ."

Hanako wa heya o sōji shita ue ni ryōri made shite-kureta.	Hanako cooked for me on top of cleaning the room.

V-ta **ue** *de* "upon finishing doing . . ."

Jūbun kentō shita ue de kimeyō.	Let's decide after full deliberation.

X o **ukibori** *ni suru* "bring X into relief, present X clearly"

Sono shōsetsu wa Nihon no seiyōka ga motarashita mujun o ukibori ni shite-iru.	The novel clearly presents the conflicts brought about by Japan's westernization.

V-stem **uru**/*eru*. See below, § 3.1C.

W

V-stem + **wa** + *suru* See ch. 4, § 5.1.2D.

wakaru *yō ni* "as you understand if you (do) . . ."

N kara (mo) or *V-te (mo)* + **wakaru** *yō ni* "as you understand from / if you do . . ."

kono shashin kara (mo) (= o mite mo) wakaru yō ni	as you understand from (if you look at) this photograph

wake See ch. 4, § 11.

[   ] **wari** *ni* "in spite of . . ."

*toshi no **wari ni** wakai*	young for his age

Y

A **ya** *B* **nado** "A, B, and so on"

V-ru **ya (inaya)** "as soon as, immediately after"

A **yara** *B* "A, B, and so on; A or B or something like that"

yara with a repeated interrogative word linked by *ga*:

Kono bun wa muzukashikute nani ga nani yara wakaranai.	This sentence is so difficult that I can't make anything of it.

| *Kurakute dare ga dare yara miwake ga tsukanakatta.* | Since it was dark it was difficult to tell who they were. |

yarikirenai See **shikata** *ga nai.*

V-stem **yasui.** See below, § 3.2.

X no **yochi** *ga aru* "There is room for X."

[ ] **yō da/na/ni** (=*mitai da*) "it seems/looks as if . . ." See also ch. 4, § 14.2.

| *Dōzō no kao ga waratte-iru yō ni mieta.* | The face of the statue looked as if it were smiling. |

V-ru/nai **yō** *ni iu/chūi suru* "tell/warn . . . to . . ."

| *Gakusei ni chikoku shinai yō ni itta.* | I told the students not to be late for class. |

V-ru/nai **yō** *ni naru* "become, reach the point where . . ."

| *Yasashii kanji ga kakeru yō ni natta.* | I have become able to write simple Kanji. |

V-ru/nai **yō** *ni suru* "try doing . . ."

| *Mainichi taisō o suru yō ni shiteiru.* | I am trying to do exercise every day. |

. . . **yō** *ni* (at the end of an expression of a wish or prayer)

| *Tsugi no tesuto de A ga toremasu yō ni.* | Please let me get an A in the next test! |

A (= N or V/ADJ) **yori** *B (N no or V/ADJ-plain) hō ga . . .* COMPARISON: "B is larger/smaller than A"

yori ADJ/AN/ADV "more, greater degree of . . ."

N or V-ru **(yori)** *hoka/shika (ni te ga) nai* or *. . . hoka wa nai* "there is no other way than . . ." (See also *. . . igai (ni) nai*)

Akirameru yori hoka nai.	There is no choice but to give up.

X ni **yoruto.** See **ni** *yoru to*

. . . **yoshi** *da* (at the end of a sentence) "I hear/understand that . . ."

N no or *V-ru/nai* + **yotei** *da* "be scheduled to . . ."

X ni **yowai** "be poor at X"

(Sore) **yue ni** . . . "therefore . . ."

[ ] **yue ni** "because . . ." See [ ] **kara** above.

[ ]**yuen** *dearu/da* "is the reason why . . . , is how it came about that . . ."

Z

*V-***zaru o enai** "have to . . ." or "not be able to help doing . . ." (Syn. Negative + *wake ni wa ikanai.* See ch. 4, § 11.7)

Kare no yōsu ga kokkei de shitsurei da to wa omoi-nagara mo warawazaru o enakatta.	He was so funny that I couldn't help laughing, even though I knew it was rude to do so.
Yakusoku shita kara (ni wa) yukazaru o enai.	Since I promised, I must go.

. . . **zengo** "around, about . . ."

X toiu **zentei** *de* "on the assumption of X, with X as a premise"

*V-***zu** *jimai da* "end up not doing . . ."

Tōtō ikazu jimai datta.	I ended up not going after all.

*V-***zuni** or *V-zu shite*: see *V-naide*

*V-***zuni** *wa irarenai* "not be able to help doing . . ." See **zaru** *o enai,* above.

Hachi ni sasareta tokoro ga kayukute kayukute dōshite mo kakazu ni wa irarenakatta.	It was so terribly itchy where I got a bee-sting that I just couldn't help scratching.

2. Idioms using V-te forms

2.1 Idiomatic Phrases

There are quite a few expressions in Japanese that involve *V-te* forms. These should not be confused with *V-te* functioning as a component of a multiple predicate, and simply have to be learned individually.

N or [   ] (*no*) + *ni* **atatte**   "when/upon doing . . ."

Kaigi o kaisai suru no ni atatte kaku daihyō no aisatsu ga atta.	Upon the opening of the conference each representative gave a speech of welcome.

. . . *o/wa* **betsu toshite** (or . . . *tomokaku toshite*)   "quite apart from . . ."

Hiyō wa betsu toshite sonna mezurashii tokoro eno tsuā ni sanka suru hito ga iru darō ka.	Quite apart from the cost, I wonder if anyone would go on a tour to such an exotic place.

. . . *o* **fukumete**   "including . . ."

. . . *ni* **hanshite**   "in contrast to, contrary to . . ."

hatashite . . . *ka*   "is it really that . . . ?"

. . . *o* **hete**   "through, via . . ."

. . . *ni/to* **hirei shite**   "in proportion to"

Kaku chiiki no gakkōsū ni hirei shite shikin ga wariaterareru.	Funds are allotted in proportion to the number of schools in each district.

kaette "on the contrary, contrary to expectation" or "all the more"

. . . *ni* **kangamite** "in view of X"

. . . *ni* **kanshite** "regarding, about . . ."

X **kara shite** "the very X, especially X" or "even X, not to mention X"

Kono ronbun wa dai kara shite mazui.	This paper is bad, especially its title.

[ ] **kara to itte** *betsu ni/nanimo V-ru koto wa nai* "It isn't necessary to do . . . simply because . . ."

Taifū ga kuru kara to itte betsu ni kowagaru koto wa nai.	Just because a typhoon is approaching you needn't be so frightened.

karōjite "barely, narrowly"

Karōjite shi o manukareta.	I barely escaped death.

. . . *ni* **kuwaete** "in addition to . . ."

mashite . . . let alone . . .

Eigo ga dekinai. Mashite doitsugo nado tondemo nai.	I can't speak English, let alone German.

. . . *o* **megutte** "regarding, about . . ."

. . . *o* **mezashite** "aiming at . . ."

. . . *to* **miete** "apparently because . . ."

Atsui to miete kodomo wa shatsu o nuide-shimatta.	Apparently because he was hot the child took off his shirt altogether.

. . . o **moto ni shite** "based on . . ."

ima **motte** "still"

Gakusei no toki wa amari pa tto shinakatta ano otoko ga ano yō ni shusse suru to wa ima motte fushigi da.	It is still a wonder that a man who as a student was not at all outstanding became such a success.

N o **motte** "with, using"

N o **motte** *shite wa/mo* "with/using/by way of N"

*mae***motte** "beforehand, in advance"

Kai no hinichi ga kimattara maemotte shiraseru koto ni natte-iru.	We are supposed to let (people) know in advance when the meeting date is decided.

mattaku **motte** "utterly, totally"

Kodomo ga dōro ni gomi o suteru no o oya ga damatte mite iru to wa mattaku motte yurusenai.	It is quite unforgivable that the parents don't say anything when children throw trash on the road.

mazu **motte** "before all else"

Mazu motte oya ga kōshū dōtoku no mohan o miseru-beki da.	Before all else (= ahead of everyone) parents should be models in public morality.

. . . o/de **motte** "using . . . , with/in . . ."

Kirisuto wa ai o motte hito ni taisuru koto o oshieta.	Christ taught to relate to others with love.

. . . o/de **motte** *shite mo* "even with . . ."

Tsui shi-gojūnen gurai mae made wa igaku no chikara o motte shite mo haibyō kanja o tasukeru koto wa dekinakatta.	Until 40 to 50 years ago tuberculosis patients could not be saved even by the power of medical science.

. . . o **nozoite** "except for . . ."

Byōki no mono nimei o nozoite wa zen'in ga shingaku shita.	Except for the two who were ill everyone went on to the next class.

N, V-ru ni **oite** "in, at"

shakai ni oite	in society
shinri o tankyū suru ni oite	in pursuing the truth

There is a special honorific usage which shows the topic of a sentence by inserting *ni* **okarete**/*okaserarete wa* or *ni araserarete wa*:

heika ni okarete wa	his imperial highness

. . . ni **ōjite** "in proportion to, in response to, in compliance with"

Kinzoku nensū ni ōjite bōnasu ga shikyū sareru.	A bonus is provided in proportion to one's years of continuous service.

N or *V-ru ni* **shitagatte**/**tsurete** "(in proportion) as, in accordance with . . ."

Seichō suru ni shitagatte/tsurete kangaekata ga kawaru.	As one grows up one's way of thinking changes.

Shite

1. (QUANTITY of people) + **shite**

futari shite	both of them
fūfu shite	as a (married) couple
kazoku shite	the entire family
minna shite	everyone together

2. *N (kara)* **shite**. See above, **kara shite**.

3. QUANTITY (TIME) + *ni* **shite**

isshun ni **shite**	in just a moment/blink
ichiya ni **shite**	in just a night

4. *N o* **shite** *V-(a)shimeru* "make N do . . .) See ch. 3, Example 8.

5. *N ni* **shite *(kara ga)*** *(= N kara shite)* "even N"

Oya ni shite (kara ga) kō dakara kodomo ga hikōka suru no wa muri mo nai.	It is easily understood that the children become juvenile delinquents since even their parents are like this.

6. *N ni* **shite wa** . . . "not as (well) as one would expect from N"

Chanpion no Jon ni shite wa mazui shiai datta.	John did not play as well as one would expect from a champion.

7. *V-zu* **shite** = *V-naide* "without doing . . ." See *V-zuni* in § 1, above.

8. *N ni arazu* **shite** "if . . . is not N"

Kare wa gakusha ni arazu shite ittai nani de arieyō ka.	If he is not a scholar, what in the world could he be?

. . . *ni (****shite****) mo* See ch. 4, § 7.5A, and also above, § 1, . . . **ni seyo**.

. . . *ni* **sokushite**/*sotte* "going along with, in conformity with"

. . . *ni* **taishite** "regarding/opposing . . ." (See ch. 3, § 5.2.)

. . . *ni/to* **terashite** "in comparison with"

. . . *ni* **tomonatte** "(in proportion) as . . ." See . . . *ni shitagatte* above.

. . . *tomokaku* **toshite** See above, § 1, ***tomokaku*** *toshite*.

. . . *o* **tōshite** (= . . . *o* **tsūjite**) "through . . ."

Viza wa sono kuni no taishikan o tsūjite mōshikomu.	We apply for a visa through the country's embassy.
Terebi o tsūjite Nihongo o benkyō suru.	I study Japanese by [watching] television.

. . . *ni* **totte** "for . . ."

Yōji ni totte hahaoya wa sekai no chūshin da.	For a small child the mother is the center of the world.

N or [*] *(toiu) koto ni* **tsuite** "about, regarding"

> * When the predicate is *V*, *(toiu) koto* may be omitted.

ni **tsurete** See above, *ni* **shitagatte**.

. . . *ni* **watatte** "throughout . . ."

Taifū no tame (ni) kyūshū chihō ga kōhan'i ni watatte higai o uketa.	Because of the typhoon damage was sustained throughout a vast area of Kyūshū.

. . . *ni* **yori/yotte** "by, with" 'or "depending on"

Sankōsho ni yori shiraberu.	I check by/using a reference book.
Sankōsho ni yori setsumei ga chigau.	The explanation is different, depending on the reference book.

2.2 Idiomatic constructions

V-te **bakari irarenai** "one cannot just be doing . . ."

Samukute mo/samukutatte sutōbu ni atatte bakari irarenai.	Even if it's cold I can't just be hanging around the heater.

V-te **hajimete** "only if/when . . ."

Oya ga shinde hajimete sono arigatasa ga wakaru.	One becomes truly thankful for one's parents only when they die.

V-te **irai** "since"

| *Kani ni atatte irai kani ga kirai ni natta.* | Since getting food-poisoning from crab I came to dislike it. |

*V-te **kara*** "after doing . . ." (distinguish from *V-ta kara* "because")

| *Tabete kara dekakeru.* | I will go out after I eat. |

See also ch. 1, § 3.2.1.

*V-te **koso*** "only if (one does) . . ."

| *Yakusoku wa hatashite koso imi ga aru.* | Promises are meaningful only if one keeps them. |

*V-te **ma** mo nai* "not be long since . . ."

| *Kare wa koko e koshite-kite ma mo nai.* | It hasn't been long since he moved here. |

*V-te **made** suru/shite* "even to the point of . . ."

| *Kanojo wa okane o karite made shite tomodachi o tasuke-yō to shita.* | She tried to help out her friends even to the point of borrowing some money (for them). |

*V-te **mo** V-nakute **mo*** "whether one does . . . or not"

| *Sono hon wa yonde mo yomanakute mo dochira demo ii (kamawanai/kankei nai).* | It doesn't matter whether you read that book or not. |
| *Ame ga futte mo furanakute mo shiai wa okonawareru.* | Regardless of whether it rains or not the game will be played. |

For *V-te mo V-te-mo*, see ch. 4, § 13.

*V-te **shibaraku** suru to* "shortly after . . ."

| *Uchi e kaette shibaraku suru to denwa ga natta.* | Shortly after I got home the telephone rang. |

*V-te mita **tokorode*** or *V-ta tokorode* + negative (see ch. 4, § 10.3)

V-te **yamanai** "do nothing but"

Kodomotachi no shiawase o inotte yamanai.	I do nothing but pray for happiness for my children.

3. Compounds using V-stem

Many of the items in this section come from a list compiled by my colleague Mrs. Kakuko Shoji.

3.1 V-stem + V

A. BEGIN, CONTINUE, AND FINISH

V-stem + *hajimeru* or *dasu* "begin (doing) . . ."

hon o yomi-hajimeru/dasu	begin reading a book
Akanbō ga naki-dashita.	The baby suddenly began crying.

The *dasu* here connotes abruptness. Compare with

Kumo ga dete-kita.	Clouds began to appear.

The beginning of the occurrence in this case is gradual in comparison with the examples above with *-hajimeru* or *-dasu*. See ch. 4, § 2.5.3 for *V-te kuru*.

V-stem + *kakeru* (Vt)/*kakaru* (Vi) "begin doing . . ."

Hon o yomi-kaketara denwa ga natta.	As I began to read the book, the telephone rang.
Tonari no hito ni hanashi-kaketa.	I spoke to the person next to me (= began a conversation).
Sono ie no tokoro o tōri-kakaru to ii ongaku ga kikoete-kita.	As I began to pass by the house, I could hear pleasant music.

V-stem + *tsuzukeru/tsuzuku* "continue (doing)"

aruki-tsuzukeru	keep on walking
Hon o yomi-tsuzuketa.	I kept on reading the book.
Ame ga furi-tsuzuita.	It continued raining.

Note that the use of *-tsuzuku* is limited.

V-stem + *oeru/owaru* "finish doing . . . , be finished"

| *Shōsetsu o kaki-oeta.* | I finished writing a novel. |
| *Shōsetsu ga kaki-owatta.* | The novel is finished (= the writing is finished). |

Note that we cannot say *Ame ga furi-oeru/owaru* for "It stops raining." (See next example.)

Vi-stem + *yamu*(Vi) "stop*"

      * Usually of a natural phenomenon such as rain or snow, or else a sound.

Ame ga huri-yanda.	It stopped raining.
Kaminari ga nari-yanda.	It stopped thundering.
Kodomo ga naki-yanda.	The child stopped crying.

V-stem + *ageru/agaru* "complete doing . . . , be completed"

yōfuku o nui-ageta.	I finished sewing the clothes.
yōfuku ga nui-agatta.	The clothes are finished (= the sewing is finished).
Sora ga hare-agatta.	The sky cleared up (completely).

B. UP, DOWN, IN, OUT

V-stem + *ageru/agaru* "up"

Ishi o mochi-ageta.	I lifted up the stone.
Jiken ga mochi-agatta.	An event took place (= arose).
Kodomo wa tachi-agatta.	The child stood up.

V-stem + *orosu/oriru* "down"

Okujō kara machi o mi-orosu.	I look down on the town from the rooftop.
Sonna tokoro kara tobi-oritara abunai.	It would be dangerous to jump down from such a place.

V-stem + *kudasu/kudaru* "down"

hito o mi-kudasu	look down on others
heri-kudaru	be humble

V-stem + *komeru/komu* "in"

Atari ittai ni koi kiri ga tachi-komete-ita.	A thick fog has enveloped (= closed in) the entire area.
Amedama o nomi-konde-shimatta.	I have swallowed a candy.
Kare wa sono toi ni kotaerarenakute, kangae-konde-shimatta.	Being unable to answer the question, he ended up lost in thought.

V-stem + *ireru/iru* "in"

Nihonjin wa gaikoku kara yoi tokoro o tori-ireru no ga umai.	The Japanese are good at taking in good things from foreign countries.
Dorobō ga oshi-itta.	A burglar broke into the house.

V-stem + *dasu/deru* "out"

nige-dasu	run away
omoi-dasu	to recall
nuke-deru	sneak out
Niwa kara yoso no inu o oi-dashita.	I chased someone's dog out of the yard.

Sotto uchi o nuke-dete soto e deta.	Quietly I sneaked out of the house.

C. OTHERS

V-stem + *akiru* "get tired of"

mi-akiru	get tired of looking
tabe-akiru	get tired of eating

V-stem + *au* "mutually, do . . . with each other"

hanashi-au	talk to each other

V-stem + *awaseru* "put together, combine, adjust"

mōshi-awaseru	agree to do . . .
kumi-awaseru	combine

V-stem + *akasu* "do . . . through the night"

hanashi-akasu	talk through the night

V-stem + *atsumeru* "gather"

hiroi-atsumeru	glean
yobi-atsumeru	call together

V-stem + *chigaeru/chigau* "differ, not agree"

kaki-chigaeru	make an error in writing
mi-chigaeru	mistake (A for B), fail to recognize (someone)
iki-chigau	miss each other
kui-chigau	go wrong with a person, clash, be at cross purposes

V-stem + *eru* or *uru** "obtain, be able to . . ."

Sō kangae-uru.	It is possible to think so.

> * The classical equivalent of *-eru* is *-u*. Vowel Verbs whose roots end in *-e* take *-uru*; otherwise either form (*-eru* or *-uru*) may be used. The negative form is *-enai* for both *eru* and *uru*:

Sonna koto wa ari-enai.	That is not possible.

V-stem + *fukumeru* "include, bear in mind"

ii-fukumeru	inculcate
toki-fukumeru	persuade

V-stem + *fuseru* "turn down, conceal"

kumi-fuseru	hold someone down
machi-buseru	ambush

V-stem + *hateru* "exhaust"

komari-hateru	be totally perplexed
tsukare-hateru	be exhausted

V-stem + *harau* "pay/clear out"

tori-harau	take away
furi-harau	shake off

V-stem + *hiromeru* "spread"

ii-hiromeru	spread the word

V-stem + *horeru* "fall in love"

kiki-horeru	be absorbed (in music)
mi-horeru	look admiringly

V-stem + *kaeru/kawaru* "change"

nori-kaeru	transfer (transportation)
ki-kaeru	change clothes
kaki-kaeru	rewrite
torikaeru	exchange
umare-kawaru	be reborn, make a fresh start

V-stem + *kaesu/kaeru* "redo"

kuri-kaesu	repeat
yomi-kaesu	reread
tori-kaesu	take back
iki-kaeru	come back to life
furi-kaeru	look back

V-stem + *kakusu* "hide"

ōi-kakusu	cover
oshi-kakusu	try to conceal something

V-stem + *kaneru* "be unable to, be difficult to do"

deki-kaneru	be unable to do
ii-kaneru	be difficult to tell

V-stem + *kanenai* "be possible that . . ."

. . . byōki ni nari-kanenai	. . . [he] might fall ill

V-stem + *kiru* "cut," "do (something) completely"

ii-kiru	declare
omoi-kiru	give up

tachi-kiru	break off (a relationship)
shinji-kiru	trust completely
komari-kiru	be sorely perplexed, be at a loss
uri-kiru	sell out

V-stem + *kireru* "be cut," "be done completely"

suri-kireru	be worn out
uri-kireru	be sold out
shi-kirenai	be unable to finish doing
tabe-kirenai	be unable to eat up
*machi-kirenai**	can hardly wait
*yari-kirenai**	be unable to bear

* These are used as single verbs and are not used in the affirmative form.

V-stem + *kosu/koeru* "go beyond"

oi-kosu	to surpass, get ahead
nori-kosu	pass (one's stop)
nori-koeru	go over, overcome
tobi-koeru	jump over

V-stem + *konasu* "digest," "manage to do (something) well"

yomi-konasu	read throughly
Kimono o umaku ki-konasu no wa muzukashii.	It is difficult to wear a kimono well.

V-stem + *korosu* "kill"

hiki-korosu	kill by running over
kiri-korosu	slay
shime-korosu	suffocate

V-stem + *kowasu/kowareru* "break"

tataki-kowasu	smash up
buchi-kowareru	be broken
buchi-kowasu	ruin

V-stem + *kumu* "combine"

iri-kumu	get complicated
shi-kumu	plot
tori-kumu	tackle

V-stem + *kurasu* "do . . . day and night"

asobi-kurasu	live in idleness
naki-kurasu	live in sorrow

V-stem + *makuru* "tuck, roll up"

ii-makuru	talk a lot (so that the other person doesn't have a chance to)
kaki-makuru	write an enormous amount

V-stem + *mawasu/mawaru* "(go) around"

mi-mawasu	look around
aruki-mawaru	walk around

V-stem +*meguru* "turn, surround"

kake-meguru	run around

V-stem + *miru* "see, look"

aogi-miru	look up
nozoki-miru	glance at

V-stem + *modosu* "return"

harai-modosu	give a refund
maki-modosu	rewind

V-stem + *motsu* "hold, possess"

kake-motsu	hold two or more positions concurrently
tori-motsu	mediate

V-stem + *naosu/naoru* "redo, do again"

kaki-naosu	rewrite
yomi-naosu	reread
i-naoru	change one's attitude

V-stem + *narasu/nareru* "be accustomed to"

kai-narasu	tame (an animal)
sumi-nareru	get used to a place
kaki-nareru	get used to writing (with)

Note that *nareru* may also be attached to a noun:

te-nareru	be skillful
yo-nareru	see much of life

V-stem + *nogasu* "let . . . go"

mi-nogasu	overlook
kiki-nogasu	miss hearing . . .

V-stem + *nokosu/nokoru* "leave/remain"

ii-nokosu	leave a message

tori-nokosu	leave behind
i-nokoru	stay

V-stem + *nuku* "go through, penetrate"

mi-nuku	see through
tae-nuku	endure through
kiri-nuku	cut out

V-stem + *otosu/ochiru* "fall, drop"

mi-otosu	overlook
kaki-otosu	miss (something) while writing
furi-otosu	shake off
tori-otosu	drop something
koroge-ochiru	roll down
yake-ochiru	burn down

V-stem + *okosu/okiru* "raise/cause"

daki-okosu	help (someone) sit up
yobi-okosu	call
hiki-okosu	cause
tobi-okiru	jump out (of the bed)

V-stem + *okureru* "be late for"

nori-okureru	miss (a train, bus, plane)

V-stem + *okuru* "send"

kaki-okuru	write a person
mi-okuru	see someone off

V-stem + *saku* "tear"

hiki-saku	tear up
kiri-saku	sever by cutting

V-stem + *saru* "leave"

hashiri-saru	leave running
sugi-saru	pass

V-stem + *semaru* "draw near, urge"

oshi-semaru	draw near
sashi-semaru	be imminent

V-stem + *shiru* "know"

omoi-shiru	learn a lesson
mi-shiru	be familiar

V-stem + *sobireru* "miss the chance to . . ."

ii-sobireru	miss a chance to say something
kiki-sobireru	miss a chance to hear something

V-stem + *sokonau* "fail to do"

kaki-sokonau	make a slip of the pen
mi-sokonau	misjudge

V-stem + *sonjiru* "fail to do"

kaki-sonjiru	make a slip of the pen
shi-sonjiru	make a mistake

V stem + *sugiru* "do something too much"

nomi-sugiru	drink too much
ne-sugiru	sleep too much

Note that *sugiru* can also be attached to ADJ-stem and AN:

atsu (Adj)-sugiru	too hot
hade (AN)-sugiru	too bold/gay/bright

Related Construction:

V/Adj/AN stem + *sugiru kirai ga aru*   "have a tendency to overdo . . ."

Jiman shi-sugiru kirai ga aru.	He has a tendency to be boastful.

V-stem + *sugosu*   "do excessively"

ne-sugosu	oversleep
omoi-sugosu	worry too much

(Note that this usage is more limited than V-stem + *sugiru*: one cannot say *nomi-sugosu* or *asobi-sugosu*.)

V stem + *tariru*   "be sufficient (Vi)"

ne-tariru	have enough sleep

V stem + *tameru*   "do . . . a lot (so that the results accumulate)"

Naganen kakete kaki-tameta mono o hon ni shita.	I made the things I had written all those years into a book.

V-stem + *tateru/tatsu*   "stand"

kaki-tateru	arouse
tsumi-tateru	save/reserve money
tobi-tatsu	fly up
waki-tatsu	boil up, be in an uproar
furui-tatsu	rouse oneself

V-stem + *tomeru/tomaru* "stop"

kaki-tomeru	note/jot down
yobi-tomeru	call (a person) to stop
tachi-domaru	stop, pause, halt

V-stem + *toru* "take"

kaki-toru	write down
kiki-toru	catch what someone says

V-stem + *tsugu* "succeed"

katari-tsugu	hand down (stories) from generation to generation
tori-tsugu	mediate

V-stem + *tsukeru/tsuku* "attach"

oshi-tsukeru	force, press
fumi-tsukeru	trample
oi-tsuku	catch up with
tobi-tsuku	jump on to
omoi-tsuku	think of

V-stem + *tsukusu/tsukiru* "be exhausted"

ii-tsukusu	describe exhaustively
shiri-tsukusu	know everything
moe-tsukiru	burn out

V-stem + *ukeru* "receive"

machi-ukeru	wait for
mi-ukeru	look/appear

V-stem + *utsusu* "copy"

kaki-utsusu	copy

V-stem + *wasureru* "forget"

ii-wasureru	forget to tell
keshi-wasureru	forget to turn off

V-stem + *watasu/wataru* "hand over"

ii-watasu	tell, sentence (legal)
nagame-watasu	look over
iki-wataru	spread
hare-wataru	clear up

V-stem + *yaru* "give, dispatch, do"

mi-yaru	look at
nage-yaru	leave untouched

V-stem + *yoseru/yoru* "drop in, approach"

seme-yoseru	come to attack in vast numbers
tori-yoseru	get, order from, send for
tachi-yoru	drop by
mochi-yoru	bring

V-stem + *yuku* or *iku* "go"

sari-yuku	go away
sugi-yuku	pass

There are numerous verb compounds many of which have become independent verbs in which the first verb in the stem form acts as a prefix. Some examples are:

furi- "shake" as in *furi-muku* "look back"
oshi- "push" as in *oshi-komu* "push in"
tori- "take" as in *tori-kakaru* "take up, begin"
uchi- "strike" as in *uchi-kiru* "call off (a meeting, negotiation, etc.)"

3.2 Other V-stem Compounds and Phrases

V-stem + *yasui / nikui* "be easy/difficult to do (an action)"

Kono pen wa kaki-yasui	This pen is easy to write with.

V-stem + *gatai*, "be difficult to do . . ." (more abstract than the above)

Kotoba de wa ii-gatai.	It is difficult to express in words.

One **cannot** say *Kono kotoba wa hatsuon shi-gatai.* "This word is difficult to pronounce." The correct form is: . . . *shi-nikui.*

> Note that *arigatō* "thank you," derives from *ari-gatai* "difficult to exist/have, precious"—hence the meaning "grateful."

V-stem + *bae* ga suru* "appear attractive"

> * *Bae* derives from the verb *haeru* "look attractive."

Sono doresu wa ki-bae ga suru.	That dress looks nice when worn.
Kono e wa piano no ue ni kakeru to mi-bae ga suru.	This painting looks nice when hung above the piano.

V-stem + *de* (substance) *ga aru* "be substantial"

Kono ryōri wa tabe-de ga aru.	This dish is substantial (= a solid meal).
yomi-de ga aru hon	a book that takes time and effort to read

V-stem + *dōshi da* or *-ppanashi** "keep doing"

Denwa ga nari-dōshi/ppanashi datta.	The telephone kept on ringing. (= There were many phone calls)

    * *Dōshi* derives from the verb *tōsu* "let something go through," which is the transitive counterpart of *tōru* "go through." *-ppanshi* derives from the verb *hanasu*, "to release, let go."

V-stem + *gachi da* "tend to . . ."

Ano gakusei wa yasumi-gachi da.	That student tends to miss classes.

V-stem + *gai ga aru* "be worth doing . . ."

iki-gai ga aru jinsei	a life worth living

V-stem *kata* "a way of doing something"

yomi-kata	way of reading
yuniiku na kangae-kata o suru	to think in a unique way

V₁-stem + *mo sureba* V₂-stem *mo suru* "not only do V_1 but also V_2"

Gorufu mo sureba tenisu mo suru.	He not only plays golf but also tennis.

V-stem *nagara* See ch. 4, § 2.6.

V-stem + *ni* PURPOSE See ch. 4, § 7.5.

V-stem/N + *ni (tori)***kakaru** See above, § 1.

V-stem + *ni* V-*ru* See above, § 1: V-stem **ni**.

V-stem *sae sureba* See ch. 4, § 12.2B.

V-stem + *shidai* "as soon as"

Shigoto ga sumi shidai renraku suru.	I will contact you as soon as I finish my work.

Cf. *shidai* (N) "order, the state of things"; *shidai ni* (Adv) "gradually"

4. Grammar lists

ageru	raise (**trans.**)		*agaru*	rise (**intrans.**)
akeru	open		*aku*	open
amasu	leave, save		*amaru*	remain
ateru	hit, guess		*ataru*	be hit
atsumeru	gather		*atsumaru*	be gathered
azukeru	entrust		*azukaru*	be entrusted with
chijimeru	shrink		*chijim(ar)u*	be shrunk
dasu	take out, serve		*deru*	come out, appear
fuku	blow, breathe		*fuku*	blow (wind)
fuyasu	increase		*fueru*	increase
hajimeru	begin		*hajimaru*	begin
herasu	decrease		*heru*	decrease
horobosu	defeat		*horobu/ horobiru*	perish, be ruined
ikasu	let live		*ikiru*	live, be effective
ireru	put in, insert		*hairu*	enter, be put in
kaesu	give back to, return		*kaeru*	go back, return

kakeru	hang, fasten, lock, spend	*kakaru*	be hung, fastened, locked
kakusu	hide, conceal	*kakureru*	hide
kawakasu	dry	*kawaku*	get dry
kesu	erase, extinguish, turn off	*kieru*	be erased etc., disappear
kimeru	decide	*kimaru*	be decided
kobosu	spill	*koboreru*	be spilled
kudaku	break	*kudakeru*	be crushed
kuwaeru	add	*kuwawaru*	join
kogasu	scorch	*kogeru*	be scorched
machigaeru	(make a) mistake	*machigau*	be in error
mageru	bend	*magaru*	be bent, turn
masu	increase	*masu*	increase
mawasu	rotate, pass around	*mawaru*	rotate, revolve, go around
mazeru	mix	*majiru*	be mixed, merge
mitsukeru	find	*mitsukaru*	be found
moyasu	burn	*moeru*	burn
mukeru	face toward	*muk(a)u*	face, go toward
nagasu	let flow	*nagareru*	flow
naosu	correct, repair, cure	*naoru*	be corrected, repaired, cured
narasu	tame, accustom to	*nareru*	get accustomed to
natsukeru	make someone attached to	*natsuku*	become attached to
nobasu	stretch	*nobiru*	stretch
nokosu	leave	*nokoru*	be left
noseru	put on top, load	*noru*	get on, ride on

nurasu	wet		*nureru*	get wet
oeru	finish		*owaru*	end
okosu	raise, cause, waken		*okiru*	happen, get up
orosu	lower, put down, unload		*oriru*	get off, go down
otosu	drop		*ochiru*	fall
sageru	lower, hang		*sagaru*	go down, be hanged
shimeru	close, fasten		*shimaru*	be closed, be fastened
shizumeru	calm		*shizumaru*	calm down
sodateru	raise		*sodatsu*	grow up
sugosu	pass, spend (time)		*sugiru*	pass by, pass (time)
susumeru	advance		*susumu*	advance, proceed
taosu	knock down		*taoreru*	fall over
tateru	erect, build		*tatsu*	stand, be built
tobasu	let something fly		*tobu*	fly
todokeru	deliver		*todoku*	reach, be delivered
tomeru	stop		*tomaru*	stop
tozasu	close		*tojiru*	close
tsukeru	attach		*tsuku*	be attached
tsumeru	stuff		*tsumaru*	be stuffed
tsunag(er)u	connect		*tsunagaru*	be connected
tsutaeru	convey		*tsutawaru*	be conveyed, transmitted
tsuzukeru	continue		*tsuzuku*	continue
ukaberu	float		*ukabu*	float
umeru	bury/fill		*umaru*	be buried/filled
utsusu	transfer, move		*utsuru*	move, be transmitted
utsusu	copy		*utsuru*	be copied/reflected

wakasu	boil		*waku*	boil up
watasu	pass over		*wataru*	cross over, be passed over
yaku	burn, bake		*yakeru*	be burned, baked
yameru	stop, quit		*yamu*	stop (rain/snow/sound)

4.2 *-i* (Vowel) Verbs

abiru	bathe
akiru	get tired of
dekiru	be able to, be ready
furubiru	to become old
hikiiru	lead
hiru	get dry
horobiru	be ruined Vi (Vt *horobosu*: Consonant V)
ikiru	live
iru	be, exist [accent on *ru*]
iru	shoot (an arrow) [accent on *i*]
iru	cast (metal) [accent on *i*]
kabiru	become moldy
kaerimiru	look back on
kangamiru	take into inconsideration (*X ni kangamite* "in view of X")
kariru	borrow
kiru	wear (clothes) [accent on *ru*]

kobiru	flatter
kokoromiru	try
koriru	learn by experience
kuchiru	decay, rot
kuiru	regret
michiru	become full Vi (Vt *mitasu*: C. V.)
miru	see, look, observe
mochiiru	use
mukuiru	reward
niru	resemble
niru	boil, cook
nobiru	stretch, grow Vi (Vt *nobasu*: C. V.)
nobiru	extend, be postponed
obiru	wear, be tinged with
ochiru	fall, drop Vi (Vt *otosu*: C. V.)
oiru	grow old
okiru	get up, occur Vi (Vt *okosu*: C. V.)
oriru	get off, go down Vi (Vt *orosu*: C. V.)
sabiru	rust
sabiru	be desolate
shiiru	force, press
shimiru	penetrate into
shimiru	freeze
sugiru	pass Vi (Vt *sugosu*: C. V.)

tariru	suffice
tojiru	close
tojiru	bind, file
tsukiru	be exhausted
wabiru	apologize
wabiru	be grieved

There is also a group of Sino-Japanese Vowel Verbs that take *-jiru/zuru* and whose negative forms are *-jinai/zezu.*

amanjiru	be contented with
anjiru	worry
benjiru	discern, speak
chōjiru	grow up, excel
danjiru	discuss, negotiate
danjiru	decide, judge
dōjiru	be agitated
enjiru	perform, act
fūjiru	seal, enclose
gaenjiru	consent
genjiru	deduct, lessen
ginjiru	chant, recite
hajiru	feel ashamed
hōjiru	report, requite
hōjiru	heat, roast
hōjiru	present, dedicate
jōjiru	multiply, take advantage of
junjiru	apply correspondingly

junjiru	sacrifice one's life
kanjiru	feel
karonjiru	belittle
kenjiru	present, dedicate
kinjiru	forbid
kōjiru	worsen
kyōjiru	amuse oneself
meijiru	command
menjiru	dismiss, exempt
ninjiru	appoint
ōjiru	respond, comply
omonjiru	value
ronjiru	discuss, argue
sakinjiru	precede, anticipate
sanjiru	go
sanjiru	disperse, squander
senjiru	boil, decoct
shinjiru	trust, believe
shōjiru	emerge
sonjiru	damage, injure, hurt
soranjiru	memorize
tenjiru	change, turn, rotate
tenjiru	drop, ignite
tōjiru	throw, cast
tsūjiru	get through
utonjiru	be cold toward
yasunjiru	content oneself
zonjiru	know, think

4.3 Momentary Verbs

aku	open
amaru	be left over
ataru	be hit
chiru	fall, scatter
deru	depart, appear
furu	fall (rain/snow)
fureru	touch
hairu	enter
hajimaru	begin
hanareru	separate
horobiru	be ruined
iku	go
kaeru	go back
kakureru	hide
kawaku	become dry
kekkon suru	marry
kieru	disappear, go off (electricity)
kimaru	be decided
kogeru	be scorched
komu	become crowded
kowareru	break
kuru	come
machigau	be in error
majiru	be mixed
mitsukaru	be found

motsu	have, hold, own
naoru	be cured, repaired
nareru	get accustomed to
naru	become
natsuku	become attached
nokoru	remain
noru	get on, ride on
nureru	get wet
nyūgaku suru	enter school
oboeru	memorize
ochiru	fall
okiru	get up
oriru	get off
owaru	end, be over
rikon suru	get divorced
saku	boom
sameru	wake up, cool down
shimaru	shut, close
shinu	die
shiru	acquire knowledge of
shizumaru	calm down
shuppatsu suru	depart
sotsugyō suru	graduate
sugiru	pass by
suku	become less crowded
sumu	be over
suwaru	sit
tatsu	erect, stand

taoreru	fall down
todoku	reach, be delivered
tomaru	stop
tōchaku suru	arrive
tsukiru	be exhausted
tsuku	arrive
tsuku	attach, go on (elec.)
tsumaru	be stuffed
tsunagaru	be connected
tsutawaru	to be conveyed
umareru	be born
umaru	to be buried/filled
utsuru	be transmitted, move
wakaru	understand
waku	boil up
wasureru	forget
yakeru	be burned
yameru	quit, give up
yamu	stop falling (rain/snow)

4.4 Adjectival Nouns

Note that the antonyms of some ANs are Adjs.

an'i na	careless, not thorough
anka na	inexpensive (= *yasui*)

atataka na	warm (*suzushii* "cool")
aware na	pitiful
baka na	stupid
benri na	useful, convenient
betsu na	separate, different (*betsu* may take *no* as N)
binbō na	poor, not rich
dame na	no good (*yoi/ii* "good")
daiji na	important
daijōbu na	all right
date na	dandyish, showy
fuben na	inconvenient
fujiyū na	handicapped
fujun na	impure; irregular
fujūjun na	disobedient
fukuyoka na	round, fleshy
fukuzatsu na	complicated
fumeiyō na	dishonorable
futsugō na	inconvenient
ganko na	stubborn
gehin na	vulgar, indecent, unrefined
genki na	healthy, peppy (*byōki*[N] *no* "sick, ill")
gōjō na	stubborn, obstinate
hade na	bright, bold
hanayaka na	gay, flowery (*wabishii* "lonely, dreary")

hanzatsu na	complicated
haruka na	distant (in time or space) (*chikai* "near")
hen na	strange, eccentric
heiki na	nonchalant
heta na	clumsy, poor, unskillful
hima na	free, having spare time (*isogashii* "busy")
hogaraka na	cheerful, clear
idai na	great
igai na	unexpected
iikagen na	perfunctory
ijiwaru na	mean
ijō na	abnormal
inki na	gloomy, melancholic
iki na	chic, smart, stylish
iya na	disagreeable, unpleasant
jama na	in the way (obstructing)
jimi na	subdued, quiet
jiyū na	free, liberal
jōbu na	durable, healthy
jōzu na	skillful, proficient
jōhin na	refined, sophisticated
junjō na	naive
jūnan na	soft, flexible, supple (*katai* "hard, inflexible")
junsui na	pure
jūjun na	obedient
kantan na	simple

kasuka na	subtle, minute
kawaisō na	pitiful
kekkō na	fine
kirei na	pretty, clean (*kitanai* "dirty")
kirai na	that (one) dislikes
kiraku na	carefree
konnan na	difficult, hard, troublesome
kōka na	expensive (= *takai*)
kōtsugō na	favorable, convenient
majime na	serious, grave
mame na	diligent, hardworking
manzoku na	satisfying
mare na	unusual
meikaku na	clear
meiryō na	clear
meiwaku na	disturbing
mijuku na	inmature
mottomo na	reasonable, understandable
migoto na	beautiful, splendid (*misuborashii* "shabby")
mucha na	unreasonable, irrational
muda/mueki na	useless, wasteful
muri na	unreasonable, impossible
nigiyaka na	busy, noisy, festive (*sabishii* "lonely, desolate")
nonki na	carefree
nyūwa na	gentle, mild

odayaka na	calm, gentle, mild (*kewashii* "steep, severe")
okubyō na	cowardly, timid
onwa na	gentle, mild
oroka na	stupid
raku na	easy, confortable (*kurushii* "painful, hard")
reisei na	calm, cool, level-headed
rikō na	smart
rippa na	fine, great, handsome (*misuborashii* "shabby")
sakan na	vigorous, energetic, lively
seijitsu na	sincere
seikaku na	accurate
sekkachi na	hasty, impatient
shisso na	simple, plain, homely
shitsurei na	rude, impolite
shizuka na	quiet (*urusai* "noisy")
shōjiki na	honest
sōjuku na	precocious (*okute* [N] *no* "slow to mature")
suki na	that (one) likes
sunao na	gentle, mild, obedient
suteki na	nice, neat
taihen na	hard, troublesome
taisetsu na	important, precious
takumi na	skillful
tanjun na	simple

teinei na	polite
tekitō na	appropriate, suitable
tsūkai na	very pleasant, delightful
yabo na	unrefined, not stylish
yōki na	merry
yukai na	pleasant, joyful
yutaka na	rich (*mazushii* "poor")
yūeki na	useful, beneficial
yūkan na	brave
yūmei na	famous
zeitaku na	luxurious, extravagant

...-*teki*, ...-like (as in *kihon-teki* "basic")

attō-teki na	overwhelming
bunka-teki na	cultural
chihō-teki na	local
den'en-teki na	rural
hikan-teki na	pessimistic
hōken-teki na	feudalistic
inshō-teki na	impressive
kindai-teki na	modern
koten-teki na	classical
minshu-teki na	democratic
rakkan-teki na	optimistic
shakai-teki na	social
seiji-teki na	political

shinpo-teki na	progressive
tokai-teki na	urban

Nouns that take *-teki* may also be used with a following *no*. In these cases the meanings may be slightly different: *shakaiteki na mondai* "social problems," and *shakai no mondai* "problems in a society"

The following are examples of ANs using foreign words:

(abu)nōmaru	(ab)normal
ereganto na	elegant
furesshu na	fresh
modan na	modern
rakkii na	lucky
shikku na	chic
sumāto na	slender, stylish
yuniiku na	unique

4.5 Conjunctions

The following is a list of conjunctions commonly used at the beginning of a sentence in written discourse. Since there are not many of them, the student may find it most efficient simply commit them to memory.

dakara or *dearukara (shite)*	therefore
denakereba	if not this, then
keredomo	however
mata	and, moreover, on the other hand
mottomo	(This is true,) but
(sore wa) naze ka toiu to	if I state the reason why

nazenara(ba)	the reason is, because
sate	well, now, so; in the meantime
shikamo	moreover
shikaruni	however
shikashi(nagara)	but, however
shitagatte	therefore, consequently
sokode	so, therefore
sōkatoitte	even so
sorekara	and then
sore ni (= sono ue/sarani [ADVs])	besides, furthermore
sorenishitemo	even so
soretomo	or (else)
soreyue(ni)	therefore
soshite	and
sunawachi/torimonaosazu/ tsumari	that is (to say), in other words
tadashi	but, only, however
tahō (de wa)	on the other hand
tokorode	by the way
tokoroga	however
tsuite wa or *tsukimashite wa* [polite]	so, therefore, such being the case
yue ni	therefore

5. Old kana

---

1 は , ひ , ふ , へ , ほ are used for わ , い , う , え , お : いはれる for いわれる , いひます for いいます , いふ for いう , いへば for いえば , いはば for いわば ("so speak"), いはゆる for いわゆる , あひ for あい ("put together, in between; meet, encounter"), いへ for いえ ("house"), うへ for うえ ("on, above"), いきほひ for いきおい ("power, strength"), and so on.

2 わ , ゐ , う , ゑ , を , for わ , い , う , え , を : ゐる for いる , ゑる for える , ゑむ for えむ ("smile"), をる for おる ("to be"), あゐ for あい ("indigo blue"), ゑ for え ("a picture"), をんな for おんな ("woman"), and so on.

3 おほ for おお : おほきい for おおきい ("big"), おほひ for おおい , ("a cover"), おほやけ for おおやけ ("public").
あう for おう : さう for そう ("so"), かうむる for こうむる ("be affected"), まうす for もうす ("say-HUMBLE"), すまう for すもう ("Sumo wrestling").
えう for おう : V-ませう for V-ましょう , でせう for でしょう , せう for しょう ("small, less; summon, disappear, laugh"), ぜうぜつ for じょうぜつ ("loquacity"), てふ for ちょう ("a butterfly, a notebook")

4 くわ for か : くわびん for かびん ("a flower vase"), いっくわん for いっかん ("one volume, volume one"), くわがく for かがく ("chemistry"), ぐわんねん for がんねん ("first year of the reign of [the emperor . . .]").

5 ぢ for じ and づ for ず : ぢめん ("the ground"), はぢ ("shame, disgrace"), ぢき ("soon"), まづ ("first, firstly"), つづく ("continue").

...about the authors

SETSUKO AIHARA was born in Japan and received a degree in International Relations from International Christian University in Tokyo. After receiving an M.A. in Teaching Japanese as a Second Language from the University of Hawaii, she went on to study linguistics, and has taught Japanese there at various levels for over twenty years. She is the co-translator of *The Self-Overcoming of Nihilism* by Nishitani Keiji and of various philosophical essays.

GRAHAM PARKES teaches philosophy at the University of Hawaii. He is the other translator of *The Self-Overcoming of Nihilism* and editor of the anthologies *Heidegger and Asian Thought* and *Nietzsche and Asian Thought*.

本書で使用された例文の出典リスト
(各行頭の数字は、本書の掲載ページです)

『日本の名著7 〝道元、正法眼蔵(抄)〟』責任編集玉城康四郎、©1974 中央公論社
　P．90ローマ字「人が悟りを得るのは………ものである。」(原著P．122)

"Modern Japanese for University Students, Part 2" ©1974 国際基督教大学語学科日本
語研究室、国際基督教大学売店
　　P．95ローマ字「教育学者………という。」(原著P．132)
　　P．100ローマ字「それをこうした………歌うのです。」(原著PP．101-102)
　　P．104ローマ字「大学から帰る道で………そうである。」(原著P．79)
　　P．110ローマ字「誰が最初に………かもしれない。」(原著P．119)
　　PP．114-115ローマ字「ことに〝はにゅうの宿〟………思うのです。」(原著P．107)
　　P．120ローマ字「ただちょっと………あげてみたのです。」(原著P．128)
　　P．143「どっちがいいか、………決めました。」(原著P．30)
　　P．150「歌の声にひかれて、………すわっているのです。」(原著P．100)
　　P．151「満州国においては、………いだき始める様になった。」(原著P．150)
　　P．159「この妻の労苦に対して………それだけであった。」(原著PP．79-80)
　　P．160「アフリカ大陸の………効率は良いわけである。」(原著P．86)
　　P．169「十月末のある朝の……ぼう然とながめていた位だ。」(原著P．141)
　　P．171「急に私の後ろから………子供の声がした。」(原著P．143)
　　P．173「子供はお茶のはいったことを知らせに来たのだ。」(原著P．143)
　　P．177「しかし、原住民の中で………越えて行きました。」(原著P．98)
　　P．189「私が結婚したのは、………苦しかったであろう。」(原著P．79)

『西谷啓治著作集、第8巻』 ©1986 西谷啓治著、創文社
　　P．126「その魂は………魂である。」(原著P．82)
　　P．132「フォイエルバッハによれば………ものであり、」(原著P．36)
　　P．133「之に反して………固い底をもっている。」(原著P．261)
　　P．134「氏自身、………と言っているが、」(原著P．180)
　　P．139「ニイチェと………ものとなっている。」(原著P．5)
　　P．143「私は祝福する者なり、然りを言う者となった。」(原著P．82)
　　P．144「現代の無神論は、………軸を一つにしている。」(原著P．286)
　　P．148「運命に身を委せる………還るということであった。」(原著P．80)
　　P．154「そこに、そのヨーロッパの………知られるであろう。」(原著P．54)
　　P．157「併し、そのような………両者は軸を一つにしている。」(原著P．280)
　　P．158「従って虚無は、存在するものに対する否定ではない。」(原著P．164)
　　P．161「また憤怒が起こっても、………霧散して了う。」(原著P．260)
　　P．162「彼が反対せざるを得なかった………からであった。」(原著P．263)
　　P．163「彼(ドストエフスキー)の天才は………追求したのである。」(原著P．265)
　　P．163「そこからスティルナーは、………標榜したのである。」(原著P．109)

P．164「さきにマルキシズムや………ということである。」（原著P．287）

P．165「併しながら、………と言えるであろうか。」（原著P．287）

P．166「スティルナーも、………証明しようとした。」（原著PP．109-110）

P．181「例えばニイチェは………それを克服する。」（原著P．42）

P．185「宗教に於けるこのような………この非本質性の否定である。」（原著P．277）

『適応の条件』　©1972　中根千枝著、現代新書300、講談社

P．137「もちろん、それらのシステムは、………もっている。」（原著P．5）

P．141「言語が異なるばかりか、………ことではない。」（原著P．3）

『毎日新聞記事1989年11月より』　©1989　毎日新聞社

P．138「マスコミの………引っ込んでいたい。」

P．140「自己資本比率は、………目標達成に近付くが、」

P．173「自己資本比率の数字を………対処することにしている。」

P．174「この国際統一基準の………詰めて来た。」

"Modern Japanese: A Basic Reader, Vol.2 "　©1967　by Howard Hibbett & Gen Itasaka, Harvard University Press, Cambridge, MA.

P．146「日本の歴史で………続いていることです。」（原著P．110）

P．175「明治維新以後西洋の………からとも言えよう。」（原著P．138）

P．178「誰もまだ自殺者自身の………によるものであろう。」（原著P．88）

『午後の曳航』　©1986　三島由紀夫著、新潮社

P．179「母子は次第に洛陽丸に近づいて、………ふくれ上がった。」（原著P．29）

P．180「彼女は女であることの………存在だった。」（原著P．41）

P．190「夜、開け放した窓からは、………夢の中に現われた。」（原著P．11）

『ハワイは沈みつつ西へ動く』　©1986　竹内均著、ＰＨＰ研究所第一出版部

P．186「しかしこのハワイ島の………はっきりと現われる。」（原著P．64）

『日本文化史』　©1971　家永三郎著、岩波新書367、岩波書店

P．192「和歌は依然として………終っていたとみとめられる。」（原著P．75）

P．194「これは、やはり日本文化史上………であったといえよう。」（原著P．108）

『観阿弥と世阿弥』　©1976　戸井田道三著、岩波新書719、岩波書店

P．194「大森彦七のような………許されていいのではあるまいか。」（原著P．45）

P．195「おおよそのことは、………といっていいであろう。」（原著P．64）

『仮面の解釈学』　©1987　坂部恵著、東京大学出版会

P．196「わたしが以下に………ねらいとするものではない。」（原著P．124）

P．197「欧米語あるいは日本語の………わたしも知らぬではない。」（原著P．125）

以　上